This is an annual. That is to say, it is substantially revised each year, the new edition appearing in late March of each year. Those wishing to submit additions, corrections, or suggestions for the 1982 edition, should submit them prior to September 1, 1981, using the forms provided in the back of this book.

D1025727

Other Books by
Richard N. Bolles

Where Do I Go From Here With My Life?
(co-authored with John C. Crystal)

*The Three Boxes of Life, and How
To Get Out of Them*

What Color Is
Your Parachute?

1981 Edition
Revised and Enlarged

What Color Is Your Parachute?

A Practical Manual
for
Job-Hunters
& Career Changers

•

Richard Nelson Bolles

Ten Speed Press

What Color Is Your Parachute? is published by
Ten Speed Press, Box 7123, Berkeley, CA 94707.
You may order single copies prepaid direct from
the publisher for $14.95 + $.75 per copy for
postage and handling (clothbound), or, $6.95 +
$.50 per copy for postage and handling (paper).

© 1981, 1980, 1979, 1978, 1977, 1976, 1975,
1972 by Richard Nelson Bolles
Library of Congress Catalog Card No. 81-50471
ISBN 0-89815-046-9 paper
ISBN 0-89815-047-7 cloth

Beverly Anderson Graphic Design
Type set by Type & Graphics
Printed by Consolidated Printers, Inc.
Berkeley, California

Why This Book Was Written,
Commonly Called

THE INTRODUCTION,
OR   PREFACE

NCE UPON A TIME, I was struck by a thought: some people are more successful than others at job-hunting or changing careers. Why? What do they do, that the rest of us don't do? Are there any common steps or principles that seem to guide their search, from which the rest of us could learn?

It was an intriguing problem. Coming from a family of journalists (my brother was the reporter slain in Arizona back in 1976, and our father and grandfather were also journalists) I decided to investigate. That investigation was lent some urgency by the fact that a number of my friends at the time were out of work, and begging me for some clues as to what they should do. Moreover, I myself had been unemployed two short years previously, so I remembered the challenge of that experience.

Well, I traveled around the country for two years, covering some 65,000 miles and talking endlessly to job-hunters, agency counselors, career experts, employment specialists and the like. When I was done, I sifted down what I had discovered, and published the results — in the form of this book.

Thinking it would enjoy only a modest readership, I self-published the thing, at first. It soon threatened to swallow up my life, in its popularity. Luckily, a very fine publisher, Phil Wood by name, stepped forward and offered to take the publishing task off my hands. The rest is history: the book went on to become what it currently is, the best-selling book on job-hunting and career changing in the history of this nation.

I want to underline that this is not a book of *my* ideas about how you should go about job-hunting. It is the distillation of the experience of literally millions of successful job-hunters. Blue-collar job-hunters. White-collar job-hunters. Male job-hunters. Female job-hunters. Young job-hunters. Older job-hunters. Highly verbal job-hunters. Very shy and often so-called low verbal job-hunters. I am only the reporter of their experience.

I also want to underline that it was not my purpose to compare or evaluate the many job-hunting *systems* that are abroad in the land. They are the invention of gifted men and women who have thought long and hard about job-hunting problems. But, beneath systems, I wanted to get at *the principles* which successful job-hunters and successful systems had in common. As you will see in the body of the book, I discovered these principles to be four in number. Successful systems, and successful job-hunters, almost always seem to use one, two, three or all four of these principles.

Since, at my publisher's behest, this book is revised annually, I like to think of it as our annual "Report to the Nation — and Canada — About the Most Effective Job-Hunting Ideas." The book began, way back in 1970, as a monologue — I did all the talking. Now the book is a dialogue. Countless job-hunters, career-changers, and job-counselors write me during the year (my address is in the back of every book) and tell me new wrinkles, new ideas and new techniques that they found worked. These get duly incorporated into the book the following year. Thus it is now a sort of "Job-Hunters' Report to the Nation" rather than just "My Report."

This information is drastically needed. Job-hunting is a repetitive activity in the Western world. According to a recent study made by the U.S. Department of Labor, the average job tenure for all workers in 1978 was 3.6 years. That means the average worker goes job-hunting once every 3.6 years in the U.S. (The figures are probably not substantially different in other parts of the Western world.)

Our society has taken pity on the job-hunter and career-changer, and invented all kinds of helps for you, when you are in that plight: federal-state employment agencies, private employment agencies, classified ads, job counselors, computerized job banks, and so forth. None of these works very well; in fact, the number of people who turn to any one of them, without getting a job as a result, is simply mind-blowing. Even when they do work, they only at best rescue you from your present predicament (maybe), but often in jobs which are vastly below your abilities, and which bore you out of your mind. And — what is worse — they give you not a clue as to how you should go about your job-hunt the next time. . . and the next time. . . and the next time; i.e., every 3.6 years, on an average.

There is an ancient saying: "Give me a fish, and I will eat for today; teach me to fish, and I will eat for the rest of my life." It is time in our society when we thought it worthwhile to try a noble experiment: to stop giving the job-hunter a fish, half a fish, or no fish at all; and instead to teach you how to fish.

This book is an attempt, through print, to teach you how to fish with respect to the most difficult task any of us faces in life: namely The Job Hunt. This book is an attempt to, in other words, empower you as job-hunter or career-changer, so that no matter how many times you have to go about the job-hunt during your life (probably ten to fifteen or more times, if you are typical), you will know how to do it.

The principles in this book, as I have said, were discovered through the interviewing of successful job-hunters. But many of them are indebted for these principles, though they know it not, to some of the pioneering thinkers in this field, whose ideas as I since discovered have influenced people's consciousness more than they know: John Mills of Western Electric, whose ideas were first published in 1924, A. W. Rahn also of Western Electric, who published his ideas in 1936, Jules Payot who wrote in France of his ideas early in the 1940s, and then subsequently — in this country — Bernard Haldane, Sidney Fine, Harold L. Sheppard and A. Harvey Belitsky (who did a pioneering study on blue-collar job-hunters), John Crystal, John Holland, Richard Lathrop, and Nathan Azrin.

I want to express to John Crystal especially a word of undying gratitude. John is not only a genius about job-hunting, but he is also very gracious and humane. He took the time and trouble to explain to me, when I first began this research, what is wrong with the whole job-hunting process in this country, why it is essentially Neanderthal, and what can or could be done about it. He suggested some organizing principles for the data I was collecting, which principles became the cornerstones of Chapters 5, 6, and 7 in this book.

No book can be written nowadays unmindful of people's increased sensitivity to the issue of sexism in language. 1960 was the year that I myself first protested, in print, such language; but I am frank to say that twenty years later I do not think we are anywhere near a final solution to the problem. Everytime we achieve a semblance of non-sexism, English — in its cadence and majesty — lies mortally wounded. Sample: "The odds are ten to one that you've figured out someone who'll refer you, and act as your link to him or her; but even lacking that referral you can still tell him or her that you want to talk to him or her about some of the problems of the organization, and what you've discovered that might be helpful to him or her." Casey Miller and Kate Swift in their excellent new book, *The Handbook of Nonsexist Writing*, have cogently argued from history that part of the solution is in using "they" as a singular pronoun ("Anyone using this beach after 5 p.m. does so at their own risk."), as indeed it always was by Thackeray, Goldsmith, Eliot, Shaw and Whitman, until in a more sexist age it was decided that agreement in number was more important than agreement in gender. Now the situation is reversed, these authors argue, and agreement in gender is more important than agreement in number. Thus "they," normally plural, can serve as singular, even as in an earlier time "you," normally plural, also became singular. That is the usage followed throughout this book.

My concluding plea: if you are a worker today, you will be a job-hunter tomorrow. If you are a job-hunter more than once, you will almost inevitably turn into a career-changer as well. Learn how to take self-management of your job-hunt and your career-change, without going back to college necessarily for arduous retraining, and without putting your fate totally in someone else's hands.

Learn how to fish.

Whether you be sixteen or sixty, you are setting out on what can be a challenging, exciting, even if somewhat difficult,

journey. The light-hearted tone in much of this book is not intended to deny the seriousness of all this for your life and your
being; but it is intended hopefully to make the journey a little
lighter and more, well, fun. Why should job manuals be dull?
Why should your job-hunt be anything less than an adventure —
in enjoyment, in risk-taking, in growth and in success?

Peace and shalom.
R.N.B.

November 25, 1980

Contents

*airy Godmother,
where were you
when I needed you?*

Cinderella

CHAPTER ONE

A Job-Hunting We Will Go

Okay, this is it.
You've been idly thinking about it, off and on, for
some time now, wondering what it would be like.
To be earning your bread in the marketplace.
Or maybe you're already out there,
And the problem is choosing another career,
The old one having run out of gas, as it were.
Anyhow, the moment of truth has arrived.
For one reason or another, you've got to get at it —
Go out, and look for a job, for the first time or the twentieth.
You've heard of course, all the horror stories.
Of ex-executives working as taxi-drivers
Of former college profs with two masters degrees
working as countermen in a delicatessen.
Of women Ph.D.s who can only get a job as a secretary.
And you wonder what lies in store for you.

Of course, it may be that the problem is all solved.
Maybe you're going to "drop out" and just go
"do your own thing." The subsistence-survival game.
Or, if not, maybe some friend has button-holed you
and said, "Why not come and work for me?"
So, your job-hunt ends before it begins.
Or, it may be that you came into your present
career after a full life doing something else, and
You know you're welcome back there, anytime;
Anytime, they said.
And, assuming they meant it,
no problem, right?
So long as that's what you still want to do.
But for the vast majority of us,
that isn't how it goes.
Not for us the Horatio Alger role;
ah no! In retrospect it seems
We play a kind of Don Quixote; and
the job-hunt is our windmill.

Those who have gone the route before,
all say the very same thing.
This is how we go about it, when our time has come:
We procrastinate,
That's what we do.
Busy winding things up, we say.
Actually, if the truth were known,
we're hoping for that miracle,
you know the one:
that if we just sit tight a little longer,
we won't have to go job-hunting, no
the job will come hunting for us.
Right in the front door, it will come.
To show us we are destiny's favorites,
And that God loves us.
But, it doesn't, of course, and
eventually, we realize that time
and money
are beginning to run out.

Time to begin in earnest.
And all of our familiar friends immediately
are at our elbow, giving advice —
solicited or unsolicited, as to what we should do.
"Jean or Joe, I've always thought you would make a great teacher."
So we ask who they know
in the academic world,
and, armed with that name,
we go a-calling. Calling, and
sitting, cooling our heels
in the ante-room of the Dean's office,
until they ask, at last,
"And what can I do for you, Mr. or Ms. ?"
We tell them, of course, that we're job-hunting.
"And one of my friends thought that you ..."
Oops. We watch the face change,

And we (who *do* know something about body language),
    Wait to hear their words catch up with their body.
        "You feel I'm 'over-qualified'? I see.
            "Two thousand applications, you say, already in hand
                For one hundred vacancies? I see.
                No, of course I understand."
                Strike-out. Back to the drawingboard. More advice.
                "Jean or Joe, have you tried the employment agencies?"
                "Good thinking. No, which ones should I try?
                The ones which deal with professionals? Which ones are they?
                Okay. Good. Down I'll go."
                And down we do go.
            Down, down, down, to that employment agency.
        The ante-room again.
    And those other hopeful, haunted faces.
    A new twist too: our first bout
  with the Application Form.
    "Previous jobs held.
  List in reverse chronological order."
  Filling all the questions out. Followed by
 That interminable wait.
And then, at last, the interviewer,
She of the over-cheerful countenance, and mien —
She talks to us. "Now, let's see, Mr. or Ms.,
What kind of a job are you looking for?"
"Well," we say,
"What do you think I could do?"
She studies, again, the application form;
"It seems to me," she says, "that with your background
—it is a *bit* unusual—
    You might do very well in sales."
        "Oh, sales," we say. "Why yes," says she, "in fact
            I think that I could place you almost immediately.
            We'll be in touch with you. Is this your phone?"
                We nod, and shake her hand, and that is the
                    Last time
                        We ever hear from her.
                            Gad, this isn't an honest world, after all.
                                Strike out, number two.

Now, our ballooning hopes that we would quickly land a job
  are running into some frigid air,
    So we decide to confess at last
      Our need of help — to some of our more successful friends
      in the business world (if we have such)
      Who *surely* know what we should do
      At this point. The windmill is tiring us. What would they suggest
      that Don (or Donna) Quixote do?
     "Now, what kind of a job are you looking for?"
    Ah, *that*, again! "Well, you know me well, what do you think
    I can do? I'll do almost anything,"
  we say, now that the hour of desperation is snapping at our heels.
  "You know, with all the *kinds* of things I've done —"
we say; "I mean, I've done this and that, and here and there,
It all adds up to a kind of kaleidoscope;
Well, anyway, there must be *something* you can suggest!"

"Have you tried the want-ads?" asks our friend.
"Or have you gone to see Bill, and Ed, and John, and Frances and Marty?
Ah, no? Well tell them I sent you."
So, off we go—now newly armed.
We study the want-ads. Gad, what misery is hidden in
Those little boxes. Misery in miserable jobs which are built
As little boxes.
We dutifully send our resume, such as it is,
To every box that looks as though
It might not be a box.
And wait for the avalanche of replies, from bright-eyed people
Who, seeing our resume, will surely know
Our worth; even if, at this point, our worth seems
In question in our own eyes.
Avalanche? Not even a rolling stone. (Sorry about that, Bob.)

Time to go see all those people that our friend said we
ought to see.
You know: Bill, and Ed, and John, and Frances and Marty.
They seem slightly perplexed, as to why we've come,
And in the dark about exactly
Just exactly what they can do for us.
We try to take them off the hook; "I thought, friend of my friend,
Your company might need—of course, my experience *has*
Been limited, but I am willing, and I thought perhaps
that you..."

The interview drags on, downhill now, all the way
As our host finishes out their courtesy debt,
A debt not to us but to the friend that sent us; and we go.
Boy, do we go! over hill and valley and dale,
Talking to everyone who will listen,
Listening to everyone who will talk
With us; and thinking that surely there must be
Someone who knows how to crack the job-market;

This job-hunt seems the loneliest task in the world.
Is it this difficult for other people?
The answer is *YES*.

Are other people *this* discouraged, and desperate
And frustrated, and so low in self-esteem after
A spell of job-hunting?
The answer, unhappily, is
YES, YES, *YES.*

8

*Well, yes, you do have
great big teeth; but, never mind
that. You were great to at
least grant me this interview.*

Little Red Riding Hood

CHAPTER TWO

Rejection Shock

OUR NEANDERTHAL
JOB-HUNTING PROCESS

Sure, the preceding account of the job-hunt is rather bleak. But it has happened, is happening, and will continue to happen to countless millions of job-hunters in just the fashion described (or even worse). Including you and me.

Is it because we are different from other job-hunters? No. This happens to about 95% of all the people in this country who get involved in the job-hunt, at one time or other in their lives.

Let us put the matter simply and candidly: The whole process of the job-hunt in this country is Neanderthal. (Say it again, Sam.)

In spite of the fact that nearly every adult American man and, presently, some 45 million women have been or will be involved in the job-hunt at some time in their lives, we are condemned to go about the job-hunt as though we were the first person in this country to have to do it.

Year after year, our 'system' condemns man after man and woman after woman to go down the same path, face the same problems, make the same mistakes, endure the same frustrations, go through the same loneliness, and end up either still unemployed after an inordinately long period of time, or —

what is much more likely — underemployed, in the wrong field, at the wrong job, or well below the peak of our abilities. Neanderthal, indeed!

And when we turn to the "experts" in this field to say, "Show me a better way," we are chagrined to discover that the genuine experts (who *do* exist) are few and far between, and awfully difficult to find; while most of those whom the world accounts as experts (so-called "personnel people" or "human resource developers") are — in their quiet, meditative moments, and in their heart of hearts — *just as baffled by this job-hunt, and just as aware that they haven't yet come up with the answer to it, as we are.*

"Let's put it this way—if you can find a village without an idiot, you've got yourself a job."

From *The Saturday Review*, August 8, 1977. Reprinted by special permission.

This is never more clear than when *they themselves* are out of a job, and have to join the multitude in "pounding the pavements." You would think that they would absolutely be in their element, and know just precisely what to do. Yet the average executive (even the personnel executive) who yesterday was screening, interviewing, hiring any number of people, is just as much at a loss as anyone else *to know how to go about the job-hunt systematically, methodically, and successfully.*

Very often, the best plan they can suggest to themselves is the best plan they could suggest, in the past, to others: "The numbers game." That's right, the numbers game. It sometimes has a somewhat more sophisticated title (like, say, *systematic job search*), but in most cases this is what it comes down to, and this is what a number of experts are honest enough to call it.

THE NUMBERS GAME

In its original evolution, someone must have worked it all out, *backwards*. It wouldn't have been all that difficult. The logic would have gone like this:

For the job-hunter to get a job they really like, they need to have two or three job offers to choose among, from different employers.

In order to get two or three offers, the job-hunter probably ought to have *at least* six interviews at different companies.

In order to get six interviews he or she must mount a direct mail campaign, sending out x resumes to prospective employers, with covering letters, or whatever other kind of mail will titillate prospective employers and their screening committees (personnel department, executive secretaries, et al); like: telegrams, special delivery letters, or whatever. So, how many is "x"? Well surveys have indicated that each 100 resumes sent out will get 1-2[1], or 2-3[2] or 3-4[3] invitations for the job-hunter to come in for an interview, — the figure varying depending on which expert you are talking to, listening to or reading.

Consequently, the conclusion of this game is that you should send out at least 500 resumes, with some experts saying 1,000 or 1,200, and others saying that there is no limit: send out 10-15 each day, they say, keeping a card-file on them, recording the outcome — responses, completed interviews and so forth.

In a nutshell, that is The Numbers Game — the best that the

---

1. Executive Register, 72 Park Street, New Canaan, Conn. 06840, cited this figure.
2. Albee, Lou, *Job Hunting After Forty*, cites this figure (on his page 137).
3. Uris, Auren, *Action Guide for Executive Job Seekers and Employers*, cites this figure (on his page 149).

personnel system in this country has been able to come up with (except for a creative minority — more about them, later).

You like?

Most of the books you can pick up at your local bookstore for a fiver, or so, will sell you this game.

Most of the job counselors you can go to (paying fees up to $3,000 or higher) will sell you little more than this game — with maybe a little psychological testing and video-taped interview-role-playing thrown in.

Most of the personnel people in whose offices you may sit, will counsel you for nothing, . . . but *in this game.*

There may be a few variations here and there: and sometimes the old game is hidden under an exquisitely clever new vocabulary, so it sounds like a very different system. But you will suddenly awake to realize it is, in the end, The Little Ol' Game We've All Come To Love and Know So Well: Numbers.

HOW WELL DOES IT WORK?

Now, let's face facts: no matter how much of a gamble it sounds, for some people this numbers game works exceedingly well. They luck in. They end up with just the job they wanted, and they are ecstatically happy about the whole thing . . . especially if they were engaged in only aimless job-hunting behavior prior to stumbling upon this plan. This works just beautifully, by contrast — *for some people.*

For other people, this numbers game works passably. They end up with a job of sorts, and a salary, even though in retrospect it is not really the kind of work they had been hoping for, and the salary is quite a bit below what they really needed or wanted. But . . . a job is a job is a job. Parenthetically, the one thing that the job-hunt 'system' in this country does, and does exceedingly well, is scaring people to the point where they are more than willing to lower their self-esteem and hence their expectations as to what they will settle for. So, the numbers game works passably, so far as some people are concerned.

But for the vast majority of people who use this 'system' (some 80-95% of them, we guess) it just doesn't work at all — and most especially for those who are essentially aiming at a new career. Despite notable exceptions, as a group second-careerists have the most difficulty with this system.

Thus, some job-hunters have sent out 400, 500, 600, 700, 800 resumes or more, without getting one single invitation to come in for an interview. Only the polite acknowledgment ("thank you for yours of the sixteenth. We regret . . .") or the polite turndown ("we will however keep your resume on file (in the wastebasket!) and should anything . . ."), or — no answer whatsoever.

PEOPLE-IN-THE-FORM-OF-PAPER

Nor, from the *company's* point of view, is it difficult to see why. Some companies receive as many as 250,000 resumes in a year. And even small companies may receive as many as ten to fifteen a week. The employment world floats on a sea of resumes, as some experts have observed.[1] Hence, in dealing with resumes at employers' headquarters, the key word for the personnel department (and executive secretaries) is not selection, but *elimination*. (Of course, if you're agriculturally minded — or Biblically minded — you may prefer: *winnowing the crop*.) Here, to a particular organization, flows in this endless stack of People-in-the-Form-of-Paper, day after day. If you're working there, what do you do with the stack? Well, of course. You go through it, to see if you can get the stack down to more manageable size. You look to see who you can eliminate.

Who gets nominated for this dubious honor? Well, $140 a week file-clerks who are applying for a President's job. And $140,000 a year Presidents who are willing to settle for file-clerks' jobs. And resumes so poorly written you can't tell anything about the men or women behind them. And resumes so slickly written (usually by a hired professional) that you

---

1. Snelling, Robert, *The Opportunity Explosion*, p. 129.

can't tell anything about the men or women behind them. And...people applying for a job for which they look as though they have not had the necessary qualifying experience or credentials. Those resumes which have the greatest difficulty in getting through this Screening Process are those belonging to Zig Zag people, would-be career-changers who've accumulated a lot of experience in their old Zig profession, and now are trying to Zag. Their resumes, unless they are done extremely cleverly, find this Screening Out Process is a killer.

Well, all in all, how likely is your resume to survive the Process? A study of a number of different companies revealed that those companies sent out only one invitation to an interview for every 245 resumes that they received *on an average.* But this average represented a range between companies which consented to one interview for every 36 resumes they received, and companies which sent out only one invitation to an interview for every 1,188 re-sumes they received.[1] In terms of the first process that resumes are subjected to, therefore, the Screening Out Process searches for reasons to eliminate 35 out of every 36 resumes if we are lucky; or for reasons to eliminate on up to 1,187 out of every 1,188 resumes received if we're dealing with a tough company market.

You are of course free to doubt these statistics and decide they are simply unbelievable. Or, you may want to make your resume *the one that gets through.* Or, you may want to know a better system altogether than the Numbers Game. We will try to point out aids for all three groups: the Doubters, the System-beaters, and the Alternatives-seekers.

---

1. Deutsch, Shea & Evans, Inc. quoted on page 73 in *Electronic Design 16.*

REJECTION SHOCK

But, first of all, every job-hunter owes it to him- or herself to *understand* the system. What it is. How it works. What its limitations are. What its out-and-out defects are.

Why? Well, first of all, to save yourself from Rejection Shock. Rejection Shock occurs when you set out to look for a job, confidently follow all the instructions that you are given about the Numbers Game (via books, articles, friends and paid professionals) only to discover that none of this works *for you* and after a lengthy period of time you are still unemployed. You then go into Shock, characterized by a slow or rapid erosion of your self-esteem, a conviction that there is something wrong *with you,* leading to lower expectations, depression, desperation and/or apathy. This assumes, consequently, all the proportions of a major crisis in your life, your personal relations and your family, leading to loneliness, irritability, and withdrawal, where divorce is often a consequence and even suicide is not unthinkable.[1] *(One major executive career counselor did a survey of 15,000 clients, and discovered that 75% of them were either facing, in the midst of, or just out of, a marital divorce.)*[2]

Rejection Shock also occurs when you set out to look for a job, confidently follow all the instructions you are given about the Numbers Game, only to discover that this only *partially* works for you, and after a lengthy period of time (often) you have gotten a job in which you are *under-employed.* You are in the wrong field, or at the wrong job, or well below the peak of your abilities. You go into Shock, consequently, because you feel under-valued, ill-at-ease, underpaid and poorly-used, and you think you must be content with this under-employment *because something is fundamentally wrong with you.* In the midst of Shock, as you are, it never occurs to you that perhaps something is fundamentally wrong with *the whole job-hunting 'system' in this country.*

A NATIONAL TRAGEDY

It should be every job-hunter's high purpose to avoid not only the obvious devil of Un-employment, but also the less-

---

1. See Albee, Lou, *Job Hunting After Forty.*
2. In a study conducted by J. Frederick Marcy and Associates.

obvious devil of Under-employment, with every resource that is at your command. And, more than that, to determine to help others to understand the 'system,' so that they, too, may be spared the blight of these two devils.

Insiders estimate that, currently, 80% of our working people are Under-employed.[1] Or more. This is a national tragedy. But people submit to it because they regard Under-employment as preferable to Un-employment. They prefer pounding a typewriter to pounding the pavements.

And in this instinctive fear, they are quite right. Insiders again and again bring forth statistics which reveal that those who regard the job-hunt as an occasion for leaping to a better job are taking a big gamble, and especially so if they are either on in years (polite euphemism) or unemployed, or both. Witness these statistics with regard to men in particular:

Of the several thousand middle-aged men who lose their jobs this month, one year from now 80% will be unemployed, under-employed (at lesser salary than before), or eking out a private income, estimates one insider.[2]

Three million people are trying to get better jobs (at over $30,000 a year), and of these, 75% will not succeed in finding them — estimates another insider.[3]

A year from now, 20% of those middle-aged men who lose their jobs will still be unemployed.[4]

The cause *in large measure:* failure to understand the job-hunting system in this country.

The result: Rejection Shock.

Tragedy.

HOW TO USE THE NUMBERS GAME, INSTEAD OF BEING USED BY IT

A second reason why every job-hunter ought to understand the numbers game, in all its parts, is you may want to use *some*

---

1. California State University at Fullerton, in its *CP & PC News*, reported a sixteen year study of 350,000 job applicants, which concluded that 80% were in the wrong jobs. As did Herbert Greenberg, president of Marketing Survey and Research Corporation (*The Futurist*, August, 1978).

2. Albee, *op. cit.*, p. 3.

3. John C. Crystal.

4. Albee, *op. cit.*, p. 3.

parts of it to *supplement* your main program outlined in chapters 4 through 7.

A study of *The Job Hunt* by Harold L. Sheppard and A. Harvey Belitsky[1] revealed that the greater the number of auxiliary avenues used by the job-hunter, the greater the job-finding success. It makes sense, therefore, to know of *all* the avenues open to you, how they work and what their limitations are, so that you can choose *which* avenue or avenues you want to use, and *how* you want to use them. You will then be in the driver's seat about these matters, as you should be.

The parts of this game most commonly described are:

- mailing out your resume
- contacting executive search firms
- answering newspaper ads
- placing newspaper ads
- going to private employment (or placement) agencies
- going to the federal/state employment agency
- contacting college placement firms
- using executive registers or other forms of clearinghouses
- making personal contacts through friends, personal referrals and so forth.

Let us look at the virtues, and defects, of each of these, in rapid succession; to see why they usually don't work — and how you might get around their limitations. I will quote some statistics as I go along, in order to *illustrate* the aforementioned defects. You will note that some of these statistics are not, ahem, *current* — to put it gently. That's because the most recent study about this-or-that part of the numbers game was done some years ago, and no-one has thought to repeat that study since that time. But, *hey,* we're lucky to be able to refer to *any* study — even one that was some years back. And besides — believe me — the numbers game hasn't changed that much, since the studies cited. So, on with our exciting story.

---

1. In their book, *The Job Hunt: Job-Seeking Behavior of Unemployed Workers in a Local Economy.*

HEADHUNTERS, OTHERWISE KNOWN AS EXECUTIVE SEARCH FIRMS

If you play the numbers game, and especially if you pay someone to guide you in it, you will be told to send your resume to Executive Search firms. And what, pray tell, are *they?* Well, they are recruiting firms that are retained by employers. The very existence of this thriving industry testifies to the fact that employers are as baffled by our country's Neanderthal job-hunting 'system' as we are. Employers don't know how to find decent employees, any more than we know how to find decent employers. So, what do employers want executive recruiting firms to do? They want these firms to hire away from other firms or employers, executives, salespeople, technicians, or whatever, who are employed, and rising. From this, you will realize these head-hunting firms help create, and are dealing with, known vacancies. That's why, in any decent scatter-gun sending out of your resume, you are advised — by any number of experts — to be sure and include Executive Search firms. Not surprisingly, there are even a number of enterprising souls who make a living by selling lists of such firms.

You can get lists of such firms from:

1. The American Management Association, Inc., 135 West 50th Street, New York, NY 10020, in a list entitled *Executive Recruitment Organizations and Executive Job Counselling Organizations.* $2.

2. Performance Dynamics, Inc., Publishing Division, 300 Lanidex Plaza, Parsippany, NJ 07054 has a list entitled *The Performance Dynamics Worldwide Directory of Job-Hunting Contacts: A Guide to 2400 Employment Recruiters.* $9.95; $12.50 for the executive list. Prices subject to change.

3. Consultants News, Templeton Road, Fitzwilliam, NH 03347 has a Directory of Executive Recruiters which lists 1,224 search firms and offices in the U.S. and abroad. $10., prepaid. Updated annually.

The question is: do you *want* these lists, i.e., are they going to do you any good?

Well, let's say you regard yourself as at executive level, and so you decide to send recruiters your resume (unsolicited — they

EXECUTIVE RECRUITERS

Name: Executive recruitment consultants, executive
    recruiters, executive search firms, executive de-
    velopment specialists, management consultants.
Nicknames: head-hunters, flesh peddlers, body
    snatchers, talent scouts.
Number: estimated by James H. Kennedy, editor of
    Consultants News, to total 1,224.[1]
Volume of business: they have combined billings of
    more than $300 million a year, currently.[1]
Number of vacancies handled by a firm: each staff
    member can only handle 6-8 searches at a time
    (as a rule)[2]; so, multiply number of staff that a
    firm has (if known) times six. Majority of firms
are one-two staff (hence, are handling 5-10 current openings); a few are four to five staff
(20-25 openings are being searched for); and the
largest have staffs handling 80-100 openings.

didn't ask you to send it, you just sent it). The average Executive Recruitment Firm or Executive Search Firm may get as
many as 100 to 300 such resumes a week. Or letters. And, as we
see above, the majority may be handling five to ten *current
openings*, for which they are looking for executives who are
presently employed and rising.

Well okay, that Executive Recruiter is sitting there with 100
to 300 resumes in his or her hands, at the end of that week —
yours (and mine) among them. You know what's about to
happen to that stack of People-in-the-Form-of-Paper. That old
Elimination, Winnowing, or Screening Process again. Your

1. *Business Week*, May 5, 1980.
2. Butler, L. A., *Move In and Move Up*, pp. 160-61.

chances of surviving? Well, the first to get eliminated will be those who a) are not presently executives, or b) employed as such, or c) rising in their firm.

That's why even in a good business year, many experts say: *Forget it!* It is worth noting, however, that to every generalization there are exceptions; and *some* recruiters try to be helpful to job-hunters, even if the recruiter has no opening for them, by giving the job-hunters what they can: helpful advice, a steer in the right direction, a referral to some good job-hunting book (ahem!) and the like.

For further reading on this subject, see *Confessions of A Corporate Headhunter*, by Allan J. Cox (Pocketbooks, 630 Fifth Avenue, New York, NY 10020. 1974, 1973. $1.50, paper).[1]

ANSWERING
NEWSPAPER ADS

Experts will advise you, for the sake of thoroughness, to study the newspaper advertisements *daily* and to study *all of them, from A to Z* — because ads are alphabetized, in some sections, according to job title; and there are some very strange and unpredictable job titles floating around. Then if you see an ad for which you might qualify, even three quarters, you are advised to send off:

        a) your resume, OR
        b) your resume and a covering letter, OR
        c) just a covering letter.

In short, you're still playing the Numbers Game, when you answer ads. And the odds are stacked against you just about as badly as when you send out your resume scatter-gun fashion. How badly? (Better sit down before reading further.) A comparatively recent study conducted in two sample cities revealed (and I quote) "that 85 per cent of the employers in San

---

1. The job-hunter must be wary about firms which have the word "search" or "recruiter" in their title, as this does not necessarily mean a) that they really are recruiters, or b) that they can or will use such facilities (even if they have them) to aid you ... glittering promises (mostly verbal) notwithstanding. *The Los Angeles Times* back in November 1970 reported the indictment of an executive employment agency, for example, which ran ads saying "our clients are hungry for executives." In point of fact, however, records revealed that allegedly only one client of a total of 361 was ever placed.

Francisco, and 75 per cent in Salt Lake City, did not hire any employees through want ads" in a typical year. Yes, that said *any* employees, *during the whole year.*[1] Well, then, why are ads *run?* For the fascinating answer to that, read "Blind Ad Man's Bluff" in David Noer's *How to Beat The Employment Game.*[2]

NEWSPAPER ADS

Where Found:

    1. In the business section of the Sunday New York Times (Section 3) and the education section (Section 4); also in Sunday editions of Chicago Tribune and Los Angeles Times.

    2. In the business section (often found with the sports section) of your daily paper; also daily Wall Street Journal (especially Tuesday and Wednesday's editions).

    3. In the classified section of your daily paper (and Sunday's, too).

Jobs Advertised: usually those which have a clear-cut title, well-defined specifications, and for which either many job-hunters can qualify, or very few.

Number of Resumes received by Employer as Result of the Ad: 20-1,000, commonly.

Time It Takes Resumes to Come In: 48-96 hours. Third day is usually the peak day, after ad is placed.

Number of resumes NOT Screened Out: Only 2-5 out of every 100 (normally) survive. In other words, 95-98 out of every 100 answers are screened out.

---

1. Olympus Research Corporation, *A Study To Test the Feasibility of Determining Whether Classified Ads in Daily Newspapers are An Accurate Reflection of Local Labor Markets and of Significance to Employers and Job Seekers.* 1973. From: Olympus Research Corporation, 1290 24th Avenue, San Francisco, CA 94122.
2. Ten Speed Press, Box 7123, Berkeley, CA 94707. $4.95. Or at your local library.

THINGS TO BEWARE
ABOUT NEWSPAPER ADS

Blind ads (no company name, just a box number). These, according to some insiders, are particularly unrewarding to the job-hunter's time.

Fake ads (positions advertised which don't exist)—usually run by placement firms or others, in order to garner resumes for future use.

Phrases like "make an investment in your future" which mean you *have to put money down* (often quite a lot of thousands) to buy in, on the job.

Phone numbers in ads: don't use them except to set up an appointment. Period. ("I can't talk right now. I'm calling from the office.") Beware of saying more. Avoid getting screened out over the telephone.

Of course, you may be one who still likes to cover all bets, and if so, you want to know how *your* resume can be the one that gets through the Screening Process. (Let's be honest: answering ads *has* paid off, for *some* job-hunters.)

Most of the experts say, *if* you're going to play this game:

1. All you're trying to do, in answering the ad, is to get invited in for an interview (rather than getting screened out). Period. So, quote the ad's specifications, and tailor your resume or case history letter (if you prefer *that* to a resume) — so that *you* fit their specifications as closely as possible.

2. Omit all else from your response (so there is no further excuse for Screening you out).

3. *If* the ad requested salary requirements, some experts say ignore the request; others say, state a salary range (of as much as three to ten thousand dollars variation) adding the words "depending on the nature and scope of duties and responsibilities," or words to that effect. If the ad does not mention salary requirements, *don't you either.* Why give an excuse for getting your response Screened Out?

PLACING ADS YOURSELF
IN THE NEWSPAPER

Sometimes job-hunters try to make their availability known, by placing ads themselves in newspapers or journals.

PLACING ADS

Name of Ads (Commonly): Positions wanted (by the job-hunter, that is).

Found in: Wall Street Journal, professional journals and in trade association publications.

Effectiveness: Very effective in getting responses from employment agencies, peddlers, salesmen, and so forth. Practically worthless in getting responses from prospective employers, who rarely read these ads. But it *has* worked for some job-hunters.

Recommendation: If you take odds seriously, you'd better forget it. Unless, just to cover all bets, you want to place some ads in professional journals appropriate to your field. Study other people's formats first, though.

Cost: Varies.

ASKING PRIVATE EMPLOYMENT
AGENCIES FOR HELP

PRIVATE EMPLOYMENT
AGENCIES

Number: Nobody Knows. There are probably at least
8,000 private employment or placement agencies in the U.S.

Specialization: Many specialize in executives, financial, data processing, or other specialties.

Fees: Employer; or job-hunter may pay *but only
when and if hired.* Fees vary from state to state.
Tax deductible. In New York, for example, fee
cannot exceed 60% of one month's salary, i.e., a
$15,000 a year job will cost you $750. The fee
may be paid in weekly installments of 10% (e.g.,
$75 on a $750 total). In 80% of executives'
cases, employer pays the fee.

Contract: The application form filled out by the
job-hunter at an agency *is* the contract.

Exclusive handling: Generally speaking, don't give it,
even if they ask for it.

Nature of business: Primarily a volume business, requiring rapid turnover of clientele, dealing with
most-marketable job-hunters, in what one insider has called "a short-term matching game."

Effectiveness: In 1968, spokesman for Federal Trade
Commission announced average placement rate
for employment agencies was only 5% of those
who walked in the door. (That means a 95%
failure rate, right?)

PRIVATE EMPLOYMENT
AGENCIES continued

<u>Loyalty</u>: Agency's loyalty in the very nature of things must lie with those who pay the bills (which in most cases is the employer), and those who represent repeat business (again, employers).

<u>Evaluation</u>: An agency, with its dependency on rapid-turnover volume business, usually has not time to deal with *any* problems (like, career-transitions). *Possible exception for you to investigate:* a new, or suddenly expanding agency, which needs job-hunters badly if it is to get employers' business.

ASKING THE
FEDERAL-STATE
EMPLOYMENT SERVICE
FOR HELP

UNITED STATES
EMPLOYMENT SERVICE

Old Name: Was called USTES—United States Training and Employment Service, 2,400 offices in the country, used by 10.9 million yearly, in 1965, or 14% of the work force at that time; used by 9.9 million in 1970, or 11.5% of the work force.[1] Today, who knows?

Services: Most state offices of USES not only serve entry level workers, but also have services for professionals. Washington, D.C. had most innovative one. Middle management (and up) job-hunters still tend to avoid it.

(Footnote is on next page.)

UNITED STATES
EMPLOYMENT SERVICE
continued

Nationwide Network: In any city (as a rule) you can
inquire about job opportunities in other states
or cities, for a particular field. Also see Job Bank
(page 30.)

Openings: 8.3 million job vacancies listed with USES
in 1965; 6.7 million vacancies listed with them
in 1970.

Placements: Of the 10.9 million who used USES in
1965, allegedly less than 6.3 million (or 59%)
found placement. Of the 9.9 million who used it
in 1970, allegedly less than 4.6 million (or 46%)
found placement.[1] A survey in one area raised

some question about the quality of placement,
moreover, when it was discovered that 57% of
those placed in that geographical area by USES
were not working at their jobs anymore, just 30
days later.[2] (That would reduce the placement
rate to 20%, at best; an 80% failure rate. It's
probably closer to 13.7% placement rate, hence
an 86.3% failure rate.)

1. Quoted in the excellent study prepared by The Lawyer's Committee for Civil Rights
Under Law, Sarah Carey, Assistant Director, and The National Urban Coalition: *Fall-
ing Down on the Job: The United States Employment Service and the Disadvantaged,*
June, 1971.

2. The San Francisco Bay Area, for the period January 1966 thru April 1967, as reported in *Placement and Counseling In a Changing Labor Market: Public and Private
Employment Agencies and Schools.* Report of the San Francisco Bay Area Placement
and Counseling Survey, by Margaret Thal-Larsen. HR Institute of Industrial Relations,
UC Berkeley, August, 1970.

COLLEGE
PLACEMENT
CENTERS

COLLEGE PLACEMENT OFFICES

<u>Where Located</u>: Most of the 3,173 institutions of higher education in this country (1,211 are two-year community colleges, while 1,962 are four-year institutions) have some kind of placement function, however informal.

<u>Helpfulness</u>: Some are very good, because they understand that job-hunting will be a repetitive activity throughout the lives of their students; hence they try to teach an empowering process of self-directed job-hunting. Other offices, however, still think they have done their job if they have helped "each student find a job upon graduation," through the use of recruiters, bulletin board listings, and the like; i.e., if they help their students with this one job-hunt this one time.

<u>Evaluation</u>: Visit, to see whether they teach skills in "management by initiative," or only in "management by invitation." Not likely to be terribly helpful with alumni, though some, like UCLA's, are.

SUBSCRIBING TO
REGISTERS OR
CLEARINGHOUSES
OF VACANCIES

REGISTERS OR CLEARING-HOUSE OPERATIONS

These are attempts to set up "job exchanges" or a kind of bulletin board where employer and job-hunter can meet. The private clearinghouses commonly handle both employer and job-hunter listings, charging each.

Types: federal and private; general and specialized fields; listing either future projected openings, or present ones; listing employers' vacancies, or job-hunters' resumes (in brief), or both.

Cost to Job-Hunter: ranges from free, to $75 or more.

Effectiveness: A register may have as many as 13,000 clients registered with it (if it is a private opera-

tion), and (let us say) 500 openings at one time, from employer clients. Some registers will let employer know of every client who is eligible; others will pick out the few best ones. You must figure out what the odds are. A newer register *may* do more for you than an older one.

Loyalty: For most private registers, company pays the fee (like, 20% of first year's gross salary) if they hire a register client. As in case of private placement agencies, loyalty probably goes to those who pay bills, and offer repeat business.

continued

This is a very popular idea, and new entrants in the field are appearing constantly. On the following cards, we list some examples:

REGISTERS ETC.
continued

General Clearinghouse Listing Present Vacancies:
The State Employment Offices in over 43 states, comprising over three-quarters of the Nation's population, have allegedly set up a computerized (in most cities) *job bank* to provide daily listings of job openings in that city. If every employer cooperated and listed every opening they had, each day, it would be a great concept. Unhappily, employers prefer to fill many jobs above $11,000 in more personal, informal ways. So the Job Bank remains a rather limited resource for such jobs. *Can be a helpful research instrument*, however. A summary of the job orders placed by employers at Job Banks during

the previous month is published under the title of "Occupations In Demand At Job Service Offices." Available from: Consumer Information Center, Pueblo, Colorado 81009.
A Clearinghouse of Newspaper Ads: The idea of someone reading on your behalf the classified sections of a lot of newspapers in this country, and publishing a summary thereof on a weekly basis (or so), is not a new idea — but it is apparently growing increasingly popular. Problem: how old the ads may be by the time you the subscriber read them. That is the sum of the following times: a) the time it took for the hometown paper, in which the ad first appeared, to be sent to the town in which the clearing-

REGISTERS ETC.
continued

house operates; plus b) the time the clearinghouse held on to the ad, — especially if it just missed "last week's" edition of the clearinghouse Report; plus c) the time it took, after insertion in the Report, before the Report came 'off the press'; plus d) the time it took for the clearinghouse's Report to get across the country to you (discount this last, if you live in the clearinghouse's backyard; otherwise give this Large Weight, especially if it is not sent First Class/Airmail — or have you forgotten about our beloved Postal Service?); plus e) the time it takes to get your response from your town to the town in which the ad appeared.

You'll recall from page 21 that most classified ads receive more than enough responses within 96 hours of the ad's first appearing; how likely an employer is to wait for you to send in your response many days, or even weeks, later, is something you must evaluate for yourself — and weigh that against the cost of the service. If you want it, there are several places offering this service. Among the most reliable: The Wall Street Journal publishes a weekly compilation of "career-advancement postions" from its four regional editions. $2.50 an issue, available on some newsstands, or order from: National Business Employment Weekly, c/o The Wall Street Journal, 22 Cortlandt Street, New York, NY 10007.

REGISTERS, ETC.
continued

Clearinghouses for Junior and Community College Vacancies: The American Association of Junior Colleges is now sponsoring a job placement program for two-year college teachers, which is essentially a register. It costs $20, for individuals interested in teaching in a junior or community college to register. Address: AACJC Career Staffing Center, P.O. Box 298, 621 Duke St., Alexandria, Virginia 22314. Phone (703) 549-8020. Your name gets sent to 900 colleges, in December and April.

Community College Job Listing Service: Registrants are sent a list of vacancies in their field, each June. Their condensed resume is sent to community colleges in all the states they designated. P.O. Box M-1007, Ann Arbor, Michigan 48106. $25.

Registers in the Church: Intercristo is a national Christian organization that lists over 23,000 jobs, covering 4,600 vocational categories, available within about 700 Christian organizations in the U.S. or overseas. Their service, called Intermatch, costs the job-hunter $25. In 1979, one out of every twelve job-hunters who used this service found a job thereby. Their address is 19303 Fremont Avenue North, Seattle, WA 98133, and they have a toll-free telephone number: (800) 426-1342.

Other Registers or Clearinghouses: Are these registers or are they not? If job-listings exist all by themselves, they tend to be legitimately called "registers." If they exist within the framework of a journal or magazine which also contains other material, they tend to be called "ads." The following list straddles both sides: [1]

For Social Occupations: Volunteers for Educational and Social Services, 3001 S. Congress Ave., Austin, TX 78704 publishes a list of jobs available. The National Association of Social Workers, Personnel Information, 1425 H Street, N.W., Suite 600, Washington, DC 20005 publishes a listing of clearinghouses, called *Job Opportunities in Social Work*. The Family Service Association of America, 44 E. 23rd Street, New York, NY 10010 publishes *Social Casework*, a journal which includes listings of jobs with social agencies.

For Jobs with Youth or Children: The Child Care Personnel Clearinghouse, Box 548, Hampton, VA 23669 publishes a biannual list called *Help Kids*. The Child Welfare League of America, 67 Irving Place, New York, NY 10003 publishes *Child Welfare*, which includes job ads for people who want to work with children.

For Jobs Outdoors: The Association of Interpretative Naturalists, 6700 Needwood Rd, Derwood, MD 20855 publishes a monthly listing of jobs; the list costs $10. The Natural Science for Youth Foundation, 16 Holmes Street, Mystic, CT 06355 publishes a bi-monthly job-listing, called *Opportunities*; the list costs $15. Colorado Outward Bound School, 945 Pennsylvania Street, Denver, CO 80203 publishes a nationwide "Jobs Clearing House" list.

---

1. My thanks to my friend, John William Zehring, Director of Career Planning and Placement at Earlham College, for help with this list.

One final word about registers: the very term "clearing-house" or "register" can be misleading. The vision: one central place where you can go, and find listed every vacancy in a particular field of endeavor. *But, sorry, Virginia; there ain't no such animal.* All you'll find by going to any of these places is *A Selected List* of some of the vacancies. But only some.

So far as finding *jobs for people* are concerned, these clearinghouses and agencies (like employment agencies) really end up finding *people for jobs*. (Think about it!) Heart of gold though they *may* have, these agencies serve employers better than they serve the job-hunter.

And yet there are always *ways* of using such registers to gain valuable information for the job-hunter and to suggest places where you may wish to *start* your information interviewing (about which, more in chapter 6. So, at the least, the Federal job bank (if there is one in your city), and perhaps a relatively inexpensive Register (if there is one in your particular field) can serve as *auxiliaries* to your job-search.

OTHER IDEAS

Your Resume in a Book: Some organizations circulate small booklets which are essentially mass distribution of people's resumes, in precise form. Forty-Plus Clubs do this, through their *Executive Manpower Directory*. So do some of the executive registry places. Evaluation as to its worth to you as job-hunter: well, it's a gamble, just like everything else in this Numbers Game system. A real gamble, if you are trying to start a new career. You have to boil your resume down to a very few words, normally. And then decide if you stand out. If not, forget it. If yes, well...maybe.

OTHER IDEAS

Off-Beat Methods: Mailing strange boxes to company
presidents, with strange messages (or your resume) inside; using sandwich board signs and
parading up and down in front of a company;
sit-ins at a president's office, when you are
simply determined to work for *that* company,
association, or whatever. You name it — and if
it's kooky, *it's been tried.* Sometimes it has paid
off. Kookiness is generally ill-advised, however.
$64,000 question every employer must weigh: if
you're like this *before* you're hired, what will
they have to live with *afterward*?

To summarize the effectiveness of all the preceding methods in a table (you do like tables, don't you?), we may look at the results of a survey the Bureau of the Census made. The survey, made in 1972 and published in the *Occupational Outlook Quarterly* in the winter of 1976, was of ten million jobseekers.

USE AND EFFECTIVENESS OF
JOB SEARCH METHODS

Method	Usage*	Effectiveness Rate**
Applied directly to employer	66.0%	47.7%
Asked friends about jobs where they work	50.8	22.1
Asked friends about jobs elsewhere	41.8	11.9
Asked relatives about jobs where they work	28.4	19.3
Asked relatives about jobs elsewhere	27.3	7.4
Answered local newspaper ads	45.9	23.9
Answered nonlocal newspaper ads	11.7	10.0
Private employment agency	21.0	24.2
State employment service	33.5	13.7
School placement office	12.5	21.4
Civil Service test	15.3	12.5
Asked teacher or professor	10.4	12.1
Went to place where employers come to pick up people	1.4	8.2
Placed ad in local newspaper	1.6	12.9
Placed ad in nonlocal newspaper	.5	***
Answered ads in professional or trade journals	4.9	7.3
Union hiring hall	6.0	22.2
Contacted local organization	5.6	12.7
Placed ads in professional or trade journals	.6	***
Other	11.8	39.7

   * Percent of total jobseekers using the method.
  ** A percentage obtained by dividing the number of jobseekers who found work using the method, by the total number of jobseekers who used the method, whether successfully or not.
*** Base less than 75,000

Well, anyway, Mr. or Ms. Job-hunter, this just about covers the favorite job-hunting system of this country *at its best*. (Except personal contacts, which we give special treatment — Chapter 6.)

If it works for you, right off, *great!* But if it doesn't, you may be interested in *the other plan* — you know, the one they had saved up for you, in case all of this didn't work? Small problem: with most of the experts in our country, *there is no other plan.* And that is that.

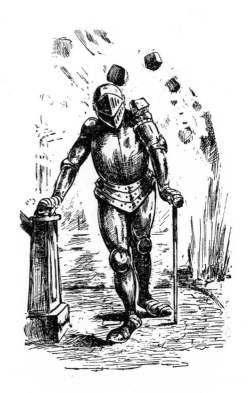

Any new theory first is attacked as absurd; then it is admitted to be true, but obvious and insignificant; finally—it seems to be important, so important that its adversaries claim that they themselves discovered it!—

William James

CHAPTER THREE

You Can Do It!

YOU *CAN* DO IT

If you decided to hop around in this book, rather than reading it from the very beginning, the odds are great that this is one of the first chapters you decided to look at—right?

So for those who have just joined us, we will summarize what has transpired thus far in our saga. Through all the preceding pages, two facts have stood out—like Mt. Everest—above all others:

(1) The whole job-hunting system in this country is a big fat gamble, in which the dice are loaded against *any* job-hunter who wants more than "just a job." *Any* job-hunter.

(2) The job-hunting system in this country poses especial difficulties for *all those who seek to change careers* — And that is, according to statistical studies, four out of every five job-hunters, before their life is through.

Now, on with our story.

There are a few heroes in this country, who belong to what might be called "the creative minority" in this whole field. They are a very diverse group. Some of them live in the big city; some out in the country. Some teach and do research at universities; others are professional career counselors. But, despite these outward differences, these unsung heroes have at least two denominators in common, maybe three:

First of all, they have refused to accept the idea that the job-hunting system has to be as bad as it is, or as much of an outright gamble as it is.

Secondly, instead of just criticizing the system, they have sat down and figured out how it could be done better. (They are pragmatists, before they are theoreticians.) And, not too surprisingly, they have all come up with methods which are strikingly similar to one another.

Third, in spite of widely teaching their methods over a number of years and in a number of places to the everlasting benefit of job-hunters near and far, they have been *studiously ignored* by the "manpower / human resources development /

personnel / experts" in this country, from the Federal government on down (or up, depending on your point of view).

For *any* job-hunter, this creative minority and their insights are important.

But when it comes time for you to seek another career, you will discover this creative minority and their insights are absolutely crucial.

THE CREATIVE MINORITY'S DIAGNOSIS

What, then, is it that makes the present job-hunting system in this country so disastrous? That was the question which the creative minority, wherever they were, first asked themselves. What are the fatal *assumptions* that are so casually made by job-hunters everywhere, to their ultimate detriment and hurt? To the creative minority, the fatal assumptions seemed to be these:

√ *Fatal Assumption No. 1: The job-hunter doesn't need to work very hard at the job-hunt, and can settle for devoting just a few hours a week to the task, since something will always turn up eventually anyway; moreover, the job-hunter can pretty well "go it alone" while hunting.* Not true, said the creative minority. There are people who have been on the unemployment rolls for two years or more because they gave their job-hunt just "a lick and a promise," confident that "something will turn up." Common sense, as well as actual experiments, demonstrate that the harder you work at the job-hunt, the shorter will be the length of your unemployment — other things being equal. Experience dictates that you can't wait for something to come to you; you must go to it. Moreover, experience dictates that it is easier, by far, to keep your nose to the grindstone with respect to the job-hunt, if you solicit the company and support of other job-hunters or at least of other friends.

√ *Fatal Assumption No. 2: The job-hunter should remain somewhat loose (i.e., vague) about what he or she wants to do, so that they are free to take advantage of whatever vacancies may be available.* Good grief, said the creative minority, this is why we have so great a percentage of Under-employment in this country. If you don't state just exactly what you want to do, first of all to yourself, and then to others, you are (in effect) handing over that decision to others. And others, vested with such awesome responsibility, are either going to dodge the decision or else make a very safe one, which is to define you as capable of doing only such and such a level of work (a safe, no risk diagnosis).

√ *Fatal Assumption No. 3: The job-hunter should not spend any time identifying the organizations that might be interested in him or her (no matter in what part of the country they may be), since employers have all the initiative and the upper hand in this whole process.* Nonsense, said the creative minority. This isn't a high school prom, where the job-hunters are sitting around the edge of the dance-floor, like shy wallflowers, while the employers are whirling around out in the center of the floor, and enjoying all the initiative. In many cases, those employers are stuck with partners (if we may pursue the metaphor) who are stepping on their toes, constantly. As a result, although the employer in theory has all the initiative as to whom they choose to dance with, in actuality they are often praying *someone will pay no attention to this silly rule, and come to their rescue by cutting in.* And indeed, when someone does take the initiative with the employer, rather than just sitting on the sidelines with *I'll-be-very-lucky-if-you-choose-me* written all over their face, the employer cannot help thinking *I-am-very-lucky-that-this-one-has-chosen-me.* People who cut in are usually pretty good dancers.

√ *Fatal Assumption No. 4: Employers see only people who can write well.* Pretty ridiculous, when it's put that way. But, said the creative minority, isn't that just exactly what our present job-hunting system is based on? To get hired, you must get an interview. To get an interview, you must let the personnel department see your resume first. Your resume will be screened out (and the interview never granted), if it doesn't make you sound good. But the resume is only as good as your writing ability (or someone else's) makes it. If you write poorly, your resume is (in effect) a Fun House mirror, which distorts you out of all proportion, so that it is impossible to tell what you really look like. *However, no allowance is made for this possibility, by personnel departments, except maybe one out of a thousand.* Your resume is assumed to be an accurate mirror of you. You could be Einstein or Golda Meir, but if you don't write well (i.e., if you write a terrible resume) you will not get an interview. Employers only see people who can write well. Ridiculous? You bet it is. And, say the creative minority, this is an assumption which is long overdue for a rest. It just doesn't have to be this way.

THE CREATIVE MINORITY'S PRESCRIPTION

Once the fatal assumptions of the present system were accurately defined, it wasn't all that difficult to create a new prescription. Once you have said that the fatal assumptions are: that the job-hunter doesn't need to work very hard at the job-hunt, that the job-hunter should stay vague, that employers have all the initiative as to where a job-hunter works, and that employers only see people who write well, the prescription almost writes itself, as to *the new assumptions that are the key to success:*

Key No. 1: You must decide that job-hunting will be for you a full-time job (unless you are currently employed, in which case you will still give it every spare hour possible); and that you will use group support in your job-hunting as much as you can.

Key No. 2: You must decide just exactly what you want to do.

Key No. 3: You must decide just exactly where you want to do it, through your own research and personal survey.

Key No. 4: You must research in some depth the organizations that interest you and then approach the one individual or committee in each organization who has the power to hire you for the job that you have decided you want to do.

"Organization" is used here as an all-inclusive term embracing businesses, industry, colleges, government, agencies, associations, foundations, churches or whatever.

For any job-hunter who wants more than "just-a-job," is rather seeking that job which employs their abilities and interests at the highest level possible, the above prescription of the creative minority is crucial.

But for the job-hunter who is trying to strike out in some new directions, or who must of necessity do some different things than they have done heretofore, the prescription of the creative minority is careerwise *a matter of life and death.* It will be a rare career-changer, indeed, who seeks employment without paying attention to these steps in the job-hunting process, and does not wind up Unemployed or, worse, Under-employed.

THE DEMAND
FOR THIS KNOWLEDGE

According to a study published by Future Directions for a Learning Society, more than 40 million Americans are currently in some stage of career transition or job-change.[1] It is hardly any surprise then, that social scientists and futurists as well as vocational experts are continually telling us that workers must be prepared to change careers several times in their lives.

Some careers have a certain limit, such as baseball players or opera singers, after which the person *has* to change careers. Some careers have a high "burn-out rate," such as traveling salespeople, teachers, and the like. They are jobs which some people, at least, cannot find the energy and enthusiasm to do for more than a certain number of years, after which the person *wants* to change careers. And some careers get phased out by our society, such as buffalo-skinners, buggy whip makers, blacksmiths, and such. It is true there are still a few people around, who are practicing the trade; but by and large the career has been phased out by society and history. After which, those who practiced that craft are *forced* to change careers. And then, some careers are still around, affording employment to a large number of people — but historically showing a dramatic decrease in numbers, compared to those who were once thus employed. The American farmer, of old, and the American automobile assembly-line worker presently, are examples which spring instantly to mind. In which case, career change is forced

1. Aslanian, Carol B., and Brickell, Henry M., *Americans in Transition: Life Changes As Reasons for Adult Learning.* 1980. Also: Arbeiter, Solomon; Aslanian, Carol B.; Shmerbeck, Frances A.; and Brickell, Henry M., *40 Million Americans in Career Transition; The Need for Information.* 1978.

upon those displaced — a bitter pill when they see others still thriving in the career they once loved.

Career change is also an issue for those who are forcibly retired, as at a certain age, but still want to work creatively at *something*. And it is an issue for those who voluntarily retire, as from the military, but at such a young age (comparatively) that they feel they *must* seek a career.

It is not difficult to understand why the number of Americans in transition at any given moment is 40 million. And the statistics in Canada and other countries are probably similar.

It has, unhappily, taken our educational system — particularly higher education — a painfully long time to become aware that its average student is going to change careers two or three times in their lifetime. We still, as a learning society, train people to do just one thing, encourage them to become specialists — and then we wonder at their agonized cry when they discover, one day, that their specialty is no longer what they can, or want to, do. Our country's only solution for them, at that moment, is to urge that they go back to school and get retrained all over again for another specialty. Never mind how much time it takes, or how much money. Never mind whether they are re-tracing their steps, picking up skills which they already possess. And never mind how short-lived this new specialty of theirs may turn out to be, in terms of the market-place and its demand. This is still the solution that our country typically urges, from Congress on down, when faced with the problem of career change. Band-aids.

CAREER AND LIFE PLANNING:
AN OVERVIEW OF THE ART

In protest against this shortsightedness, there has grown up a field called by many names, but known generally as *career and life planning*. The purpose of this new "art" — for that is what many regard it as being, rather than a science — is to take a longer view of your life — so that you can avoid short-term, band-aid thinking. It involves building in Alternative Options into any plans that you make, from the very beginning. Like: in high school or college.

The art is really just the systematic teaching of the four principles outlined above, along with some expansion of their major ideas, and the application of them to other arenas besides work.

You can find this new art being practiced everywhere. Its popularity has snowballed in recent years. You will find it in college courses, night schools, weekend seminars, workshops, conferences, human growth centers, displaced homemakers centers, annual conventions, on tape, in books, and — like that.

Given the present course of history, it seems that career and life planning is something we are all going to have to do quite a bit of, unless we want to be helpless victims, tossed on the stormy sea of change hither and yon. Actually, it's not all that hard to get involved with career and life planning. Because, if you go about identifying *what it is you want and what it is you want to do* — not only for the immediate present but at least a little bit beyond that — you *are* doing life planning. The minute you think out, or write down, some short- or long-term goals for yourself, you are into it. All that the art does is to systematize it, give you some tools for getting at it, and give you the benefit of other people's experience.

Unhappily, some of what passes for career planning in this country, taught by good-willed people at that, is not very well thought out. Some people think that because it's called "career and life planning," it *must* be good. Let's be clear about that, right now: *there is no magic in the name.* Some people have gone away to seminars or courses billed as — well, there are a whole list of possible names:

LONG RANGE CAREER DEVELOPMENT

LONG TERM HELP IN CAREER PLANNING

FULL CAREER PLANNING

STUDYING YOUR CAREER PATTERNS

FULL CAREER PROGRAM

CRITICAL ASSESSMENT OF ONESELF AND ONE'S FUTURE

LONG RANGE ACTION PLANNING

SELF-COUNSELING AND PLANNING

SELF-CONFRONTATION AND DESIGN

DEALING WITH WHAT I WILL BECOME, AS

WELL AS WITH WHAT I WILL DO.

HUMAN RESOURCES PLANNING

VOCATIONAL DEVELOPMENT PROCESS

LONG RANGE LIFE PLANNING

Anyway, by whatever name, people attending seminars or courses in this "art" have come back "happy"— but just as confused and uncertain about what they want to do as they were before they went.

So, before we turn to our four principles — distilled from the experience of successful job-hunters and career-changers and from successful career planning *systems* — let us set this definition clearly before us, and keep it before us, as we go:

For you, career and life planning is useless, unless at the end of your homework, you are very definite about exactly what you want to do—for at least the immediate future.

*L*ife is what happens while
you're making other plans.
— Tom Smothers

CHAPTER FOUR

You Must
Keep At It

THE FIRST KEY
TO CAREER PLANNING
AND JOB-HUNTING

First *means* first, as in "most important." This is the first key because it is the most important. It is to this that I always point, when people say to me, "Well, you've studied successful job-hunters and successful job-hunting systems: what, in your opinion, is the most important secret of successful job-hunting or career-changing?"

The answer is simple: keeping at it. Successful job-hunters are those who keep at the task of job-hunting, with a vengeance. Successful job-hunting systems are those which have figured out a way to help the job-hunter keep at it.

I first noticed this factor, when several job-hunting systems were brought to my attention, each of which had a fantastically high success rate. I studied their characteristics, supposing that I would find certain common denominators. I did not. They were as different as night and day. Some spent all their time getting the job-hunter to do homework. Some spent all their time getting the job-hunter to turn up "leads" to prospective employers. Some spent all their time rehearsing, and video-taping, the actual hiring-interview. Yet, despite such diversity, all reported a very high success rate. Why? I asked myself.

Upon examination, it turned out that all of them had one characteristic in common, which I had at first overlooked. All of them treated job-hunting as, in itself, a full-time job. All of them had the job-hunter come in, Monday through Friday, from 9 in the morning, until 4 or 5 in the afternoon. Some even had the job-hunter punch in, on a timeclock, at the beginning of the day, and punch out, on a timeclock, at the end of each day . . . just as they might do at a real job.

Thus did I begin to suspect that it was the very act of keeping at it, that was the most important aspect of any "system." I still believe that. Simple logic would suggest that the more time you spend out on the street job-hunting, the more doors you will knock on. The more doors you knock on, the more employers you are likely to see. The more employers you get in to see, the more interviews you will have. The more interviews you have, the more job-offers you are likely to receive. The more job-offers you receive, the more likely it is that one of these will be a job you like the sound of. Thus, you accept that offer, and your job-search is successfully concluded.

Let us suppose that when you are job-hunting, you decide — on the basis of the above argument — that you will go out job-hunting from 9 a.m. to 5 p.m. every day, Monday through Friday. Within four weeks, then, you will have spent seven hours a day (an hour off for lunch) for twenty days job-hunting, or a total of 140 hours. Contrast this with the behavior of the average job-hunter, who — according to the Census Bureau — in two-thirds of the cases, spends less than five hours a week in job-search activities. In four weeks, that adds up to only twenty hours of job-hunting.[1]

Small wonder, then, that two additional studies revealed that the average job-hunter contacts only six potential employers directly in the period of a month, and in one-third of the cases, only ten potential employers in a period of seven weeks. [2]

If you decide to treat your job-hunt or career-change as a full-time job, and devote full-time to it, you will be spending seven times as many hours upon it, as do two-thirds of all job-hunters. Thus, you increase your chances of success seven-fold. Not six potential employers contacted in person during a month's time, but — potentially — forty-two. Not ten employers contacted in seven weeks time, but — potentially — seventy.

And, as you will recall from the table on page 36, applying directly to an employer is *the single most effective* method of job-hunting.

Let me give all this theory some substance by relating to you not *The Tale of Two Cities* but *The Tale of Two Job-hunters in the Same City*. Joan and Ralph were job-hunters, who lived in the same city. What was of interest was that they were both trying to change careers, to go into a field they had had no experience in, both of them had similar backgrounds, had similar degrees of expertise, and were of similar ages. And both of them were job-hunting at the same time. Joan went out every day, Monday through Friday. Eight-thirty found her leaving her

1. Robert G. Wegmann, "Job Search Assistance Programs: Implications for the School," in *Phi Delta Kappan*, December 1979, p. 271ff.

2. Robert G. Wegmann, "Job-Search Assistance: A Review" in the *Journal of Employment Counseling*, December 1979, p. 212.

house each morning. Nine o'clock found her knocking on the office door, without appointment, of the first employer — or potential employer — on her list. That employer would usually suggest someone else she ought to visit, and in many cases, would make an enabling phone call to prepare the way for her, while she was still there in that office. She continued calling, with an hour off for lunch, all day long. She repeated this sort of schedule each day of the week. Within ten days, she had four bona fide job offers, one of which she accepted, because it was precisely what she was looking for. Ralph, on the other hand, had been conducting his job-search for nine months, without success. He had done all the exercises in this book, knew what his skills were, and what kind of job he wanted — in the same field as Joan's — but he only devoted an hour or two to his job-hunt, two or three days each week. The rest of the time was spent on errands, cleaning house, visiting his friends, and complaining how impossible it was to find a new career in today's job market. Most of the time that he did devote to his job-hunt was spent in sending out resumes, with covering letters, and then anxiously visiting his mail box each afternoon to see if anyone had replied.

Now, I would not like to be misunderstood as claiming that if you devote full-time to your job-hunt you will have a job in ten days. Though that *does* happen. Nor would I like to be misunderstood as claiming that if you don't devote full-time to the hunt, you will be out of work nine months. Though *that* does happen. But, flukes and luck aside, there often is a direct correlation between the amount of time devoted to the job-hunt, and the speed with which you will find not just *a* job, but *the* sort of job that you are most anxious to find. And that is that.

JOB-HUNTING
WHILE YOU ARE STILL
EMPLOYED

All of the foregoing, of course, assumes that you are unemployed, and hence have complete freedom as to how you allot your time. But what do you do about the job-hunt or career change, if you are presently holding down a full-time job?

Good question. That is the case in which many find themselves. How many? Well, the government, bless its heart, did a study of job-hunting among employed workers about five years ago, and discovered that in a typical month (it was May of 1976) 4.2% of all employed workers, or nearly one out of every twenty, went looking for another job sometime during that month. In actual numbers, that represented 3,269,000 people who were job-hunting while still employed.[1] If the same percentage obtains today, it means 4,074,000 are employed but job-hunting.

I would like to point out two things about this finding. First of all, it means that one-third of all job-hunters are conducting the search while they are still employed. (How did that conclusion get reached? By assuming that those unemployed and seeking work are as the government says — 8,019,000 at this writing — and adding to that figure the number above of 4,074,000, which yields a total of 12,093,000 job-seekers currently — of which 4,074,000, or one-third, are job-hunting while still employed.)

Secondly, if over 4 million are thus job-hunting in a typical month, one can imagine how much larger that figure would be for an entire year. This helps to explain the statistics uncovered

---

1. *The Extent of Job Search by Employed Workers.* March, 1977. Special Labor Force Report 202. Published by the U.S. Department of Labor, Bureau of Labor Statistics; available from any of their regional offices.

in other studies, which reveal that the average non-agricultural firm in this country has to hire — in a typical year — as many new people as it has employees. In other words, a firm with three employees will probably have to hire two or three employees each year. A firm with 100 employees will probably have to hire 90 new employees each year. That's on the average. If you want a more detailed breakdown, it works out like this: the average retail firm with say 100 employees may have to hire 136 new people each year; the average firm dealing in services and having say 100 employees may have to hire 111 new employees each year; the average financial institution, 74; the average manufacturing firm, 65; the average transportation or public utilities company, 32; and the average construction company, a whopping 202 new employees for every 100 it currently has.[1]

It is this job-hunting behavior on the part of employed workers which helps to create so many vacancies — thus increasing every job-hunter's chance of success so dramatically.

How do employed job-hunters go about their search? You guessed it: the same way unemployed job-hunters do. According to the government's study, 70% of all employed job-hunters contacted an employer directly. But, back to our original question: how do you find time to do the job-hunt if you are presently holding down a full-time job? We have asked employed job-hunters how they did it, and the sum of their advice to you — based on their experience — is:

(1) Determine to keep at it, with every spare hour you can find. Press evenings, weekends, lunch hours and the like, into the service of your job-hunt.

(2) Use evenings and weekends to do the original homework, figuring out what your skills are and what it is you want to do, as well as where you want to do it. Later on in your job-search, use evenings and the weekend also to write thank you notes, send out letters, and the like.

(3) For the actual calling upon potential employers, if they are in the city where you presently work, press your lunch hours into service. If you "brown-bag it," you will have time to

---

1. Wegmann, *op. cit.*, pp. 208-209. Wegmann quotes statistics for one quarter of the year, which I have multiplied by four. It is arguable that a quarter may not be typical; hence I have used the word "may" in describing annual hires.

make and keep one appointment, particularly if your intent is to make the interview no longer than twenty minutes — a good idea, in any case, for the exploratory or information interview. People take lunch hours at all different times: 11:15 a.m., 11:45, 12 noon, 12:30, 1 p.m. While you are on your lunch hour, somebody you want to see hasn't gone to lunch yet, or has just come back. Sometimes you can move your lunch hour — if the place where you are presently working is flexible about that — to the 11 a.m. to 12 noon time slot.

(4) Press late afternoons into service. Many people you will want to see are on an executive or management level, and they often do not get away from their offices promptly at 5. It is appropriate to estimate how long it will take you to get across town to them, and ask them if they could see you that long after your quitting time, on a particular day.

(5) Press holidays into service. Holidays fall into two classes: those which everyone observes, like Christmas and New Year's Day; and those which some people observe, like Washington's Birthday, etc. In the case of the latter kind of holiday, if you have it off, you will sometimes be able to visit the people you want to see, because they do not have it off.

(6) Press Saturdays into service. Sometimes the people you want to see work on Saturday, or are occasionally willing to set up appointments for Saturday.

(7) Press your sick-leave into service. In some organizations, workers accumulate sick-leave, and have the right to take it as time off. If that is the case with you, use such days off judiciously, to visit potential employers who interest you.

(8) Press your vacations into service. If you are dead-serious about the importance of your job-hunt or career change, it is not too great a sacrifice to devote one year's vacation time to your job-hunt. This is especially important if you are trying to secure employment in a distant city. Schedule your vacation in that city, and make arrangements and appointments, by letter and phone, ahead of time (see chapter six, on how to research a place at a distance).

(9) If you have sufficient savings, the following stratagem may be one you would like to consider in addition to all the above: if you have a whole list of people and places you need to visit, and you require a concentrated period of time in which to do this, and cannot wait until your vacation time, you have the

right to ask your present employer if you can have a leave of
absence without pay. So long as the time requested is no longer
than a week or so, and so long as it is scheduled at the
convenience of the employer (i.e., not in the week that they
need you the most), this request will often be honored. You can
give, as the reason, the simple truth: Personal Business.

Should you feel guilty about job-hunting while you are still
employed? Well sure, if you want to. But there is no need.
One-third of all job-hunters are doing the same thing: it is a
common practice in our economy. Nothing odd-ball about it.
Moreover, remember these simple truths: Your employer has
certain rights, including the right to fire you at any time, for
sufficient cause; moreover, they have the right to prepare for
this act of firing ahead of time, laying the groundwork, transfer-
ring part of your work to other colleagues, etc. You, as employee, likewise have certain rights, including the right to quit
at any time, for sufficient cause; moreover, you have the right
to prepare for this act of quitting ahead of time, laying the
groundwork through interviewing and job-searching.

JOB-HUNTERS
ANONYMOUS

The secret of success for all job-hunters — employed or
unemployed — is (to use my rich skills at overkill): keeping at
it. Devoting every hour you can to the task. Having said that,
however, we can press on to our next truth about job-hunting
or career-changing. Namely: it is very difficult to mount a
sustained effort when you are job-hunting all by yourself.
Motivation flags, energies get diluted, and frequently — to use a
common expression — we run out of gas.

It is no wonder then that during the past decade, one of the
most interesting developments within the field of job-hunting
has been the rapid growth of job-hunting groups. Even as we
have seen, in this country, the spawning of Alcholics Anonymous, Overeaters Anonymous, and the like, so now we are seeing the springing up of a kind of Job-hunters Anonymous:
job-hunters seeking out their fellow job-hunters, and banding
together for the purpose of helping each other with the task.

It is as though job-hunters were saying: well, if I can't keep at
this task all by myself, I'll find a support-group which will help
me to keep at it.

These group-job-hunting organizations vary widely in their program, scheduling and techniques. But all of them are indebted, in one degree or another, to:

Nathan Azrin's Job-Finding Clubs or Job Clubs, which were spawned in Carbondale, Illinois, thence New York City (Harlem), New Brunswick, Milwaukee, Wichita and Tacoma, and now in many places throughout the country;

and/or Charles Hoffman's Self-Directed Placement Corporation (SDP) which began in San Diego, then commenced similar operations in Tucson, Indianapolis and Baltimore;

and/or Joseph Fischer's and Albert Cullen's Job Factory, in Cambridge and Worcester, Massachusetts;

and/or Forty Plus Clubs, which were founded in New York City, Philadelphia, Washington D.C., Chicago, Milwaukee, Houston, Denver, Los Angeles, the Bay Area (Oakland) of California, and Hawaii;

and /or similar job-hunting groups, such as have existed for years — created and run by the government (as, through CETA programs), or by various professional societies (such as IEEE, AIAA, etc.), or by various career professionals (Bernard Haldane, John Crystal, etc.).

Group-job-hunting is clearly an idea whose time has come.

NATHAN AZRIN'S
MODEL
FOR GROUP-JOB-HUNTING

The most popular model, by far, is currently Nathan Azrin's idea of Job-Finding Clubs. The idea is being replicated throughout the country; at this writing there are 100 such clubs.

Dr. Azrin started these clubs in Carbondale, Illinois, when he was Director of Research at the Anna State Hospital in Anna, Illinois (he is currently on the staff of Nova University, in Fort Lauderdale, Florida). The idea was subsequently tested across the country by the Department of Labor, with (in my opinion) spectacular success.

If you are interested in the history of that success, you can write to the National Technical Information Service, Springfield VA 22151, and for $5.25 they will send you Report PB 287-332: "Final Report to U.S. Department of Labor: The Job Finding Club," Nathan H. Azrin, Ph.D., Principal Investigator.

If you are job-hunting or career-changing and want to become a member of a group based on the Azrin model, there are three ways you can go about doing this:

(1) You can inquire from your local federal/state employment office, and/or your county CETA office, and/or (Dr. Azrin's) National Office of Program Development, Robert A. Philip, Director, 202 Canterbury Drive, Carbondale, IL 62901, as to whether or not there is a Job-Finding Club already in existence in your area. If so, find its address, and go join.

(2) If there is no Club in your area, the National Office of Program Development will (for a fee) train some professional in your area in how to set up such a Club.

(3) If you and some other job-hunters in your area have no funds for such training, but want to set up a Job-Finding Club after the Azrin model on your own, there is a manual which you can get

that will give you complete instructions. It is called the *Job Club Counselor's Manual*, and is available for $14.95 from University Park Press, 233 East Redwood Street, Baltimore, MD 21202. There is also an earlier description of how to set up such a club available from the National Technical Information Service (address above), at a cost of $9.25; it is called PB 291-558, "Accompaniment to the Final Report to U.S. Department of Labor: The Job-Finding Club," Nathan H. Azrin, Ph.D., Principal Investigator.

If, as a job-hunter, you find there is no job-club or job-hunters anonymous of any kind in your community, and you decide to band together with some other job-hunters, good for you! Even if you design your own club and your own program, it's probably going to be effective and infinitely more helpful than if you were to go about your job-hunt, or career-change, all by yourself. The mutual teamwork and support will, in all likelihood, help you to keep at the job-hunt and treat it as a full-time job — which is the point of it all.

However, there are reasons for taking Dr. Azrin's model very seriously. It is based on experience. That experience was that there were a number of problems which were defeating job-hunters — of every age, sex, race, educational and economic background. Inasmuch as Dr. Azrin is one of the original behavioral-modification psychologists in this country, he analyzed these problems, and each feature of his system was designed in response to a problem. That is to say, each feature was designed to stamp out or remove a problem. Everytime you omit one of the features of his model — either through not knowing the model, or knowing it but desiring to "cut corners" — you automatically readmit the problem which that feature was designed to eliminate.

By way of illustration, his model of the Job-Finding Club is designed around the buddy system. In order to implement that system, a telephone with an extension is mandated. The point of having both the telephone and the extension, is that the buddy can listen in on your conversation with a potential employer, and give you feedback later on how you could have improved the conversation over the phone. Then, later, you can listen in on the extension, while your buddy is making similar phone calls, and later give feedback. Eliminate the "phone-with-extension" feature, and you automatically eliminate the feedback. Eliminate the feedback and you readmit the original problem: namely, that job-hunters often don't know how to handle themselves on the phone, and hence keep repeating their poor performance — precisely because no one is there to give them immediate feedback.

OTHER KINDS OF RESOURCES
YOU CAN DRAW UPON

But it may be that in your case there is no group-job-hunting support system available, and you can't (or won't) get one started. Yet you still want some kind of support and help. What then?

Well, there are other kinds of help besides groups. There are individual helpers that you can turn to, and there are also books.

But to take advantage of these, there are two essential rules:

1. You must know what kind of help you need, and this is best discovered by first trying to do the job-hunt using your own resources: namely, your brain and your wits.

2. You must know what various resources can do to help you, and what they can't do.

TYPES OF RESOURCES

Let us begin by outlining the kinds of help that you might need and want:

HELP WITH PARTICULAR PARTS
OF THE JOB-HUNTING PROCESS.

[1] Help with deciding just exactly what it is you
     want to do (Chapter 5):
     A) In the way of vocation (what kind of
         exterior furniture do you want?)
     B) In the way of personal growth (what to
         do with your interior furniture?)

[2] Help with informational interviewing to help
     you decide just exactly where you want to
     do it (Chapter 6).

[3] Help with researching at length the organizations
     that interest you and learning how to approach
     the man or woman who has the power to hire
     you for the job you want (Chapter 7).

HELP WITH THE WHOLE PROCESS OF THE
JOB-HUNT (all of the above).

NOW, LET US LOOK AT WHAT RESOURCES THERE ARE, AND JUST WHAT THEY CAN AND CANNOT DO FOR YOU

I. *Your own research.* This is to be preferred above all resources, for any number of reasons. First of all, knowledge which you gain for yourself is more ingrained than knowledge that is simply handed to you by others. Secondly, the job-hunt process rightly understood is itself a preparation for, and training in, skills you will need to exercise once you get the job; to deprive yourself of the opportunity to get valuable practice in these skills during the job-hunting process, is to make it just that much more difficult for yourself on the job. Thirdly, even if you pay money (and a whole lot of it) to one kind of professional agency or another, there is no guarantee that they will do the process any better than, or even as well as, you would do it yourself.

> **MORAL**: *Every investment of your money is a gamble unless you have first tried to do it on your own, know what you did find out, what you did not find out, and therefore what kind of help you now need from others.*

II. *Books, pamphlets and other printed material.* If you need help this is the first resource to check out. (You already know that, or why are you reading this?) This kind of resource is inexpensive, and may give you just the extra push you need, to get past whatever bottleneck is holding you up, if information, a clue, a glimmer is all you need. If *this* book, after you have thoroughly read and tried it, just doesn't do it for you, there are a multitude of other resources listed in Appendix B.

III. *Free professional help.* People rush off to press money into the hands of paid professionals when if they would just stop to analyze exactly what they need at that moment they might discover there is professional help available at no cost. Examples of such help: your local librarian, resources at a nearby university or college, the chamber of commerce, business friends, and fellow alumni from your college or high school who live in your area (write your school and ask for their alumni list).

IV. *Professional help for a fee.* A. From a college or university. Example: vocational testing often is given for a modest fee. Recommended if you have tried all the techniques in the next chapter of this book first, without getting any satisfactory answers. B. From your own professional group. For example, if you are a clergy person there are a number of church career development centers around the country. These are able to give help in certain specific areas. Check out Appendix C. C. From the business-consultant world: (1) those which will accept anyone as a client, and (2) those which concentrate on serving specialized vocational groups.

YOUR FAMILY OR FRIENDS

Okay, you don't want to go about the job-hunt all by yourself. You've weighed the idea of a job-club, but none is available. You've weighed the idea of getting yourself a professional counselor, but you can't afford one — or you can't find one. Does this mean, then, that you are condemned to go about the job-hunt all by yourself?

Of course not. You've still got your family and you've still got your friends.

What do you ask of them? Very simple: we'll put it the form of an exercise.

Practical Exercise (Warmup)

Decide who you know (spouse, roommate, friend, etc.) that you can take into your confidence about this. Tell them what you need to do, the hours it will take and how much you need *them* to keep you at this task. Then put down in your appointment book a regular weekly date when they will *guarantee* to meet with you, check you out on what you've done *already*, and be very stern with you if you've done little or nothing since your previous week's meeting. The more a gentle but firm taskmaster this confidante is, the better. Tell them it's at least a 20,000 hour, $250,000 project. Or whatever. It's also responsible, concerned, committed *Stewardship*.

Why 20,000 hours? Well, a forty-hour a week job, done for fifty weeks a year, adds up to 2,000 hours annually. So, how long are you going to be doing this new job or new career that you are looking for? Ten years? That means 20,000 hours. Longer than that? Even more hours. So, it's at least a 20,000 hour project.

Why $250,000? Well, figure it out for yourself. Say, you hope to start this new job or new career of yours at $14,000 a year. Even if you are forty years old, you still have thirty good years of work left in you. So, let us say that over that period of thirty years you get enough raises to make your annual salary somewhere between $18,000 and $20,000. Multiply this by thirty years, and you get a total earnings of something in the neighborhood of more than half a million dollars. Too extravagant, you say? You're going to start at $7,000, and have enough raises to make your annual salary only $10,000 per year? All right, even so, that adds up to $300,000 over the thirty years. If you've got more years ahead of you, or a higher potential salarywise, you're talking about even more money. So it's *at least* a $250,000 project that you're working on, with this job-hunt of yours.

HOW MUCH TIME
TO DO IT RIGHT?

Considering this 20,000 hour, $250,000 project that you're electing to work on, from the point of view of a steward or manager rather than just crassly, how much time do you think a good steward or good manager should put in on such a project, to be sure that the half a million is well planned, well managed and well spent? Think carefully.

And realize that trying to get the job-hunt over with, just as fast as possible, taking short cuts wherever you can, giving the whole thing as little of your time and intelligence as you can get away with, is going to cost you money. Over the next decade or two, you can deprive yourself and your loved ones of many thousands of dollars, literally — due to your shoddy job-hunt. Not to mention your own misery, at ending up — as so many do — in a miserable excuse for a job, where you are undervalued, underused and ultimately burnt-out.

So, how much time to do it right? Only you can decide. But if you decide it is a full-time job, and you are going to devote every spare hour and day to it that you possibly can — whether you are employed or unemployed — you will be demonstrating wisdom far beyond your years. This isn't *just* a job-hunt. This is your life, man. This is your life, woman.

Get your family to help. Get your friends to help. Get your priest, pastor, rabbi, guru or whatever to help. Be in charge of this Project: Job Hunt. But don't go it alone. There is no need to.

The Inquiring Reporter
asked the young woman why
she wanted to be a mortician.
Because, she said, *I enjoy
working with people.*

The San Francisco Chronicle

CHAPTER FIVE

Only *You* Can Decide:

What Do You Want To Do?

THE SECOND KEY
TO CAREER PLANNING
AND JOB-HUNTING

We come now to the homework that you MUST do on yourself, as an essential prelude to your job-hunt. That homework begins with your getting at the issue of what it is that you want to do. I said this earlier, but let me repeat it here:

> *You have got to know what it is you want, or someone is going to sell you a bill of goods somewhere along the line that can do irreparable damage to your self-esteem, your sense of worth, and your stewardship of the talents that God gave you.*

Remember this: you live half your life at your job — whatever it may be. God's world already has *more* than enough people who can't wait for five o'clock to come, so that they can go and do what they really want to do. It doesn't need us to swell that crowd. Us ... or anyone else. It needs people who know what they really want to do, and who do it *at* their place of work, *as* their work.

WHAT WILL
HOLD YOU BACK?

Can you really sit down and figure out an alternative career for yourself, based on what you really enjoy doing — without going back to school for a million years of re-training? Or can you really define your very first career, systematically? You bet you can.

Then why is this whole country in general, and our personnel system in particular, baffled as to how to go about this whole process?

Now, that is a *very* good question, particularly when the creative minority have been crying out for years that it could be done and has been done by countless numbers of ordinary people from all walks of life. It's all very simple, they have been saying ... and saying ... and saying.

There are only four things that hold people back from completing this personal homework exercise successfully:

© Copyright, 1980, King Features Syndicate, Inc. Used by special permission.

"Same career, change of career, same career... change of..."

- 1. *Lack of Purpose.* People trying to identify a first or second career for themselves are not sure what kind of things they need to be looking for.
- 2. *Lack of Tools or Instruments.* People know what kind of things they are looking for, perhaps, but they have nothing to help them go about it systematically and comprehensively.
- 3. *Lack of Motivation.* People know what kinds of things they are looking for, and they have helpful instruments so that they can do it, but the *internal push* to get at it and keep at it until it is done, is inadequate. This is usually *the* major road-block of the four. We dealt with this in our previous chapter.
- 4. *Lack of Time.* Purpose is grasped, tools are in hand, motivation is just great, but they have waited to get at this exercise until they are actually living in Desperation Gulch (just on the outskirts of Panic City) — and the amount of time needed to do this properly just does not seem to be there. So of course the exercise is done joylessly and, often, without much profit. Food meant to be savored cannot be wolfed down, without the danger of acute indigestion. Likewise, career and life planning meant to be done with much time for reflection, cannot be telescoped without the danger of erroneous judgments and conclusions.

WHAT'S GOING TO
PUT YOU AHEAD

You can sit down and work out exactly what it is that you want to do, once you resolve that *you* will not and do not lack the four prerequisites for this kind of work:

Time	Motivation	Purpose	Tools & Instruments

Of course, you aren't going to get this done just by sitting up late one or two nights. It takes longer than that. You need to make up your mind to that, before you even begin. Thoughts, like soup stock, often need to simmer for awhile — on the front burner, or on the back. So, you need to get at this homework at once, and proceed with it systematically.

Of course, the temptation is to procrastinate. And procrastination, as my grandfather used to say, sent more people to hell than whiskey.

"What do you want to do, for the rest of your life?" "Oh, I don't know; I'll figure it out when I have to."

I hate to tell you this, but the time to figure out where your parachute is, what color it is, and to strap it on, is *now* — and not when the vocational airplane that you are presently in is on fire and diving toward the ground.

But most of us typically wait until a crisis occurs. Too bad! None of us are fools. We all know that we may have to go find other work, with very short notice. But we put it off. If you have a choice, begin this homework while you are still gainfully, and somewhat happily, employed. *If you're employed, somebody wants you — and values you enough to say so, in*

the coin of the realm. If you're unemployed, there is just the breath of suspicion that perhaps no one wants you. And faced with this suspicion, many employers will choose to make no decision about you (i.e., not hire you) rather than take a gamble.

Of course, the choice may not be yours. All of a sudden you're out. You didn't see it coming. There was no warning. Or maybe there was, and you just didn't see it. Well, no sense kicking pebbles and wishing you had been wiser. You *are* unemployed. You can still do the whole process right. Just put your anger aside, stop brooding about the past, and get at this homework.

Throughout the rest of this book — here and there — you are going to find references to other books. The super-conscientious reader will, of course, want to pause at each reference, run to the library, read that book, and then continue here. Thus, the super-conscientious reader will be ninety years old before finishing *Parachute*. For most of us I recommend another plan: ignore the references to other books, do *not* go and look them up, do not bother to read them — *unless* the particular subject under discussion when that reference is given just *happens to be* your Achilles heel, and you are *desperate* for some further help with that particular area of your life. In which case, make a note to yourself and — when you're all done reading *Parachute* — you can look over those notes to see which other resources, if any, you then want to go pursue.

To illustrate what I have just said, let us suppose that you have a hunch, intuition or premonition that your problem is not that you can't get organized for your job-hunt, but rather that you can't get organized about *anything*. You may find some help in Stephanie Winston's book, *Getting Organized: The easy way to put your life in order.* (Warner Books, Inc., 75 Rockefeller Plaza, New York, NY 10019. 1978. $4.95, paper.) Stephanie is the founder and director of The Organizing Principle — an interesting job-hunt/career-change story in and of itself. Her book deals with how to organize your time, paperwork, work space, rooms in general, tasks, finances, books, clothes, etc. But, don't jot down the name of this book in your notes *unless* getting organized is *the* big problem in your life.

Practical Exercise (Cooling Down?)

If two weeks after putting down this chapter, you pick it up again, and realize you still haven't even begun this homework, deciding what it is that you want to do; and if you haven't enlisted anyone else to help you either, then face it: you're going to *have to* pay someone to aid you. Too bad, because you could do it just as well or better yourself. But better this way than no way: turn to Appendix C, choose three possible counselors or places, go ask them some questions, and then choose one. Pay them, and *get at this.*

© Copyright, 1980, United Feature Syndicate, Inc. Used by special permission.

WHAT YOU ARE LOOKING FOR

In any event, on your own — or with a *planning partner* — what is it that you are looking for, during this process? We have already indicated the long-range over-all purpose. It's worth repeating:

**Career & life planning is useless, unless
at the end of the process
you are very definite about
exactly what you want to do —
at least for the immediate future.**

But let's be even more specific than this. Any career and life planning that is worth its salt should help you to do the following things:

1. To become more aware of your goals in life. What do you want to accomplish before you die? What is your life's "mission," as you perceive it?   **Goals**

You may revise this list ten times, as life goes on *(career and life planning is, ideally, an on-going continuous process — not a single event, done once and for all)*; but as you perceive it now, what are you trying to accomplish, what are you trying to become? What's unique about *you*?

2. To inventory what skills you presently have — things you do well and enjoy. This inventory needs to be taken in terms of basic units — *building blocks, if you will* — so that as time goes on, these building blocks can be arranged in different constellations. The creative minority insists this is the very heart of planning for your various careers.   **Skills**

3. To consider and identify what Peter Drucker calls the *futurity of present decisions.* Considering where you would like to go, and what you would like to do, what time spans are built into your present decisions (e.g. if school seems required, how many years before you will finish?), and what risks are built into present decisions? The purpose of your planning is not to eliminate risks (there can be no sure movement forward without them) but to be certain that the risks you take are the right ones, based on careful thought.[1]   **Time Lines**

_____

1. If you want some help with this whole business of taking risks, there is a resource you may want to take a look at: *Risking,* by David Viscott. (Simon & Schuster, 1230 Avenue of the Americas, New York, NY 10020. 1977. $2.25.)

4. To basically decide who (or what) is controlling your career planning: accident, circumstance, the stars, the system, Providence, God (how?), your family, other people or — forgive us for mentioning this possibility — You. You see, ultimately this comes down to a question of how passive you want to be about it all. (Your life, your career, where you work, the whole bag.) Now, admittedly, we have an axe to grind here: we believe you will improve your effectiveness and your sense of yourself as a person 300% if you can learn to think (or if you already think) of yourself as *an active agent* helping to mould your own present environment and your own future, rather than a passive agent, waiting for your environment to mould you.

THE CONSTANT THREAD

But, to say that your purpose in all this homework is to find your goals, skills, time lines and who's in control, is not enough. Your deepest purpose is to identify the core of your life, the constant thread, the constancy in you that persists through all the changing world around you. As we all learned from Alvin Toffler (*Future Shock*), change is coming at us so fast that many people are going into shock (marked by apathy, withdrawal, paralysis or galloping nostalgia).

The planning outlined thus far can help you deal with such change by identifying what in your life is unchanging: your sense of life "mission," your basic skills etc. — the things that continue relatively untouched at the core of your *inner nature*. A base of constancy is necessary in order to deal with the bombardment of change that has become the hallmark of this world in which we presently live.

You build this base of constancy by: identifying the goals, values, priorities, etc., that you already have; inventorying the basic building blocks of your skills that you already have; identifying the time spans and risks that you *must* deal with in making your present decisions; and exercising your present identity as one who moulds their fate rather than letting their fate mould them.

The secret of dealing with the shock that lies in the future for you is not that you should try to nail down every plank of that future, to spell it out and then stick to it, no matter what . . . (This is what it is going to be like, and this is what I am determined it shall be. On March 4, 1988, I will be doing exactly thus and so.) That's ridiculous, even as "the Now Generation" was so quick to point out.

Rather, the secret of dealing with the future is to nail down what you have in this present — and see the different ways in which the basic units of *that* can be rearranged, anytime you choose, into different constellations that are consistent with the goals and values that direct your inner nature.

You are aiming at being able ultimately to fill in this chart:

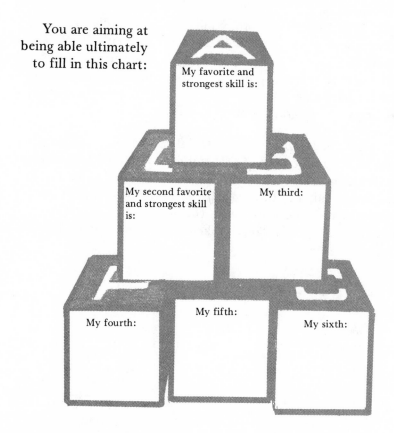

My favorite and strongest skill is:

My second favorite and strongest skill is:

My third:

My fourth:

My fifth:

My sixth:

THAT BOGEY-WORD — Skills

Now, many people just "freeze" when they hear the word "skills." It begins with high school job hunters: "I haven't really got any skills," they say. It continues with college students: "I've spent four years in college. I haven't had time to pick up any skills." And it lasts through the middle years, especially when a person is thinking of changing his or her career: "I'll have to go back to college, and get retrained, because otherwise I won't have any skills in my new field." Or: "Well, if I claim any skills, I'll start at a very entry kind of level." All of this fright about the word "skills" is very common, and stems from a total misunderstanding of what the word means. A misunderstanding that is shared, we might add, by altogether too many employers, personnel departments, and other so-called "vocational experts."

By understanding the word, you will automatically put yourself way ahead of most job-hunters. And, especially if you are weighing a change of career, you can save yourself much waste of time on the (currently popular) folly called "going back to school for retraining."

So, herewith our crash-course on skills:

According to the *Bible* of vocational counseling — the fourth edition of the *Dictionary of Occupational Titles,* (U.S. Government Printing Office, Washington, DC, 1977) — skills break down, first of all, into three groups according to whether or not they are being used with Data (Information), or People or Things. (See diagram.) Thus broken down, and arranged in a

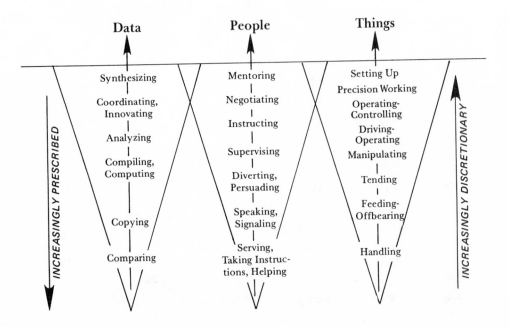

hierarchy of less complex skills (at the bottom) to more complex skills (at the top), they come out looking like inverted pyramids.

Before we explain these skills in more detail, let us look at the *most startling fact about all these skills.* It is, simply, this:

If you graded all these skills in terms of how many of their duties are prescribed in detail, i.e., by a boss, vs. how many are discretionary, i.e., left to the discretion of the employee, you would discover that the lower the skill, the *more* its duties are prescribed, with comparatively little discretion left to the employee; but, the higher the skill, the less its duties are prescribed, and the more that is left to the discretion of the employee.

This almost paradoxical meaning of the word "skill" can be easily illustrated from any, or all, of the three hierarchies on the previous page. For the sake of comparative brevity, we will take just one, namely that which deals with people. (You know, today when most people are asked what they want to do out in The World, they will almost always answer, "I want to work with people." Might as well show those of us who say this, just how varied Work with People can be.) Note, as we progress to higher levels of skills, *how it becomes harder and harder for a prospective employer (say) to draw up a job description for this skill.*

THE PEOPLE FUNCTIONS SCALE which follows, is from the *third* edition (1965) of the *Dictionary of Occupational Titles,* Vol. II, pp. 649-50, as modified and adapted by Dr. Sidney A. Fine. Thus, its skills list differs slightly from the one in the previous pictorial. Remember, as you read, each higher skill level usually or typically involves all those which preceded it.

INCREASING LEVELS OF SKILL
Beginning With
The Most Elementary Definition

TAKING INSTRUCTIONS — HELPING
Attends to the work assignment, instructions, or orders of supervisor. No immediate response or verbal exchange is required unless clarification of instruction is needed.

SERVING
Attends to the needs or requests of people or animals, or to the expressed or implicit wishes of people. Immediate response is involved.

EXCHANGING INFORMATION
Talks to, converses with, and/or signals people to convey or obtain information, or to clarify and work out details of an assignment, within the framework of well-established procedures.

COACHING
Befriends and encourages individuals on a personal, caring basis by approximating a peer- or family-type relationship either in a one-to-one or small group situation, and gives instruction, advice, and personal assistance concerning activities of daily living, the use of various institutional services, and participation in groups.

PERSUADING
Influences others in favor of a product, service, or point of view by talks or demonstrations.

DIVERTING   Amuses others.

CONSULTING
Serves as a source of technical information and gives such information or provides ideas to define, clarify, enlarge upon, or sharpen procedures, capabilities, or product specifications.   cont.

At your public library, in the current (1977) edition of the D.O.T., as the "in crowd" calls the *Dictionary of Occupational Titles*, pp. 1369-1371 you can find similar lists for Data and Things, if you think that you prefer to work primarily with them, rather than with people.

The point of all this for you, the career-changer/job-hunter, is:

1. The lower the level of skills that you think you should claim, the more the skills can be prescribed and measured and

INSTRUCTING

Teaches subject matter to others, or trains others, including animals, through explanation, demonstration, practice, and test.

TREATING

Acts on or interacts with individuals or small groups of people or animals who need help (as in sickness) to carry out specialized therapeutic or adjustment procedures. Systematically observes results of treatment within the framework of total personal behavior because unique individual reactions to prescriptions (chemical, behavioral, physician's) may not fall within the range of prediction. Motivates, supports, and instructs individuals to accept or cooperate with therapeutic adjustment procedures, when necessary.

SUPERVISING

Determines and/or interprets work procedure for a group of workers, assigns specific duties to them (particularly those which are prescribed), maintains harmonious relations among them, evaluates performance (both prescribed and discretionary), and promotes efficiency and other organizational values. Makes decisions on procedural and technical levels.

NEGOTIATING

Exchanges ideas, information, and opinions with others on a formal basis to formulate policies and programs on an initiating basis (e.g., contracts) and/or arrives at resolutions of problems growing out of administration of existing policies and programs, usually after a bargaining process.

MENTORING

Deals with individuals in terms of their overall life adjustment behavior in order to advise, counsel, and/or guide them with regard to problems that may be resolved by legal, scientific, clinical, spiritual and/or other professional principles. Advises clients on implications of diagnostic or similar categories, courses of action open to deal with a problem, and merits of one strategy over another.

demanded of you. In other words, you'll have to fit in. Conversely, the higher the level of skills that you can honestly claim, the less these skills can be prescribed and measured, and the more you will be free to carve out the job in the shape of *you* — making the fullest use of the special constellation of abilities that are yours.

2. The higher the level of skills that you can honestly and legitimately claim either with people, or data or things (or, in varying degree, with all three) the less likely it is that the kinds

of jobs you are thus qualified for will be advertised or known through normal channels; the more you'll have to find other ways of unearthing them — which is what the next chapter is all about.

3. Just because the opportunities for such higher level jobs or careers are harder to uncover, the higher you aim the fewer people you will have to compete with — for that job. In fact, if you uncover, as you are very likely to, a need in the organization (or organizations) which you like, a need which your skills can absolutely help solve, that organization is very likely to create a brand new job for you, which means — in effect — you will be competing with practically no one, since you will be the sole applicant, as it were.

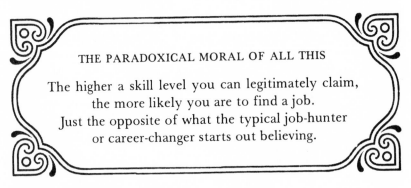

THE PARADOXICAL MORAL OF ALL THIS

The higher a skill level you can legitimately claim,
the more likely you are to find a job.
Just the opposite of what the typical job-hunter
or career-changer starts out believing.

So, now that you know you are looking for your highest level of skills, on with the homework:

- **TOOLS & INSTRUMENTS TO HELP YOU:**
  MEMORIES, FEELINGS, AND VISIONS

What you need, at this point, are some practical — some very practical — tools or instruments. So, we are going to list a lot of them. You may want to try every one. Or, you may want to approach them as a kind of smorgasbord, picking and choosing a few from among all those that are offered. Your problem, in that case: how to know which ones to choose?

If you have a reflective-type mind, it will have struck you already that long range planning must include some elements of your past, your present and your future.

The kinds of exercises which are available to you correspond to these three divisions of time.

To be sure, there is overlapping, but in terms of their major emphasis, we can categorize the following exercises in these terms:

> **YOUR MEMORIES (OF THE PAST):**
> Exercises No. 1, 2, 3 and 4.
>
> **YOUR FEELINGS (ABOUT THE PRESENT):**
> Exercises No. 5, 6, 7 and 8.
>
> **YOUR VISIONS (OF THE FUTURE):**
> Exercises No. 9 and 10.

You'll know which ones can best help YOU, by taking into account the following considerations:

If, because of pell-melling change or great stress, your memory has just taken a holiday, then we suggest you forget about the exercises that deal with your past. Or, if you are deep in apathy, (literally, *lack* of feelings; lack of *consciousness* of feelings would be a better description) the exercises dealing with the present aren't likely to be of too much help. And if you have what the Johnson O'Connor people call "low foresight," then the exercises that deal with the future aren't likely to be too fruitful for you.

If, on the other hand, your whole mind is having trouble, then we suggest you go get a *good* rest before you tackle *any* of these exercises. It may be, of course, that even with a good rest, your mind balks at the thought of doing a whole bunch of exercises. This sort of activity *always* turned you off in school, and — *like that.*

I need to point out that what may be surfacing here is the fact that your mind does better with pictures, and visualization, than it does with words and written exercises. Or, to use psychological jargon, the right-side of your brain (which thrives on pictures) may take precedence over the left-side of your brain (which thrives on words).[1] If so, draw, cut and paste, doodle, take pictures, rather than writing words, words, words.

---

1. For more about this subject, and for some possible help with visualizing — before you tackle any of these exercises — see the resources that are listed in the Bibliography, under the heading: #17. *The Nature of Your Brain, Decision-Making, and How to Stimulate Creativity* (p. 243).

Exercises 1, 2, 3, and 4 — involving
YOUR MEMORIES OF THE PAST

Career and life planning involves the past, as well as the present and future, because:

1. You are being encouraged to develop a holistic (rather than atomistic) approach to life, one which *builds upon* previous experiences, rather than rejecting them.

2. You are being encouraged to see that the drives which will dictate your future course have not been inactive up until now, but have been continually manifesting themselves in what you have done best, and enjoyed doing the most.

3. You are being encouraged to see that your life is a continuum, with a steady continuing core, no matter how the basic units or building blocks may need to be rearranged. The change lies in *the varying constellation* that these basic units are rearranged into (see page 75); but everything you enjoy most and do best will basically use the same building blocks that your past activities did.

In the light of all this, you need to look back and see when you were most enjoying life — and precisely what activities you were doing at that moment, what skills or talents you were employing, what kinds of tasks you were dealing with, what kinds of accomplishments were being done, and precisely what it was that was "turning you on."

Here, then, are some exercises and instruments designed to assist you in doing this (don't just read them as you go — *do* them):

Practical Exercise No. 1

A. Write a diary of your entire life. An informal essay of where you've been, what you've done. Where you were working, what you did there (not in terms of job titles — forget them — but in terms of what you feel you achieved).

B. Boast a little. Boast a lot. Who's going to see this document, besides you, God, and any twenty people that you choose to show it to? Back up your elation and sense of pride with concrete examples, and figures.

C. Describe your spare time, in each place where you lived. What did you do? What did you most enjoy doing? Any

© Copyright, 1980, Universal Press Syndicate. All rights reserved. Used by special permission.

hobbies? Avocations? Great. What skills did they use? Were there any activities in your work that paralleled the kinds of things you enjoyed doing in your leisure?

D. Concentrate both on the things you have done, and also on the particular characteristics of your surroundings that were important to you, and that you really enjoyed: green grass, the theater, golfing, warm climate, skiing, or whatever.

E. Keep your eye constantly on that "divine radar:" *enjoyable.* It's by no means *always* a guide to what you should be doing, but it sure is more reliable than any other key that people have come up with. Sift later. For now, put down anything that helped you to enjoy a particular moment or period of your life.

F. Don't try to make this diary very structured. You can bounce back and forth in time, if that's more helpful; then go back later, and use the questions above (and others later) to check yourself out. If you need further help with how you go about writing a diary like this, by all means get your hands on

Where Do I Go From Here With My Life? by that genius, John Crystal and friend.[1]

G. When your diary is all done, you may have a small book — it can run 30-200 pages. (My, you've done a lot of living, haven't you?) Now to go back over it, take a separate sheet of paper, and put two columns on it:

Things Which, On The Basis of Past Experience, I Want To Have or Use In My Future Career(s) (With Particular Attention To Skills)	Things Which, On The Basis of Past Experience, I Want To Avoid In My Future Career(s)

As you go back over the diary, each time you come to something you feel fits in the first column, put it there. Each time you come to something negative in your past that you feel fits in the second column, put that there.

H. When you come to a skill that you a) *enjoyed* AND b) *did well* (in *your* opinion), put it down in the first column *and underline it twice.*

I. When this is all done, go back over column one, looking primarily for skills. Choose the most important ones (*to you* — again, only your opinion counts) — choose 10, 9, 8, 7, 6, 5, but not less than five. Underline these three times.

J. Now rank them in order of decreasing importance to you. You can use the chart on page 75. Fill it in. Now you have your basic units.

K. What this exercise has left you with (hopefully) are: a) six or more building blocks that when woven together will form one coherent job description for you; b) a couple of lists which list (for your own private thinking, at the moment) some other things you want to have, or avoid, in your future employment.

So much for this exercise. If it helps, great. But maybe you are a high-school or college student or housewife, who feels you

---

1. Do remember that not everyone is helped by any one approach. So, if you want a different way of writing the diary, see *Telling Your Story: A Guide to Who You Are and Who You Can Be,* by Sam Keen and Anne Valley Fox (Signet Books, New American Library, P.O. Box 999, Bergenfield, NJ 07621. $1.50).

haven't done enough yet (work-wise) for the foregoing exercise to be very profitable; if so, there is:

Practical Exercise No. 2

List all the hobbies you have done over the years, and then organize them in terms of greatest enjoyment, on down, to see what you were doing, what skills you were using, and what results you were accomplishing. This may give you a clue to what skills you enjoy using the most when no one is telling you what to do.

You can do this same exercise, of course, with your courses in school, etc.

The above exercises, to be sure, leave you a lot of freedom to go about them however you want. But perhaps you want a little more direction and help; maybe a more systematic printed-type thing; in which case, consult the various workbooks in Appendix B under #2. Vocational or Career Planning (page 225).

Why so many workbooks? Well, there is a continuing search going on for more perfect (i.e., helpful) instruments. And each inventor of a new instrument will often claim that theirs is more effective, scientific, objective, definitive, helpful and what-have-you, than anybody else's. The truth is:

Some people are more helped by one device, and other people are more helped by other devices. You have to hunt (some) until you find the one that helps *you* the most.

One systematic printed-type thing you may like, is:

Practical Exercise No. 3

Bernard Haldane in his books[1] presents a most helpful instrument for analyzing your skills. Bernard is one of the pioneers in the whole job-hunting field in this country. His instrument consists of choosing achievements from different portions of your life (Arthur Miller[2] has you choose two achievements for

---

1. Haldane, Bernard, *Career Satisfaction and Success: A Guide to Job Freedom.* 1974. Amacom, 135 West 50th Street, New York, NY 10020. P. 66ff.
Haldane, Bernard; Haldane, Jean; and Martin Lowell, *Job Power Now! The Young People's Job Finding Guide.* 1976. Acropolis Books, 2400 17th Street, N.W., Washington, DC 20009. P. 21ff.
2. Miller, Arthur F., and Mattson, Ralph T., *the TRUTH about you: Discover what you should be doing with your life.* 1977. Fleming H. Revell Company, Old Tappan, NJ 07675. P. 145ff.

each period of your life, a period being usually five years in length). Then Bernard has you choose your ten greatest achievements and check them off against a list of skills, which he calls a "motivated skills chart." Some of the workbooks alluded to, previously, have similar kinds of lists — spinoffs from this original idea of Bernard's. Such a spinoff, or rhapsody if you will, is even to be found in The Quick Job-Hunting Map, which is in Appendix A of this book. But you may prefer to go back to the original, in which case Bernard's books (and instruments) are footnoted on page 85.

Regardless of which instrument you decide to use, where you should end up eventually is in the same place that we did on page 75. You should, that is, end up with building blocks of skills, which will form the backbone of your future job description, or your future new career.

In the previous instruments or exercises, you may be "hung up" over the idea of bragging — bragging about your achievements, accomplishments, successes, and the like. The Puritan in each of us dies hard, so it may be time for —

"FRANKLY, IT'S NOT EASY BEING A PURITAN IN THIS HEDONISTIC SOCIETY!"

Copyright © Chronicle Features, 1979, cartoon by Mal. Used by special permission.

"A SPECIAL WORD FOR PURITANS"

Puritans come in all sizes, shapes, genders, ages, and colors. Puritans allegedly believe in God; but, what a god! A Puritan believes that God didn't intend us to enjoy anything. And that if you enjoy it, it's probably wrong for you. Let us illustrate:

Two girls do babysitting. One hates it. One enjoys it thoroughly. Which is more virtuous in God's sight? According to the Puritan, the one who hates it is more virtuous.

Two Puritans met on the street. "Isn't this a beautiful day?" said one. "Aye," said the other, "but we'll pay for it."

Puritans will talk about their failures, but hardly ever about their successes — and even then, always with a feeling that "God is going to get me, for such boasting." It's too enjoyable!

Given the Puritan's belief in God, what the Puritan fails to recognize is that enjoyment, in human life, isn't a fluke. It's part of God's plan. God wants us to eat; therefore God designs us so that eating is enjoyable. God wants us to sleep; therefore God designs us so that sleeping is enjoyable. God wants to have us procreate, love, and make love; therefore God designs us so that sex is enjoyable, and love even more so. *God gives us unique (or at least unusual) skills and talents; therefore God designs us so that, when we use these, they are enjoyable.*

That is, we gain a sense of achievement from them.

So, Puritans arise; if you believe in God, believe in One who believes in you. Downgrading yourself is out — for the duration.

Practical Exercise No. **4**

When you are through with all of the above exercises, you may have a lot of data about your past life at your fingertips, but be puzzled about how you use this data to make decisions concerning your future. Indeed, one of the skills some of us never got any help with when we were going through our country's vaunted school-system, is how you go about making decisions. If this is a particular hangup for you, you will want to know that the College Entrance Examination Board has published a helpful instrument which you can get for $2.50. It is entitled *Deciding*.[1] A similar book has been published particularly for

---

1. It may be ordered from Publications Order Office, College Entrance Examination Board, Box 592, Princeton, NJ 08540. (And if, by any chance, this is to be used in a job-hunting *group*, there is also *Deciding: A Leader's Guide*, free with each thirty copies of *Deciding*.)

women: *How to Decide, A Workbook for Women.*[1] And a newer resource you may also want to get help from is Bruce Becker's *Decisions: Getting What You Want.*[2]

Exercises 5, 6, 7, and 8 — involving
YOUR FEELINGS ABOUT THE PRESENT

Maybe your memory isn't so hot, lately. If so, of course the previous exercises aren't going to be very useful to you, whatever help they may be to others. Sooooo, we press on to the present. No need for memory, here; just feelings.

But what use, you may ask, are feelings, in trying to determine what kind of work one should do? Aren't we interested only in skills, talents, and all that? Well, not exactly. You see, studies have revealed that:

1. Your interests, wishes and happiness determine what you actually do well, more than your intelligence, aptitudes, or skills do. This is the conclusion of numerous vocational psychologists (Holland, Mierzwa, Clark, Crites) and personnel people (Snelling, and others). Strength of desire outweighs everything else, they say.

Maybe the word "feelings" or "wishes" sounds just too "fantasy-like" to your ears. OK then, borrowing a word from biology, let's speak instead of "tropisms:" things which living creatures instinctively go toward, or away from. The human animal is no exception, and we each have our own personal, unique tropisms. So, ask yourself: what do you feel drawn toward, what do you instinctively go away from? Make some lists. Your own personal tropisms may be determinative for your future career.

2. If you do work that you really feel good about, and at the highest level of skills that you can legitimately and honestly claim, you are bound to do an outstanding job, and be of genuine help to others — as the creative minority (Haldane, Crystal, and others) have long been maintaining.

3. No tests or other instruments have been devised yet, that so effectively measure what you want as just *asking you* or having you *ask yourself.* As John Holland says:

---

1. Available from Avon Books, 959 Eighth Avenue, New York, NY 10019. $4.95, paperback.
2. Grosset & Dunlap, Inc., 51 Madison Avenue, New York, NY 10010. 1978. $8.95, hardcover.

"Despite several decades of research, the most efficient way to predict vocational choice is simply to ask the person what he wants to be; our best devices do not exceed the predictive value of that method."[1]

And now, on to our exercises dealing with the present. The first one, naturally enough, simply takes Holland at his word:

Practical Exercise No. 5

This exercise consists of a very simple question indeed. Write out your answer to the question: If you could have any kind of job, what would it be? Invent your own, if need be; or ask yourself the question, among all the people you know or have seen or read about, whose job would you most like to have? And why? Forget for the moment what you think you *can* do. What do you *want* to do?

You may prefer to put the question to yourself in other forms, or with time sequences: a year from now, ten years from now, twenty years from now? Try them all.

This exercise, of course, presumes that you know what makes you happy. Maybe, however, you have a much clearer idea of what makes you unhappy (a list, as it were, of "negative tropisms" — things you instinctively want to avoid). Okay, the next exercise thrives on that awareness:

Practical Exercise No. 6

Write a detailed answer to the question: "What are the things which make me unhappy?" When you are done, analyze what you've written into two columns, with the first one sub-divided:

THINGS THAT LIE WITHIN THE CONTROL OF MYSELF		THINGS THAT LIE WITHIN THE CONTROL OF OTHERS, OR FATE, OR CIRCUMSTANCE
Things which I could change thru a change in my external environment (my job, or the place where I live)	Things which I could change thru working on my interior life (what's going on inside me)	

---

1. Reprinted by permission of the publisher, from Holland, John L. *The Psychology of Vocational Choice* (Ginn and Company, Waltham, MA. 1966.) Now out of print.

Check these columns over, when you are done, reviewing the second list to be sure the things listed there *really* are beyond your control or power to alter. Then go over the first list and decide whether the priority for you is to work on your *external* furniture (environment, work, etc.) or your *internal* furniture (personal growth, emotions or spiritual factors), or *both*. List concrete resolutions for yourself, with time goals beside them. Paste the list on your bathroom mirror. Read it each morning.

If you come down, very heavily, in the previous exercise, on the need to deal with your *internal* furniture, then we suggest you go to the back of this book and read Appendix C, section VI (page 284).

"WHILE YOU'RE WAITING FOR YOUR SHIP
TO COME IN, WHY DON'T YOU DO SOME
MAINTENANCE WORK ON THE PIER?"

© Copyright, 1980, King Features Syndicate, Inc. Used by special permission.

Choosing a job is primarily a question of choosing what your *external* furniture should be. Jobs are environments, mostly "people environments," and the issue is how well these correspond to, and are compatible with, your internal furniture. In the past, our society has insisted that when your external furniture and your internal got "out of sync," that you should go get your internal furniture "rearranged," as it were. A lot of people, especially the young, are getting very impatient with this "solution." But not just the young. The increased interest in second careers these days, among those who served "honorably" in their first — clergy, doctors, aerospace engineers, physicists, executives, etc. — may be traced in large part to a new realization that where the external and internal are out of synchronization, it is easier by far (and maybe more sensible) to first try altering the external. To make the environment conform to you, rather than you to the environment.[1]

If you want to take a good hard look at the external *people* environments that are most compatible with your internal furniture, there is an exercise you may like (and a book you *must* read):

Practical Exercise No. **7**

Holland's *"The Self-directed Search"* in his *Making Vocational Choices: A Theory of Careers* (Prentice-Hall, 1973) helps to identify particular occupations you might be interested in, defined in terms of your preferred people-environments. Tremendously useful. If you want *"The Self-directed Search"* all by itself, this is available to professionals (get your clergy person, counselor, or placement officer to order it for you) from Consulting Psychologists Press, 577 College Avenue, Palo Alto, CA 94306, for around a dollar. (If you made the acquaintance of this popular and helpful instrument a long time ago, you may want to know that it has been rather substantially revised, beginning with the 1977 edition. One hundred and thirty-nine changes were made, together with the elimination of all graphs from the main instrument. The auxiliary "Occupations Finder" now has 500 occupational titles in it. And a complementary and important guide "Understanding Yourself and Your Career," by John L. Holland, has been issued for use with *"The Self-directed Search."*) These materials are helpful with all ages, but especially high-school students, and those entering the labor market for the first time.

If you want to do some hard thinking about the internal "You" that your work environment has got to be compatible with, in order for you to be happy, then we suggest you try the following exercise:

---

1. If you want to take a quick glance at the issue of external *work* environments, a most provocative book for you to browse through is: Charles A. Fracchia's *So This Is Where You Work! A Guide to Unconventional Working Environments.* (Penguin Books, 625 Madison Avenue, New York, NY 10022. 1979. $9.95, paper.)

Finding a balance between the external (work) and internal (love) is explored at length in Jay B. Rohrlich's *Work and Love: the crucial balance.* (Summit Books, Simon & Schuster Bldg., 1230 Avenue of the Americas, New York, NY 10020. 1980. $10.95, hardcover.)

Practical Exercise No. **8**

1. Take ten sheets of paper. Write on the top of each one the words: Who am I?
2. Then write, on each sheet, *one* answer to that question. At the end of the ten sheets, you'll have the same question written, but ten different answers.
3. Now go back over the ten again, and looking at each answer, write below it on each sheet *what turns you on* about that particular answer.
4. Go back over the ten sheets, and arrange them in order of priority. Your most important identity goes on top. Then, in order, on down to the identity that is *to you* of least importance, among the ten.
5. Finally, go back over the ten sheets, looking particularly at the answers you wrote (on each page) to *What turns you on?* and see if there are some common denominators.
6. If so, you have begun to put your finger on some things that your career (vocation, job or whatever) *must use* if you are to be truly happy, fulfilled, and effective — to the height of your powers.

Since this can be an eye-opening exercise, if you possess some degree of self-knowledge, but difficult if you don't, let us show how one person filled it out. This is not in any way to suggest the kind of answers you should give, but only to flesh out the instructions above — with an example from one completed exercise:

Part 1: Who Am I?

1. A man	6. A lover of good movies and music
2. An urban dweller (and lover)	7. A skilled counselor and teacher
3. A loving person	8. An independent
4. A creator	9. An executive
5. A writer	10. An enabler

Part 2: What Turns Me On About These?

1. Taking initiative, having inner strength; being open, growing, playful
2. Excitement, variety of choices available, crowds, faces
3. Feelings, empathizing, playfulness, sex, adoration given, happiness
4. Transforming things, making old things new, familiar wondrous
5. Beauty of words, variety of images, new perspectives, new relationships of ideas, words, understandings
6. Watching people up close, merging of color, photography, music
7. Using intuition, helping, seeing totalities of people, problem solving, long-term close helpful relationships

8. Making own decisions, carrying out own plans
9. Taking responsibility, wise risks, using mind, seeing totalities of problems overall
10. Helping people to become freed-up, to be what they want to be.

Part 3: Any Common Denominators?

Variety, totalities, rearranging of constellations, dealing with a number of different things and showing relationships between them all in a new way, helping others.

**Part 4: What Must My Career Use (and Include)
For Me To Be Truly Happy, Used and Effective?**

A variety of different things that have to be dealt with, with people, where seeing totalities, rearranging their relationships, and interpreting them to people in a new way is at the heart of the career.

This is but one illustration. There are many other levels that the exercise can be done at. Be as wild, imaginative, and creative as you want to be with it.

And when it is done, here are some check-back questions, to be sure you have gotten all that you can out of the exercise:

Checkback: Practical Exercise No. 8 concluded

7. What is it that, if I lost it, life would have no meaning? Is it included in the exercise above? If not, why not? (Think hard, and revise your answers, in the light of this new insight.)
8. Out of the ten identifications of myself, and the ten lists of things which turn me on, which of these *must* be included in any job I have? *Remember the world is already filled with people who have to wait until after 5 p.m. to do all the things they really enjoy.*

Those of you who feel there is too much emphasis on *doing* in our society, and not enough on *being,* should find the above exercise particularly up your alley.

Exercises 9 and 10 – involving
YOUR VISIONS OF THE FUTURE

If your memory groans at the idea of trying to remember the past, and if your feelings about yourself in the present are difficult for you to put into words, there is still another family of exercises available to you — which may help you pinpoint just exactly what it is that you want to do with your life. And they are, of course, those exercises which deal with the future.

The future. It sounds far away, mystical, and mysterious. But, as someone has said,

"We ought to be interested in the future, for that is
where we are going to spend the rest of our lives."

Most of us have our visions and dream our dreams. It's only when we come to our job, and what we want to do with the rest of our lives, that we think our visions and dreams should be shelved. In career planning there is a certain group of professionals, here and there, who love to play the game of getting you to say just what you want to do, and then "bringing you down to earth" by saying, "All right; now, let's get realistic." What they should ask is, "Are you *sure* this is what you really want?" because if it is, chances are you will find some way to do it. Remember the man who was called "The Great Imposter." Whatever he badly wanted to do, he found a way to do. Something of him lives in us all.

Never mind "being realistic." For every person who "over-dreams" — of doing more than their merits would justify, — there are four people who "under-dream," and sell themselves short. According to experts, 80% of the workers in this country are "under-employed," as we noted earlier. Trying to be "realistic" too early in your career planning becomes a prison for your mind. You are not going to do your homework very effectively if you try to keep one eye fixed on your dreams, and one eye fixed on what you *think* you know about the job market, e.g., "I'd like to be able to do this and that at my job, but I *know* there is no job in the world like that."

Granted, you may not be able to find a job that has all that you want. But why not aim for it, and then settle for less if and when you find out that you simply have to? Don't foreclose your future prematurely. You'd be surprised what you may be able to turn up (see the next chapter).

To be sure, dreams sometimes have to be taken in stages. If you want to be president of a particular enterprise, for example, you may have to work your way toward it through two or three steps. But it is quite possible you will eventually succeed — *if your whole heart is in your dream.*

If you still doubt, then maybe you'd better do a little extra-curricular reading first, like Barbara Sher's *Wishcraft: How*

to Get What You Really *Want.*[1] Whether you read this or not, when you feel that dreams once dreamed, and maybe since forgotten, are worth dusting off again, here are some exercises to help you:

Practical Exercise No. **9**

Spend as much time as necessary writing an article entitled "Before I die, I want to . . . ." (Things you would like to do, before you die.) Confess them to yourself now, and maybe you can begin to make them happen.

You may prefer to write an article on a similar topic: "On the last day of my life, what must I have done or been so that my life will have been satisfying to me?" When finished, go back over it and make two lists: Things Already Accomplished, and: Things Yet To Be Accomplished. Then make a third column, beside the one called Things Yet To Be Accomplished, listing the particular *steps* that you will have to take, in order to accomplish these things that you have listed.

1	2	3
Things already accomplished.	Things yet to be accomplished. *(Then number them in the order in which you would like to accomplish them.)*	Steps needed in order to accomplish the things in column 2

As you get involved with these exercises you may notice that it is impossible to keep your focus only on your vocation, occupation, career or whatever you want to call it. You will find some dreams creeping in concerning your leisure or your lifelong learning — of places you want to visit, some things you want to learn, some experiences you want to have, that are not on-the-job. *Don't omit these.* Be just as specific and yet holistic as possible. Incidentally, you don't have to do the above exercise just once in your life. Some experts in career and life planning suggest turning the previous exercise into a continuous one, with a list posted on your office or kitchen wall — crossing out items as you accomplish them, and adding new ones as they occur to you from month to month.

---

1. Written with Annie Gottlieb, and published by Viking Press, from whom you can order it if your bookstore doesn't have it: 625 Madison Avenue, New York, NY 10022. 1979. $9.95, hardcover.

Turning from dreams (albeit, concrete, solid dreams) to visions, let us talk of goals and purposes — for these are the visions of the future which cause men and women to set their hands to present tasks. Here is an exercise to deal with the goals that drive you (and there always are such, even if for you they are presently undefined):

Practical Exercise No. 10

Think of some practical concrete task or project in your life, hopefully in the present, that you are a) doing successfully and b) enjoying immensely. (Well, besides that!) It could be at your work, at school, at home or in your spare time. But it must be one which really "turns you on." Put down this task in the center of a blank piece of 8½ x 11 paper turned on its side. Then take the following steps:

1. Begin at the lower left hand side of the page, and write the word "why?" (do/did you want to do this), and on the line above it, indented, write that reason, goal, or purpose.
2. Then write "why?" after this answer, too; and on the line above *it*, indented even more, see if you can write an even more basic reason, goal or purpose.
3. Then write "why?" after it, and on the line above ... etc., etc., etc. Continue this exercise up the paper, until you think you have reached a purpose or goal that is rather ultimate. (You cannot think of any "why?" behind it.)
4. Now, take that most basic goal (the topmost one on the paper), and draw an arrow from it, down to the part of the paper that is beside the "task" with which you began. There, write the words "how else?" and think of what other tasks or projects would accomplish the same ultimate goal (the topmost one on your paper). In the end, your exercise will look something like this.

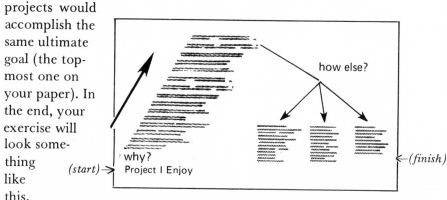

5. Repeat this schema with other projects or tasks that have really "turned you on," using a new piece of paper for each one. See if you begin to see what turns you on about life, and if you begin to see some alternate strategies (or jobs) that could accomplish the same goals. If you "run out of gas" by step four, consult some wise friend or vocational counselor (at school or wherever). This exercise, incidentally, can begin with a job you have, rather than with a task you enjoyed doing. It is particularly useful if you've lost your job, can't find any place else where you could do the same kind of work, and you're at an absolute loss to know what else to do.

IN SUMMARY: CHECK BACK

So much for our exercises. You've at least skimmed through them. Now please try them. One or two. Or (if you're the really thorough type) all of them. Do enough until they achieve your purpose — knowing exactly what you want to do. And if you draw a blank with all of them, you obviously are going to have to turn to someone for professional help. (See Appendix C.)

But let's assume you've tried some of the exercises. Here's a check list of questions to help you test how well things are going for you thus far:

Check-Back Questions:

1. Have you identified the basic building blocks (and filled the chart in, on page 75) of your strongest skills and interests? (Strongest = done best *and* enjoyed *and* feel confident about.)
Do you prefer most to be related to people, data, or things? Or all three? In what priority?
Have you avoided putting a definitive (restricting) job title on what you want to do, at least until you have done some informational interviewing? (There are many different titles for the same job, and many different jobs for the same title — don't build a box for yourself by means of a title.)

2. Are you getting locked in, in your thinking, to just one route to go in the future, or are you trying to preserve alternative options, so that you see different ways your basic skills could be utilized, and not just *one* way?
What risks are there: a) in the kind of job you might be working towards and b) in the route you are taking thereto? Have you

provided for alternative procedures, techniques and goals if those risks materialize?

When all is said and done, are you planning for a changing world, or are you assuming the world will stay still while you move? (As the experts say, *Planning without planning for change is planning for nothing but trouble.*)

3. What time spans are *built in* to the route that you have decided upon, or that you think you ought to take?

If you decide you simply *have to have* credentials, what date will you need them by, how long will it take to get them; and, when — therefore — should you start working on this? If you decide you need experience, where, how, and how long? When will you need it, how long will it take to get it, when should you start?[1]

4. Do you know what questions of life you are most earnestly seeking answers to?

Do you know now what you are after in life? Your needs? Your values? Your tropisms — the things that you instinctively (or otherwise) go *toward,* and the things you instinctively go *away from?* The things that make you happy, and the things that make you unhappy?

Which values actually hold the most attraction for you (not *should* but *do*): service, security, status, popularity, recognition, approval, affection, belongingness, acceptance, power, achievement, authority, glamour, wealth, etc.? Which rewards hold the most meaning for you?

5. In terms of the goals you are moving toward, will a change in externals (your environment, job, place of work, and so forth) be sufficient? Or do you feel that you also need some internal movement and growth? If so, in what areas?

To the extent that you can put a label on what is bothering you in your career/life at the moment, would you characterize it basically as Conflict or Frustration? Or both? Or neither? What, then? (Frustration is between an individual and their environment, and would point to the need for a new work environment. Conflict is within an individual, and points to the need for personal help and personal growth.)

---

1. If time is a continuing problem or hangup for you, you may wish to get your hands on Peter F. Drucker's *The Effective Executive.* Harper & Row, New York, NY. 1967. Excellent on time-use.

6. Do you feel that all planning of this nature is just too much work? Too long and lonely? (To sing our old song once again, how about involving your loved ones in it with you? — you might be surprised at the increased communication and its helpful benefits!)

If you don't do any planning, what will rescue you (or who) if you reach a dead-end in creativity, work and happiness? (As Ezra Pound said, *A slave is one who waits for someone else to come and free him.*)

PUTTING THE BUILDING BLOCKS TOGETHER

Okay, let's assume you pass all the above "check-backs." You know what the basic building blocks of your skills are. Now, you want to know, of course, how do you arrange them into different constellations or careers?

We begin with some basic vocabulary:

• *Jobs, positions, work, careers* are used by some people to mean different things and by other people to mean essentially the same thing. The Distinguishers vs. The Synonymists. The former generally tend to regard the word "job" as a dirty word. By job, they mean *just a job.* The Distinguishers are exquisitely careful about their vocabulary, and may look down on the Synonymists — who are not so precise. The latter feel that the framework of thinking within which a person uses particular words is of more significance and importance than the particular words they may or may not use.

• *Tasks, functions, aptitudes, abilities, skills* — another group of words used by some people to mean very different things, and by other people to mean essentially the same thing. The Distinguishers can give carefully differentiated meanings, which are all supported completely by Webster's Unabridged. The Synonymists, on the other hand, take you by the hand out onto the street and bid you listen to Everyday conversation — whereupon you discover that Everyday conversation makes no such careful distinctions between the meanings of these words, most of the time.

If you want to know the jargon, technically *a job is a flexible combination of tasks* — which can be arranged and rearranged in a number of different tantalizing ways. *A career is a flexible combination of skills* — which can be arranged and rearranged in a number of different tantalizing ways.

Turning Skills Into Careers

● Researching your skills involves trying to discover what different kinds of careers (i.e., constellations or arrangements of skills) are open to you; and then arranging these in order of priority *according to what you enjoy most.*

Now, beyond vocabulary:

How do you go about nailing this down?
Here are some *beginning* suggestions:

PRACTICAL AID NUMBER 1

The Dictionary of Occupational Titles, fourth edition: Superintendent of Public Documents, Washington, DC. 1977. Based on a concept of *functional job analysis*, the outgrowth of research from 1948-1959 directed by Sidney Fine,[1] this "Bible" of the vocational field lists some 20,000 job titles. Called by experts

1. Sidney's written works are described in Appendix B, p. 245.

either "the greatest single source of occupational information in the world" or "an unwieldy mishmash," you can locate occupations or jobs by a) physical demands, b) individual working conditions, c) interest, d) aptitude or skills, e) educational requirements, f) vocational preparation, and so forth.

Each occupation has been given a nine-digit code number. The first three digits are called *the occupational group* and describe The World of Work. The second three digits describe skills, i.e., what workers do with data, with people, and with things. The last three digits indicate the varying titles of occupations that have in common the first six digits.[1]

You are encouraged to go to your library, and browse in the D.O.T. for a while, to get the feel of it.

The point of all this research is to *be sure that you do not get prematurely locked into one field or occupation, but that you see how many alternative options are open to you.*

Our Canadian readers (or job-hunters in the U.S.A. who want a slightly different perspective) will want to look up in their library the *Canadian Classification and Dictionary of Occupations,* 1971. Vol. I and II. Published by Manpower & Immigration, available from Renouf's, 51 Sparks St., Ottawa, Ontario, Canada K1P 5R1 — or from: Canadian Government Publishing Centre, Supply and Services Canada, 45 Sacre-Coeur Blvd., Hull, Quebec, Canada K1A 059. $20. each volume.

PRACTICAL AID NUMBER *2*

A Handbook for Job Restructuring, Superintendent of Documents, U.S. Government Printing Office, Washington, DC 20402. 1970. If your library does not have this, or they cannot get it for you on an Inter-Library Loan (ask!), then I'm afraid you're out of luck, because it's out of print. Has interesting section (pp. 30-42) on "benchmarks" of various skills or aptitudes. "Benchmarks" are typical situations where, at various levels, the skill is used. If your library can find it for you, I think you will find it at least suggestive.

---

1. Counselors and others who became accustomed to the earlier third edition (1965) of the D.O.T. may want to know that there is now a book entitled *Conversion Table of Code and Title Changes Third to Fourth Edition Dictionary of Occupational Titles.* U.S. Employment Service, 1979. Available from: Superintendent of Documents, U.S. Government Printing Office, Washington DC 20402. $7.50.

PRACTICAL AID NUMBER 3

Occupational Outlook Handbook, U.S. Department of Labor, Washington, DC. Get this at your library. It gives an outline for 300 (or so) occupations. For each one, it lists: what its future looks like, nature of the work, usual training required, employment outlook, earnings and working conditions. Helpful if you don't just want to get into occupations that're closing out; but its prophecies should be taken with a large barrel (not just "grain") of salt. There is incidentally an *Occupational Outlook Handbook for College Graduates*.

The very word "outlook" (occupational or employment) ought to make you beware. "A good outlook" for a particular industry only means, if you will stop to think about it, that there is relatively little competition for the openings that exist; i.e., that there are more openings than there are bodies to fill them. On the other hand, "a bad outlook" for a particular field, or a prediction that it is going to be 'crowded,' is only another way of saying there is going to be a lot of competition. That just means you will have to follow the techniques described in this book more faithfully, that's all. Remember, time and time again men and women have gotten positions in a place where everyone told them there was No Employment At All; and they did it by following precisely the strategies described in these chapters.

PRACTICAL AID NUMBER 4

In the course of researching your skills, we urge you to consult with one or more of the following persons, to ask them: What occupations use the skills that I have?

Your *librarian* (or business librarian); *counselors* at the appropriate department of your local State Employment office; *friends* knowledgeable in the fields that interest you; *consultants* to the fields you are interested in for a list of people you might possibly want to consult with, see the *Training and Development Directory,* Paul Wasserman, Managing Editor, Second Edition, published by and obtainable from Gale Research Company, Book Tower, Detroit, MI 48226 — or see your friendly neighborhood library); and the like.

- Remember, in doing research through interviewing (just as with reading) it is *essential* that you have clearly in your own mind what questions you are trying to find answers to.

    Essentially what you are looking for, at this point, is an answer to the question: *What occupation or occupations will use as many of my strongest skills, and on as high a level, as possible? So that — at my work — I am doing what I enjoy most, and not just waiting until I get home from work to start enjoying myself.*

PRACTICAL AID NUMBER 5

In the course of researching a field we urge you to consult with a number of people who are active in it. You should not be hesitant about asking for the time of important people, even heads of companies or corporations. *If they really like their own vocation,* they should be very receptive to your desire to know more about that vocation: what they do, the various kinds of tasks and skills required, and the aspects of it that they particularly enjoy.[1]

---

1. Some employers have complained that since *Parachute* got popular, they are besieged by people wanting to take their time just to discuss what they do. They fear this is happening all over the country. We have found no evidence of this. There are 14 million employing organizations in this country — many of them having countless managers, executives, department heads and others who *might* be thus approached. This inundation is happening only to a comparative few, to those with high visibility, who are well-known and/or are leaders in their field, at least in one particular geographic area. For such employers, a word of advice: set one hour each week or every other week, when you are willing to see such people *as a group,* and don't try to see every individual inquirer by themselves. Then your secretary can simply tell them: "Ms. Vice-President will be happy to talk with you. She has set aside every Monday at 4 p.m. for that kind of sharing."

You say you freeze at the very thought of tackling interviews (even interviews *only for infomation*) with people — afraid you'll botch it up, through shyness or nervousness? Not if it's YOUR enthusiasm you're exploring — the thing in this world you're dying to know more about. But you say, "You don't know what you're asking of me. I mean, I know half the world is shy, but I've got a *terminal case* of that disease." Ah, yes, how well I know. Fortunately, there is help. First of all, a lot of research has been done on the subject of shyness by a man named Philip G. Zimbardo, and he has published his findings (and some helpful antidotes) in two paperbacks: *Shyness, What It Is, What To Do About It,* (if you're too shy to go into your bookstore to look for it, try ordering it by mail directly from Jove Publications, Inc., 757 Third Avenue, New York, NY 10017. 1977. $2.25, paper). AND: *The Shyness Workbook* (co-authored with Shirley L. Radl, and available from A&W Publishers, Inc., 95 Madison Avenue, New York, NY 10016. 1979. $5.95, paper). Secondly, when you go out on your informational interviewing, *it's perfectly kosher to take somebody with you* — anyone, though I don't particularly recommend that it be your mother, or your dog Ralph.

Well, okay, but suppose you are still nervous about The Interview — even if it isn't, at this point, for the purpose of getting hired, but only for the purpose of getting some information. Well, maybe you should browse, then, for a copy of *Contact: The First Four Minutes* by Leonard and Natalie Zunin (in your library, paperback bookstore, or directly from Ballantine Books, 201 East 50th Street, New York, NY 10022; published 1972; $1.75). That should help. After all, the harder you work on this, now, the more it's going to repay you later.

Remember, it's 20,000 hours — on up — of your time that you are trying to find out about, when you explore a possible job or career for yourself. Remember also, that you *may* be coming back to some of these men and women in a different role later on (if they are in the area you want to work in), so it would be helpful to leave a good impression behind you. In other words, dress well and conduct yourself as *quietly confident that you would be an asset to any organization you ultimately decide to serve in.*

PRACTICAL AID NUMBER

Many, if not most, fields have professional journals. Ask your local librarian to assist you in getting your hands on these. Follow all leads that they may suggest to you, as your reading of articles and ads uncovers these, for additional information.

Again, many if not most fields have professional, trade, or union associations. Your public library has all kinds of listings of such associations — yours for the asking. Such as:

Career Guide to Professional Organizations, compiled and edited by the Staff of The Carroll Press, Box 8113, Cranston, Rhode Island 02910. 1976. $8.95, paper. Classifies nearly 2,000 organizations by occupational field, with cross-references from one career field to another. Or there is:

National Trade and Professional Associations of the United States and Canada and Labor Unions, Craig Colgate, Jr., Editor, Patricia Broida, Assistant Editor. Columbia Books, Inc., Publishers, 734 15th Street., N.W., Washington, D.C. 20005. Volume XV–1980. $30.00, paper. Lists 6,000 national trade

associations, labor unions, scientific or technical societies and other national organizations — alphabetically, geographically, by budget, by key word, and by executive/directors.

Try to see what other resources there are, in the city or town where you are: Chamber of Commerce library; university libraries; libraries at appropriate businesses, etc.

PRACTICAL AID NUMBER *7*

If you decide that what you want help in researching are "alternative kinds" of work, then we suggest you look at some of what used to be called "counter-culture directories," such as "The People's Yellow Pages."

To find what there is in your own community, visit the college book store, the counter-culture 'head shop' downtown, or the American Friends Service Committee (which usually knows the resources on alternative forms of careers, quite well).

If, among the alternatives you are weighing, is perhaps part-time work, or different patterns of work, you will want to contact (on the West Coast) *The Job Sharing Project, New Ways to Work,* 149 Ninth Street, San Francisco, CA (415) 552-1000. Free information meetings about job-sharing Mondays at 12:15. Fees vary. There is also: *The Work Resource Center, New Ways to Work,* 457 Kingsley Avenue, Palo Alto, CA (415) 321-9675. Offers counseling, workshops, and information and referral services on other quality of work life issues. Fees vary. On the East Coast, there is JOB SHARERS, located at P.O. Box 1542, Arlington, VA 22210 — which maintains a talent bank of partners interested in job-sharing, as well as an information service about job-sharing, primarily directed toward employers.

There are a number of helpful booklets out, on how to split a job, etc. See page 223 ff for a list of these.

PRACTICAL AID NUMBER *8*

We have placed a number of notes on page 291 ff of this book, summarizing *some of the things* that other people have discovered (why shouldn't *you* benefit from their research?) about various fields. So, If you're interested particularly in:

- *business and management,*
- *social service or change,*
- *the education field,*
- *working in government,*
- *self-employment (counseling, consulting, writing, owning your own business, etc.)*
- *going back to school*

} turn to the Supplement which follows Appendix C, page 291.

That section won't save you from having to do your own research, but it will give you clues, at least. Then you *must* go do your own interviewing. While going on your interviewing for information, please remember that the *woods are alive* with people who will solemnly tell you *something that ain't true* as though they were sure of it with every fibre of their being. So, check and cross check and cross check again the information

that books, people, and experts give you. Let no one build any boxes for you; and watch that you don't hand them any wood with which to build one for you.

In the end, there is virtually no information you want to know, that you cannot find out. This is a *knowledge society,* and the only limits — really — lie within you, as to the amount of commitment, diligence and perseverance you want to lavish on all this. If you feel you're not cut out for research, an absolutely invaluable book is *Finding Facts Fast: How to Find Out What You Want and Need to Know,* second edition, by Alden Todd. And subtitled: *A handbook for students, political activists, civic leaders and professionals . . . based on methods used by reference librarians, scholars, investigative reporters and detectives.* [1]

PUTTING A PRICE TAG ON YOUR LIFE STYLE

Well, yes, we're going to have to talk about money, at this point. For some people, that's a *big* issue; for others, it's rather insignificant — because, well, *somehow,* they always seem to manage to survive. [2]

But I want to emphasize that we are talking about it at this point in the process, because it will help determine at what level you should do your informational interviewing, and at what level you may end up working. In other words, leaving aside the question of what money can buy, you need to know what your minimum salary requirements are going to be, before you ever start looking around to see where you want to use your talents.

If you are one of those who doesn't care much about money or possessions, but is very big on "subsistence type living," this is going to be simple. Just figure out how much you need in order to merely subsist. Housing, food, school, household furnishings, clothing, medical — and car, gas and insurance (yes, most of the subsistence people I've met seem to have a car, for

---

1. See your library, bookstore, or write directly to the publisher: Ten Speed Press, P.O. Box 7123, Berkeley, CA 94707. 1979, 1972. $3.95 — and is worth ten times that much.
2. See *Money Madness: The Psychology of Saving, Spending, Loving and Hating Money* — if money should happen to be a big problem for You. It's by Herb Goldberg and Robert T. Lewis, published by New American Library, Inc., 1301 Avenue of the Americas, New York, NY 10019. 1978. $2.25, paper.

some reason or other). Things like recreation, gifts, personal stuff and — like that — are probably academic, in your case.

If you're not into 'just subsistence,' then we suggest you make up two budgets. First: the 'rock-bottom need' budget — what you need to just survive, if you found yourself (and your loved ones) between a rock and a hard place. Second: the 'I hope' budget — what you hope you will have to live on. The categories, for both budgets, of course, include: Food — at home; Food — away; Housing — rent/mortgage, tax, insurance; Housing — furnishings; Housing — utilities and household supplies; Transportation — car payments, insurance, parking, gas, other maintenance, public transportation; Clothing — purchases, maintenance; Hairdos, toiletries; Medical — insurance, physicians visits, other, including dental; Education — tuition, books, loan repayment; Recreation; Gifts, contributions; Life Insurance; Union dues; Savings; Payments on debts; Pension contribution; Social Security; federal/state income taxes.[1]

To the two budgets add 15% more, because we all habitually underestimate our needs. Now you have your range: the amounts between which you can bargain, at the conclusion of a promising job interview, and the level at which you want to do your exploring, now.

If you're already out into the world of work, and have been for some time, you may want to fool around with making a graph of your salary history, over the years (yearly salary, plotted against time in years). If you're real good at graphs, you may want to make an overlay, of the inflation rate at the same time — that'll send you into a Depression! It may also give you the impetus to think seriously how long you want to stay where you are, without a decent further raise.

The point is, if you use the methods in these chapters, you start here — *before* you ask your librarian to help you figure out what the average salaries are in a given field, to find out if you're in the right ball park. Those average salaries incidentally,

---

1. Military are advised by the creative minority not to include their retirement pay in any way in their computations. That's extra, for emergencies. Clergy are advised that they probably make $20,000 - 30,000 — on the average — although this is hard to comprehend, until you add in all the perquisites, etc., or ask the thought-provoking question: how much would they have to pay in order to hire a layperson to do *all* my work, after I leave?

(for non-supervisory workers, at least) are found in a monthly government publication which every library should have, entitled "Employment and Earnings." At this writing, the average salary for all nonsupervisory workers in the U.S. (on private nonagricultural payrolls) was $6.07 hourly, $215.49 weekly, and $11,250.48 annually, — in case you were wondering.

Now, *if* you have done all the exercises in this chapter, and in the end you are still very hazy about what you want to do, then you will obviously need a more detailed step-by-step plan. Fortunately, such is available in a detailed Life-Planning Manual, written by John C. Crystal (and a "ghost"). You can obtain it by writing the publisher: Ten Speed Press, Box 7123, Berkeley, CA 94707. Its title: *Where Do I Go From Here With My Life?* (1974). It deals with the material covered in the next two chapters in this book, in greater step-by-step detail.

A shorter step-by-step plan is to be found in the "Quick Job-Hunting Map," which you will find in Appendix A at the back of this book. If you want it in separate form or if you want it with a more-elementary skills list (called *The Beginning Version,* whereas the one in Appendix A is called *The Advanced Version*), both are available from Ten Speed Press, Box 7123, Berkeley, CA 94707. $1.25 plus postage. This Map was invented, incidentally, in response to insistent demands from our reader(s) in Oblong, IL.

When you're done, however you did it, you should be able to say what the skills are which you most enjoy using, and (maybe) what kind of careers they point to.

Students spend four or more years learning how to dig data out of the library and other sources, but it rarely occurs to them that they should also apply some of that same new-found research skill to their own benefit—to looking up information on companies, types of professions, sections of the country that might interest them.

Professor Albert Shapero
University of Texas at Austin
Management Department

CHAPTER SIX

Where Do You Want To Do It?

THE THIRD KEY TO CAREER
PLANNING AND JOB-HUNTING

Whether it took you two weeks or two months,

whether it was done easily or only with much blood, sweat and tears,

whether you did it all on your own, or only with professional help, if you did the exercises in the previous chapter (or in the Quick Job-Hunting Map, in Appendix A) you now have identified *which skills you have that you enjoy most and do best.*

Your *priority skill* — the one you gave first place to (like, on page 75) will dictate the general kind of thing that you will be doing. Hopefully. Your *secondary skills* — the ones you gave lesser rank to (page 75, again) will help determine the more specific thing you will be doing within your general field, and perhaps give some clue as to where.

Naturally, you'll want to be narrowing this down, and also determining *at what level* your skills should (and can) be defined. But before we show you how the creative minority suggests you go about doing just that, let us look at the Third Key to your job hunt . . . career search program . . . or whatever you would like to call this whole process.

WHERE, OH WHERE

You have to decide what city, or what part of the country (or the world) you would like to work in.

You probably have one of four answers immediately trembling on the tip of your tongue:

1. I want to continue to work right where I am, because I just love it here. OR

2. I want to work in _____ , because it is my favorite spot in this country of ours. OR

3. I haven't the foggiest idea; I don't really care, either. OR

4. This is a silly exercise. Where I want to work, and where the jobs are, may be two entirely different subjects. So, why get my hopes all up, for nothing?

Since that last answer, if true, effectively wipes out the first three, let us deal with No. 4 right off the bat — and at some length — so that we understand this whole business of what is (*laughingly*) called

The Job Market

Upon hearing this very misleading term, one has visions — instantly — of some central place, like the Stock Exchange, say, where every job opening and every job-hunter can meet each other. Such a vision may dance, like a sugar plum, in the job-hunter's head; but the reality is quite different. And, much more jolting.

When you start into the *supposed* single job market, to conduct your own job-search campaign, you discover sooner or later that you actually face *fourteen million (or more) separate job markets* (for this is how many individual businesses, organizations, agencies, and foundations there allegedly are in this country). Every business or organization has its own way of going about the process of hiring — separate, independent of, and uncoordinated with, other businesses or organizations. Hence, each is a separate job-market.

THE SOURCE OF THE MYTHOLOGY

What deludes people into thinking of the whole country as a vast single job market? Two factors, at least:

First of all, the term itself. *Market* is a metaphor, at best. By analogy with the market where we shop, we have come to speak — in the world of business — of three *markets* today:

a) The market for goods and services; b) the market for capital, money, investment; c) the market for labor.

Whatever usefulness the term may have in the hands of genuine experts, as it is commonly bandied about in everyday language it often means little more than *demand,* e.g., "How's the labor market this month?" Whatever usefulness such shorthand may have among the experts, it certainly does delude the job-hunter. There is no such central market — and the generalizations made about it are downright demonic and soul-destroying to unwary and naive job-hunters.

The second factor which has deluded people into thinking of the country (as a whole) as though it were one market is the statistics that appear in the paper each month. You recall, perhaps, how an English professor once conjugated the word "lie":

LIES, DAMN LIES, AND STATISTICS

In any event, once a month (the first Friday of the month, usually, and published in Saturday's papers — if you care) the nation is alternately comforted or terrorized by *One statistic for the whole country*. It is published (naturally) by the U.S. Government (its Bureau of Labor Statistics, or BLS). And it is (naturally) the unemployment figure.

To understand it, you must be aware that there are actually three basic figures that are of interest:

1. The total number of people in the nation who want to work: e.g., 105,025,000 for August 1980.

2. The total number of people in the nation who are actually employed that month: e.g., 97,006,000 for August 1980.

3. The difference, e.g., 8,019,000 for August 1980. The last figure is the number of people who are unemployed, *as best the government can estimate*, across the entire country.

INTIMIDATING FIGURES

Prominent press coverage is always given to *this one statistic for the whole country: the unemployment figure.* The human mind is staggered by the thought of six million people being out of work. It would be even more staggered if it realized that there is good evidence that actual unemployment may be three times the government figure. The human tragedy that this represents, to each of us in the imagination of our hearts, is overwhelming.

But the press does not leave it to the imagination. Continuously, throughout the rest of the month, we are given details. For example:

New Ph.D.s having rough going in finding jobs, and the prediction that the going is to get rougher in the decade ahead.

The teaching field glutted, with some cities (such as Boston) having as many as 3,500 applicants for 350 vacancies.

The demand for engineers and scientists hitting a ten-year low.

Extensive dismissals in certain industries, such as electronics and television manufacturers, and construction companies, and advertising agencies, and clothing manufacturers, and chemical producers, and public relations, security sales, industrial psychology, and what have you.

Then, if the contemporary situation isn't bad enough, there are always some handy, long-range predictions about what technology, automation, the computers, and such, will do to various industries within the coming decade.

By the time that *You as Newspaper Reader* are ready to become *Job Hunter*, you are convinced that it is foolish of you to venture out into the so-called Job Market, because there can't be a single job left out there.

IS NO ONE HIRING?

But then, the unemployment figure doesn't really tell us anything about vacancies — as, upon sober reflection, we must realize. It only tells us how many people we are competing with (sort of) for whatever vacancies exist. That is, *assuming we all possess the skills that the vacancies call for.*

But, how many vacancies are there?

It's a relatively easy formula to figure out.

First of all, you need to take the total number of jobs in one year as compared to the previous year. For example, in July, 1979, 97.2 million people were employed. In July, 1978, that figure stood at 94.8 million.

From this, we may safely conclude that a minimum of 2.4 million new jobs were created, over a twelve-month period, sometimes by already existing businesses, and sometimes by individuals going out and inventing their own job or starting their own business.

But of course if during that same period let us say five million old jobs were phased out in various manufacturing plants and private businesses (and no one seems to know the actual figure), then actually 7.4 million new jobs would have had to have been created in order to preserve the net rise of 2.4 million. So, we must add to the minimum of 2.4 million however many such old jobs *were* phased out.

We must also add the number of jobs which fell vacant during the year at one time or another, due to the mobility of the employed, who leap from one job to another at a prodigious rate — something like 800,000 each month. (The turnover rate for office employees averaged out to be 26% in a typical year.) We have, then, revolving unemployment — much like a game of musical chairs. And, of course, while the chair is empty, *you* can compete for it as well as anyone.

What does this all add up to? It adds up to what one member of the creative minority estimates is a minimum one million vacancies or job openings each month — not counting sales or "latent" jobs. About which, more as we go on.

DURATION OF UNEMPLOYMENT, 1959-1978
(Seasonally adjusted)

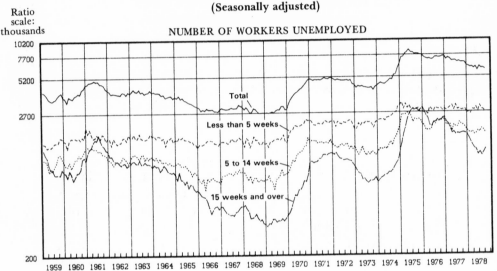

HOW MANY WANT
THE JOB THAT I WANT?

Are six million people, then (or whatever the unemployment figure is, in a given month) competing for these one million job openings each month? Well, of course you know they are not. And, for the following reasons:

1. *Musical chairs:* A lot of vacancies never have a chance to get publicized, because as soon as they exist, some employee recommends a relative; or else someone (by accident or design) walks in off the street, is interviewed, and straight-away hired.

2. *Stiff demands:* A lot of jobs call for very special skills which just may not exist in sufficient abundance, and so the jobs stay vacant for long periods of time.

3. *Low visibility:* There are a number of vacancies for which any number of qualified applicants could be found if only we

had some way of getting the information *out*. But, particularly for jobs that are at all decent, many employers prefer not to advertise the vacancy, inasmuch as they are very particular about whom they hire. Not long ago, it was estimated that there are 750,000 management vacancies each year, only 250,000 of which are filled by the end of the year. The same goes for other levels.

4. *Shying away:* Some job-hunters want relatively unskilled work, for which vacancies there are any number of applicants competing with them. These include job-hunters who are new to the job market such as unskilled teenagers, housewives, grandmothers, retired persons looking for part-time work, etc.

5. *Fictitious job-hunters:* Some people who are collecting unemployment insurance (and therefore are listed by the U.S. Government as job-hunters, which *in theory* they must be in order to collect) actually have no interest in competing for any of the one million vacancies that month: such persons as students between semesters, seasonal workers, production workers on temporary layoff, singers, actors and dancers awaiting a call, etc.

I want to repeat from our previous chapter, the paradoxical nature of the word "skills" (page 75 ff), and what this means for the job-hunter of today (whether student, housewife, mid-life changer or whatever):

(1) The higher the level of skills that you can legitimately claim, either with people, data or things (or, in varying degree,

MORE

What the job market would look like, if there were one:

Note from this illustration, there are more jobs in this country for those with the lower skill levels, than there are for men and women with higher skill levels. Depressing fact, maybe. But, there are two hopeful notes for the individual who aspires to a high skill level career— (See text.)

Level of skills required

LESS   Number of jobs in the country   **MORE**

with all three) the less these kinds of jobs are advertised or known through normal channels; the more you'll have to find ways of unearthing them — which is what this chapter you are now reading is all about. It is written for You!

(2) Just because the opportunities for the higher level jobs (or careers) are harder to uncover, the higher you aim, the less people you will have to compete with — for that job. In fact, if you uncover, as you are very likely to, a need in the organization you like (or organizations), which you can help resolve, they are very likely to create a brand new job for you, which means — in effect — *you will be competing with practically no one, since you are virtually the sole applicant,* as it were. Regardless of your age, sex, race, inexperience, lack of supposed credentials, or whatever. To repeat:

**THE PARADOXICAL
MORAL OF ALL THIS**

The higher a skill level
you can legitimately
claim, the more likely
you are to find a job.
Just the opposite of
what the typical
job-hunter or
career-changer
starts out
believing.

JOB MARKET DIAGRAMS NEVER INCLUDE
JOBS FOR WHICH NO VACANCY EXISTS

The average job-hunter — left to their own devices — is almost sure that the job-hunting task consists — in one way or another — of unearthing *jobs which someone held before, and which are now vacant. So the job-hunter searches classified ads, employment agencies, etc.*

It rarely occurs to them that if, instead, you select the organizations or companies that interest you, and do enough research to unearth their problems (and how you can help solve them) the company may be perfectly willing to create a new job, for which no vacancy exists, just because ultimately they all will save money by doing so. (Problems always cost a lot.) Heaven knows, there are enough insiders who have said — in print — that this hidden job market is what the job-hunter ought to be aiming at. Creation of new positions is the key to the professional job market, the creative minority have said again and again and again. One third of today's jobs didn't exist ten years ago. This is particularly true whenever the economy is going through some kind of paroxysm, like "the energy crisis" of 1979. New positions *must* be created.

Certainly, a little reflection will tell you why all of this is so. Pretend, for a moment, that you are an executive of some company or organization. Your organization exists in order to get a certain job done, or product produced. And it's doing a pretty good job. But *naturally* you've also got problems; who doesn't? Some of them are just minor, and of long standing — just something you live with. Others are relatively new and of major importance, maybe even in a sense a *time bomb* — if you don't solve these, they're going to break your back. All of them are costing you money, sometimes a lot of money.

Now, naturally your employees are aware of these problems — and some at least are trying to help you solve them. But, for one reason or another, they haven't succeeded. Then, into your office one morning comes some job-hunter who knows an amazing amount about your company or organization, including some of the major problems that you are facing. That person has analyzed them, and has skills which they believe can help solve them. Very soon, you believe they can too, but *there is no vacancy in your company. Will you go and try your darnedest to create a new job, in order to get your hands on this person? Regardless of their age, background, or whatever?* Provided you have the power (and our man or woman won't be talking to you if you don't) *you bet you will.* In fact, you may have been thinking for some time that you needed this new position, anyway.

KNOWLEDGE IS POWER

These facts about the nature of the "job market," the meaning of "skills," and the availability of "high level positions" are very strange.

They are also contrary to what many people, posing as experts, will tell you.

They are also (nonetheless) true.

And (consequently) they work.

Time after time, again and again, men and women who have comprehended the true nature of what they were facing in the matter of "the job market" — so called — have successfully found their first job, or made the transition from one career to another, without retraining or further post-graduate courses, and in the area of the country that *they* chose.

And this, in spite of the fact that often the geographical area they wanted to live and work in was designated as virtually a disaster area by experts, unemployment-wise and job-wise.

They realized, as we said earlier, that all that the unemployment figures tell you is how many people are competing with you for whatever vacancies there are, or for whatever new positions there might be.

But, the vacancies (or potential new positions) *are there no matter how bad the economy is.* People get promoted; people move; people die; executives get tired of dealing with the same old unsolved problems and resolve to hire *anyone* capable of solving them. Young or old; male or female. Even if they're from *Mars.*

Since the vacancies or potential new jobs really are there — wherever in the country one turns — you must choose where it is you want to focus.

That means: the place where you already are (if you love it or if you have no choice, because of family or economic pressures) or the place where you've always wanted to be or if you are absolutely without any preference, it means something like pinning up a map of the U.S. and throwing darts (one guy actually did this).

But one way or another *you* have got to do the choosing.

You should not ask another man or woman to make this decision for you, nor should you ask external events (fate, coincidence, or where the "job market" is alleged to be favorable) to decide for you.

It's your move. *Your* move.

JOB MARKET FOCUSING
(THE LASER BEAM APPROACH)

Job-hunters such as yourself, dear Reader, begin by thinking there are too few job markets (and therefore, too few jobs) "out there." Thus far, in this chapter, we have argued just the opposite. There are too many. If you try to hit them all (shotgun style) you will only diffuse your energies and your effectiveness. Better, far better, to try concentrating your energies and effectiveness. Rifle style. (For peace lovers, a nonmilitary? image would be the laser beam.) This whole process might be compared to a funneling (read the diagram on page 125 at least three times, for it summarizes the heart of this chapter):

THE CRUCIAL MATTER:

What Will Get You A Job?

Suppose the time has come when you will need an alternative career. As you think about the job-hunt, very well-meaning people will tell you that the only route is to go back to college: go learn some skill or profession other than the one you had, *they say*. Go back to school. Get retrained. Get your doctorate. *They say*.

The government, personnel experts, and many others think along these same lines: *retraining* always seems to be the answer to many well-meaning people, trying to give helpful advice. As you will discover, when that time comes. Or, have already discovered.

There is, of course, a reason for this:

People think there are only two things that you can get a job with: experience, or credentials. They figure you've got to have one or the other.

1. Experience. If you want to be a machinist, and you've done it for ten years, you have convincing experience. If you want to be a teacher, and you've taught for ten years, you have convincing experience. In other words, if you've done it long enough, many people don't care *how* you picked up the skill in the first place. However, many people, after they have identified a new career that they would *enjoy*, have to admit they have no convincing experience to prove they are good (or would be good) in that career. And since all their friends tell them their *only two means of getting a job is either experience or credentials*, the poor souls assume they therefore must go and get:

2. Credentials. Now, to be sure, there are certain fields, such as law or medicine, where the aspirant is simply going to *have* to go back to school and get the requisite training and resulting credentials, before he or she can practice. So if you have settled upon *this kind* of new career for your transition, there is not likely to be any way you can avoid the credentialing route.

With most careers, however, this is not true. No matter what others may tell you. (It is amazing how much bad advice is dispensed in our society with the sound of certainty by people who have depended either on outdated data, or on scanty sampling, or on rumor and hearsay — rather than going and

14,000,000

JOB MARKETS IN THE UNITED STATES

(that's the total number of non-farm employers)

1 You narrow this down by deciding just what area, city or county you want to work in. This leaves you with however many thousands or millions of job markets there are in that area or city. • **2** You narrow this down by identifying your Strongest Skills, on their highest level that you can legitimately claim, and then thru research deciding what field you *want* to work in, above all. This leaves you with all the hundreds of businesses/ community organizations/agencies/schools/hospitals/ projects/associations/foundations/institutions/firms or government agencies there are in that area and in the field you have chosen. **3** You narrow this down by getting acquainted with the economy in the area thru personal interviews with various contacts; and supplementing this with study of journals in your field, in order that you can pinpoint the places that interest you the most. This leaves a manageable num- ber of markets for you to do some study on. **4** You now narrow this down by ask- ing yourself: *can I be happy in this place, and, do they have the kind of prob- lems which my strongest skills can help solve for them?* **5** This leaves you with the companies or organizations which you will now, carefully plan how to approach for a job

Focusing

Down

...in your case, *the* job.

doing their own research before they solemnly tell you what you must do.) Maybe you do need credentials — if you are going to set yourself up in private practice as a marriage counselor, or consultant or such; maybe. But you ought to reach this conclusion as a result of your own intensive research first, if you reach it at all. You will discover that people have gotten jobs as full professors at Universities when they did not possess a doctorate or any other credential that everyone told them they *had* to have. Likewise with other fields. And all of this because these men and women carving out a new career for themselves just didn't believe there were only two things with which to get a job. There has got to be a third thing, they reasoned, that doesn't depend on the past at all; and that is, *to give a demonstration of your skills right in front of the prospective employer.* Impossible, you say? Not at all. You can show an employer right in their own office that you have the skill they want more than anything: namely, the skill of

3. PROBLEM-SOLVING. No matter how much it may seem that different kinds of work vary upon the surface, underneath they have this common base: they deal with one kind of problem-solving or another. Universities, community organizations, businesses — all require people good at problem-solving *no matter what title may be tacked on the person they hire, in order to justify the salary. Problem-solvers get hired,* whether they are fresh out of high school, or in their retirement years, or in between.

Now, how do you prove you are a problem-solver right before the very eyes of a prospective employer? Forget about producing convincing Experience from the past, or producing credentials from the past. Just do the most thorough-going research imaginable of the particular company(ies), university(ies), organization(s) or other "job markets" *that you have chosen as most interesting to you,* BEFORE you ever go into the office to seek the job.

Now we said this third pathway is often THE KEY to getting a job when changing careers. But it is just as important when you are setting out to find your first job, or when you are job-hunting in a field where you are already experienced. Therefore, we urge this path upon *all* job-hunters through your own most thorough-going research; we don't mean just an hour or two in the library. This is not what we are talking about, here.

> We are talking about the most thorough-going research that you have the patience and determination to do. Hour after hour; day after day. Phew! Lots of work. But the rewards: Wow.

DON'T PAY SOMEONE TO DO THIS RESEARCH FOR YOU, WHATEVER YOU DO

There are a number of reasons why *no one else* can do your research for you, in this whole process:

1. Only *you* really know what things you are looking for, what things you want to avoid if possible; in a word, what your *tropisms* are.

2. Moreover, you need the self-confidence that comes as you practice this skill of researching *before* you go after the organizations that you have chosen.

3. You will need to use this skill on the job, after you get your job, so the time spent practicing it before you get the job will pay off for literally years, thereafter.

4. Most importantly, the skills you use to find a job are close to the skills you use to do the job, after you get it. Therefore, by doing all this research — or informational interviewing, as we will call it — you are increasing your qualifications for the job itself. Thus, this conclusion: the more research you do, the more qualifications you have.

Can you do this research yourself, then?

Of course you can.

If you went to college, or even post-graduate school, which over half of the high school graduates today are doing, you know exactly how to go about Researching — since you did lots of it there.

If you only went to high school, you still did source papers and maybe even term papers. Anyway, you'd be surprised at how this kind of skill comes back, once you try to revive it.

It consists, in essence, of a skillful blend of:

WRITTEN STUFF, AND PEOPLE

In researching any part of this whole process: a) your skills; b) your field; c) your geographical area; or d) your chosen places to approach for a position, you will probably be dealing *alternately* with written material (books, journals, magazines, or other material which librarians and such can direct you to) and with people, who are experts in one aspect or another of the subjects you are researching. YOU READ UNTIL YOU NEED TO TALK TO SOMEONE BECAUSE YOU CAN'T FIND MORE IN BOOKS; THEN YOU TALK TO PEOPLE UNTIL YOU KNOW YOU NEED TO GET BACK AND DO SOME MORE READING.

Essential to your research (in either form) is that you know:

WHAT IT IS THAT YOU ARE LOOKING FOR

When You Are Reading or Interviewing About	Among The Things You May Be Looking For Are:
your skills	what kind of work uses *most* of these skills *together*
fields of possible work	which ones you will be happiest (and therefore most effective) in, because they fit in with your total Life Mission as you perceive it
geographical area that you have chosen	the kind of places that might need your skills, in the field you have chosen
places where you might want to work	to find out if there is any reason why you might *not* want to work there; to find out what problems they have *and* which problems are both urgent ("time-bombs") and ones which your skills can help solve.

© Copyright, 1979, United Feature Syndicate, Inc. Used by permission.

Interviewing
for Information Only

Beyond mechanics, it is essential for you to remember who you are, as you are going about this whole business of researching and interviewing *for information only*. The whole process will divide into two parts. Let us make clear what they are:

Part I. You are the screener. The employers and organizations are the *screenees*. You are looking them over, trying to decide which of these pleases YOU. This is for information, building of contacts, and tracking down places that interest you *only*. During this part of the process, you can even take others with you (especially if you are in high school or college and this is all new to you, or if you are a housewife coming into the market-place for the first time). After all, you are going out only to find information. You are not *yet* job-hunting. Therefore, it's perfectly okay to take someone with you, if you want to.

Part II. Having narrowed down the possibilities to four or five that really fascinate you, you now return to them in the fashion we shall describe in the next chapter, to seek an interview for an actual job there doing the thing you have decided you would most like to do. At this point *and only at this point,* you now become the Screenee, and the employers or organizations or funding-sources or whatever become the Screeners. Though, of

course, you are still keeping your eyes and ears open in case you see something dreadful that will put you abruptly back into the role of Screener and cause you to say, to yourself at least, "I have just learned this place really isn't for me." In any event, the part we are talking about in this chapter is what we have called Part I, above — where you are the Screener; and is not to be confused with Part II (next chapter) where you become the screenee. If you *feel* as though you are the Screenee in this first part of the research we are describing, you're doing something wrong — even if you have all the mechanics down pat. Just remember, as a human being you've got rights: including the right to go look at places and decide whether or not they interest you, and whether or not you could do your most effective work there if you like what they're doing.

There are resources to help you at this point; but resources are useless, unless you keep firmly in mind what kinds of questions you want the resources to help you with. These questions are best illustrated when you are:

**TRYING TO SURVEY
A FARAWAY PLACE**

The Principles of
Information-Searching
At a Distance
(But They Are The Same For
The Place Where You Live)

1 *Be clear about the different kinds of information
you are going to need for your job-hunt.*

To recapitulate, you are going to need information about the following (use this as a check-list):

a. *What your skills are (1) that you have already demon-strated; and (2) that you enjoy.* This list must be in detail, *and* clustered into families, *and* prioritized in terms of your six or so favorites. If you failed to do any of these three steps (put them in detail, clusters, and prioritized) you will *dramatically* hamper your subsequent information-search.

b. *Where you want to use these skills.* Someone who has the skill of welding can use that skill to weld the casing for a nuclear bomb, or to make a wheel for a cart. So, what do *you* want to use *your* skills with? In the service of what? To accomplish what? Simply to say you want to do welding (or whatever) is not sufficient, and will seriously hamper your subsequent information-search.

c. *What kinds of organizations are there (1) that you like in terms of their goals? and that (2) either already do use people with your skills; or (3) ought to, and perhaps could be persuaded to; and are (4) in the* geographical area (or areas) *you have focused on.* The last step above is the pre-condition for answering the other three. An overseas soldier — for example — cannot do an information-search about corporations' department of mental hygiene, until he or she has *first* selected at least an area of the country, and preferably two or three cities in that area, by name.

d. *What the names of such organizations are, in the cities you have focused upon.* The more specific and detailed you have been in step "c." above, the easier this step "d." will be. The more general you have been, the harder this step will be, e.g., "Corporations" is too general. In a particular city, that will turn out to be a very long list. But (for example) "Corporations with not more than 200 employees, which produce such and such a product" is a much shorter list, in any particular city (or country-area). Likewise, "non-profit organizations" is too general. That again will produce a long list, if your information-search is thorough. "Non-profit organizations dealing with . . . ." what? health services, consumer protection, or what? The more detailed you are, the easier it will be for you to do the information-search.

e. *What are their problems, as organizations — and particularly "in the departments or areas where I would be working?"* A lot depends on the level at which you want to work. If at the clerk or secretary level, the problems are pretty predictable: absenteeism, too-long coffee or lunch breaks, not caring about the subject-matter, not accepting your supervisor's priorities about which work needs to get done first, etc. If you want to work at a higher level, the problems are likely to be correspondingly more complex.

f. *Who there has the power to hire for the level of job you are aiming at?* It's not likely to be the Personnel Department, unless you're talking about entry-level.

Set down on paper which of the above information-searches you can do right where you are, and which ones you need others' help with, in the city of your choice.

Normally, you can do the information-search on "a." and "b." above, right where you are, since this is potentially a self-directed information-search. To aid you in doing that part of the information-search, there is the Quick Job-Hunting Map; *Beginning Version,* for high school students and others who are entering the world of work for the first time; *Advanced Version,* for those who have had considerable experience in the world of work, or who wish to change careers. (The Advanced Version as you already know, is in Appendix A, page 182.)

If, even with the Map, you have difficulty identifying your skills or where you want to use them, you may then: (1) Recruit your mate, or a friend, or business acquaintance there in your city where you presently are, to help you work through the map; OR (2) Use a professional career expert such as your college career-planning or placement office; or one of the professionals to be found in Appendix C; or one of the three hundred job-hunters or counselors who have been trained by the National Career Development Project in a two-week workshop (name of the person(s) nearest you upon request, by writing: Referrals, NCDP, P.O. Box 379, Walnut Creek, CA 94596, and enclosing a stamped, self-addressed return envelope, with a $1 cheque for postage and handling).

Now, once this is done, you are ready to go on to the other information-searches listed on the previous pages. IF there is a really good library near you, or if that library (however small and limited) is on an inter-library loan system, you can do *some* research on "c.," *some* research on "d," and some also on "f."

So, your two lists will *probably* come out looking like this:

Searches I Can Do Here	Searches Others Must Do There
a. in detail	the rest of
b.	c.
c.	d.
d. some	e. in detail
f.	f.

3 *Determine how much time you have before*
you **absolutely** *have to find a job.*

Yes, of course it would be just dandy if you could conclude your information-search — successfully — within a month. And, many people do. But it is not at all unusual for a job-hunt to take nine months (something symbolic about *that*) or longer. Soooo, how much time *do* you have before you simply *must* have your next job? At the outside limit? The earlier you can get started, the more lead-time you can give yourself, the better.

4 *Figure out if there isn't* **some** **way** *during that time*
that you could go visit the city or cities of your choice.

Does a vacation fall within the time period you have between now and when you must finally have that job? Could you visit it on vacation? Could you take a summer job there? Go there on leave? Get sent to a convention there? Get appointed to a group or association that meets there? Think it through. You will *have* to go there, finally (in almost all cases) for the actual job interview(s). If worse comes to worse, go there a week or so ahead of that interview. Better late than never, to look over the scene in person.

5 *Until you can go there, use every resource and contact*
you have in order to explore the answers to "c.," "d.,"
"e." and "f." on page 131.

It will be doubly-apparent by now, to one and all, how crucial it is for you to choose *by name* one, two or three cities or towns where you are going to (a) focus your information-search; (b) at least initially. And if it's a country-area that interests you, then at least identify that area, and the name of the city or town(s). And then, starting with the city or town that's at the top of your list, use the following resources in your information-search:

a. *The local daily or weekly newspaper.* Almost all papers will mail to subscribers anywhere in the world. So: subscribe, for a six-month period, or a year. You'd be surprised at what you can learn from the paper. Some of the answers to "c.", "d.", "e." and "f." will appear there. Additionally, you will note businesses that are growing and expanding — hence, hiring — in that city you are researching.

b. *The Chamber of Commerce, and City Hall (or the Town Hall).* These are the places whose interest it is to attract newcomers, and to tell them what kinds of businesses there are in town — as well as some details about them. So: write and ask them, in the beginning, what they have about the city or town in general. Then later, don't hesitate to write back to them with more specific questions, if need be.

c. *The local library or reference librarian, if your target city/town has one.* Yes, of course it is perfectly kosher to write to the library of your target city, asking for information that may be only there. If the librarian is too busy to answer, then use one of your contacts there to find out. "Bill (or Billie) I need some information that I'm afraid only the library in your town has. Specifically, I need to know about company x." Or, whatever.

d. *Your contacts.* Yes, of course, you know people in whatever city or town you're researching during your job-hunt-as-information-search. For openers, write to your old high school and get the alumni list for your graduating class. Then write to your college — if you went to college — and ask for the alumni list for your class, also. Subscribe to your college's alumni bulletin for further news, addresses, and hints. If you belong to a church or synagogue, write to the church or synagogue in your target city, and tell them that you're one of their own and you need some information. ("I need to know who can tell me what non-profit organizations there are in that city, that deal with x.") Or, whatever. ("I need to know how I can find out what corporations in town have departments of mental hygiene.") For further contacts, ask your family and relatives who they know in the target city or town of your choice. You know more people in that city, who could help you, than you think.

e. *The appropriate state, county, and local government agencies, associations, etc.* Ask your contacts to tell you what that appropriate agency might be. For additional help, there are directories of national addresses and phone numbers, such as: *National Directory of Addresses and Telephone Numbers,*

1980-81 Edition (by Stanley R. Greenfield, available from Bantam Books, Inc., 666 Fifth Ave., New York, NY 10019. 1977. $14.95, paper).

6 *Regard the city or town where you presently are, as a replica of the city or town you are interested in going to (at least in some respects) — so that some of the information-search can be done where you are, and then its learnings can be transferred.*

Suppose, for example, you know that you are skilled in counseling people, particularly in one to one situations, that you are knowledgeable about — and well-versed in — psychiatry, and that you love carpentry and plants. You are (obviously) at stage "c." on page 131.

What kinds of organizations does this point to?

To get at this, first translate all of your above interests into people (counseling=counselor), (psychiatry=psychiatrist), (carpentry=carpenter), (plants=gardener).

Next, ask yourself which of these persons is most likely to have the largest overview? This is often the same (but not always) as asking: who took the longest to get their training? The answer here: psychiatrist.

In the place where you presently are, then, go to see a psychiatrist (pay them for fifteen minutes of their time — if there is no other way) or go see the head of the psychiatry department at the nearest college or university, and ask them: Do you have any idea how to put all the above together in a job? And, if you don't, who might?

Eventually, you will be told by them: Yes, there is a branch of psychiatry that uses plants to help heal people.

Having found this out in the place where you live, you can then write to your target city or town to ask, What psychiatric facilities are there, there, and which ones — if any — use plants in their healing program?

Thus can you conduct your research where you are, and then transfer its learnings to the place you want to go.

For further information on how to conduct this information search more thoroughly, see *Where Do I Go From Here With My Life?* (op. cit.) pages 102-112, 120-148, the even-numbered pages particularly.

FOCUSING DOWN: TO YOUR GEOGRAPHICAL AREA

It will ultimately be *essential* for you to visit the place you want to work in (if you do not already live there). You will want to talk to key individuals *who can suggest other people you might talk to, as you try to find out what organizations interest you.* You will want to define these key individuals or contacts ahead of time, and let them know you are coming. Your list may include: friends, college alumni (if you attended college, get the alumni list from them so you can find out who lives in that area), high school pals, church contacts, Chamber of Commerce executives, city manager, regional planning offices, appropriate county or state offices in your area of interest, the Mayor, and high level management in particular companies that look interesting from what you've read or heard about them.

A new book is out, dealing with how you locate such contacts, called *Names and Numbers: A Journalist's Guide to the Most Needed Information Sources and Contacts,* by a staff member of *The Philadelphia Inquirer* (Rod Nordland). It's expensive ($24.95, in hardcover) — so I suggest you consult your local library. It has over 20,000 listings. Many job-hunters may find it helpful during their research.

When you "hit town," you will want to remember the City Directory, the Yellow Pages of your phone book, etc.

If going into a strange new geographical area is a totally new experience for you, and you have no friends there in your chosen target area, just remember there are various ways of meeting people, making friends, and developing contacts rather quickly. There are athletic clubs, Y's, churches, charitable and community organizations, where you can present yourself and meet people from the moment you walk in the doors. You will soon develop many acquaintances, and some beginning friendships, and the place won't seem so lonely at all.

Also, visit or write your high school before you set out for this new town and find out what graduates live in the area that you are going to be visiting for the first time: they are your friends already, because you went to the same school. All of these acquaintances, friends and key individuals have one common name: contacts. Yes, contacts, Contacts, CONTACTS.

Whenever anyone writes me and says that "informational interviewing may be a *great* idea for Others, but it just isn't working for Me," I know inevitably that that person just hasn't made Sufficient Use of his or her contacts. So, remember this: they are *crucial* to the success of your information-interviewing and, ultimately, your job-hunt. An interesting study about contacts has been published, and you may find some helpful ideas in it. The book is called *Getting A Job: A Study of Contacts and Careers,* by Mark S. Granovetter, and if your library doesn't have it, it can be ordered from Harvard University Press, c/o Uniserv Inc., 525 Great Road (Route 119), Littleton, MA 01460. 1974. $7.95, hardcover.

Since you are job-hunting, you may want to put a modest-sized advertisement in the paper once you go there, saying you would like to meet with other people who are following the job-hunting techniques of *What Color Is Your Parachute?* That way you'll form a kind of 'job-hunters anonymous,' where you can mutually support one another in your hunt.

You will want to follow the same process, even if you already live in the area you are interested in working in. Your search: for places that need your skills. Your aide: your contacts, and that includes *everyone* you know or meet during a typical day or week: people on the street, in the market, in the stores you patronize, the places you regularly visit, etc. Your purpose: not to find out if a particular organization wants you, but rather, whether or not *you* want them — as we keep repeating.

FOCUSING DOWN:
TO KINDS OF PLACES
IN THAT AREA

Suppose, now, you've decided that, say, being a consultant uses more of your skills than anything else. The question you then face is: should I be a consultant in education, in business, in non-profit organizations, in fund-raising, or what? It is important, as you are identifying what you like to do, that you identify in what *kinds* of places you might enjoy doing this.

It is the same with every other career or occupation. You want to be a teacher, let us say. Do you want to be one at a university, a college, a junior college, a business school, in private industry (some corporations, such as IBM for example, make large use of teachers), or where? The purpose of this section of your interviewing for information is to look at *all the options,* so that you can choose the one you prefer the most along with some possible 'plan Bs.'

You are looking for the organizations or places (colleges, institutions, agencies, etc.) where you would be *happiest* working. Why? Because the more you enjoy *what* you are doing and *where* you are doing it, the better you are going to use the talents which God gave you.

If you are not at all familiar with the business world, and want a detailed breakdown of management functions and sub-functions, so that you will gain a better idea of where you might want to target yourself, there is the *Common Body of Knowledge for Management Consultants,* available in your library or (for $13 or so) from the Association of Consulting Management Engineers, Inc., 230 Park Avenue, New York, NY 10017.

Here are the kind of questions about yourself that you are (hopefully) trying to find the answers to, as you do your research and interviewing:

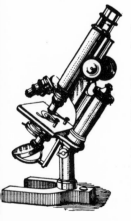

1. Do I want to work for a company, firm, agency, college, association, foundation, the government, or what?

2. Do I want to work for an older and larger organization, or get in on the ground floor of a new and smaller one, with growth possibilities?

3. Do I want to advance rapidly? If so I need an organization with solid plans for expansion — overseas or at home.

4. Do I want to work for a "going concern" or for "a problem child" type of operation. As the experts say, *a company in trouble* is a company in search of leadership. Same goes for foundations, agencies, etc. If that is your cup of tea, (well, is it?) you can probably find such places without too much investigation. Some experts say if you go for such a challenge, give yourself a time limit (say 3-5 years) and then if you can't solve it, get out.

5. Other questions: *your own personal ones* — what do I want to accomplish? what working circumstances do I want? what opportunities? what responsibilities? what kinds of job-pressures am I willing to exist under, and feel capable of handling? kinds of people to work with? starting salary? salary five years from now? promotion opportunities? (Keep these always in mind.)

It all looks, at first sight, as though this whole informational interviewing process were an awful lot of hard work. And, at first, it certainly is. Self-inventory, meaningful skills, career and life planning, job markets — there were times when we were tempted to forget the whole thing, and just go about the transition process and job-hunt in the old haphazard way that so many others do it. But, we told ourselves, *that way lies madness.* So, we kept at it. And now, we've begun to notice something: we're enjoying it. No telling just when it happened. But, we began to notice it is *fun* to travel around and talk to people. Maybe because they aren't on the spot (yet), and neither are we. And we begin to notice it is *fun* to do the research in our local library, college, or whatever.

Maybe a detective hides within the breast of each one of us. Maybe we enjoy talking to high level management and finding out that it isn't so difficult as the books *(with their long chapters on the art of conducting interviews)* make interviewing out to be. Maybe we enjoy the renewed sense of self-confidence that we are picking up, in non-stress situations. It's like solving a mystery.

Well, you with the soul of a detective, you *are* solving a mystery. Namely: in what environment will this hardy plant called *you* thrive, grow, and bloom the best? Or: if you're instinctively religious, a better form of the question for you might be, in what place can your service to the Lord best continue — without the danger of burying your talents in the ground?

That's the mystery you are unraveling.

Sure, it's fun. It's dealing with you. And by focusing down, in this fashion, you are increasingly able to concentrate your energies.

You are acting as though the organization that gets you will be darned lucky. You are even beginning to feel this is true. And, what is most strange, you are absolutely right.

FOCUSING DOWN:
GETTING ACQUAINTED

In visiting the geographical area where you most want to work, whether it is where you already are, or not, and in conducting your own personal and organizational survey of the area, you are trying to go from one person to another, building a chain of links in which each contact you see refers you to another (and hopefully sets up the appointment for you, or at least allows you to use his name).

Let's listen to an actual job-hunter describe the process:

"Suppose I arrived cold in some city, the one place in all the world I want to live — but with no idea of what that city might hold as a match and challenge for my personal talent bank. I have an economic survey to make, yes; but I also have an equally or more important personal survey to accomplish. Can this city meet my peculiarly personal needs? To find out, I meet Pastors, bankers, school principals, physicians, dentists, real estate operators, et al. I would be astonished if opportunities were not brought to my attention, together with numerous offers of personal introduction to key principals. All I would be doing is forging links (referrals) in a chain leading to my eventual targets. *The referral is the key.*"

People who haven't tried this are understandably afraid: afraid important men or women won't have time to see them, afraid they won't be able to get past the secretary or receptionist, etc. But, as was said above, referral (by one of your contacts) is the key.

Well, suppose you just can't find a referral to a particular person you want to see?

Let's listen to John Crystal, a master in this field, describe the process:

"If you really are interested in highway-carrier operations and really do know quite a bit about it, for instance, and you get to Charlotte, NC, where you learn that one small, new company is doing something really innovative and intelligent in *your* field I would guess that the chances are that its President is just as fascinated by the subject as you are. And if you called him up — Oh, yes, the secretary, well this goes for her too — and told him the simple truth about that shared interest — if he asks if you are job hunting tell him the truth, *No, not at the moment,* — but that you are *in truth* impressed by what you have heard about his bright ideas, and that you want to hear more about them, and that you just might possibly have a suggestion or two based on your own experience which he might find useful — Well, he just might invite you to lunch. And if he wants to offer you a job after a while, and many do, it's strictly *his* idea. And you do not accept it although you are always polite enough to say that you will be glad to consider it and perhaps talk it over with him again later on, after you have decided precisely what you want to do, where, with whom, etc. The key to the whole thing is this: treat the other person just as you would like to be treated yourself."

If this process has been followed religiously (so to speak) you will have at the end of your initial informational interviewing:

1. A *list* of places in your chosen geographical area *that interest you, and that look as though they have problems your skills can help solve.*

What you then want to do further research about is:

2. *Identifying in detail what those problems are,* for the manageable number of organizations you have now identified in list No. 1 above.

AN ORGANIZATION'S PROBLEMS

All organizations have money — to one degree or another. What you are looking for are *problems* — specifically, *problems that your skills can help solve; what problems are bugging this organization? Ask; look. (If you are talking to people within a*

© Copyright, 1980 NEA, INC. *Contra Costa Times.* Used by special permission.

*company or organization that looks as though it might be
interesting to you, ask them ever so gently:* What is the biggest
challenge you are encountering here?)

The problem does not have to be one that is bothering only
that organization. You may want to ask what problem is
common to the whole industry or field — low profit, obsoles-
cence, inadequate planning, etc.? Or if there is a problem that is

INTERVIEWING
FOR INFORMATION ON
AN ORGANIZATION'S PROBLEMS

How does this organization rank within its field or industry? Is this organization family owned? If so, what
effect has that on promotions? Where are its plants, offices or branches? What are all its projects or services? In
what ways have they grown in recent years? New lines,
new products, new processes, new facilities, etc? Existing political situations: imminent proxy fights, up-
coming mergers, etc.? What is the general image of the
organizations in peoples' minds? If they have stock,
what has been happening to it (see an investment broker
and ask).

What kind of *turnover of staff* have they had? What is
the attitude of employees toward the organization? Are
their faces happy, strained, or what? Is promotion
generally from within, or from outside? How long have
chief executives been with the organization?

Do they encourage their employees to further their
educational training? Do they help them pay for it?

How do *communications* work within the organization? How is information collected, by what paths does
it flow? What methods are used to see that information
gets results — to what authority do people respond
there? Who reports to whom?

Is there a "time-bomb" — a problem that will kill the
organization, or drastically reduce its effectiveness and
efficiency if they don't solve it fast?

common to the geographic region: labor problems, minority employment, etc. All you really need is one major problem that you would truly delight to help solve.

Some of these questions above will be relevant, for you; others will not be. *If you are "going after" a college, for example, some of these may have to be ignored, and some adapted.*

Some of these questions are general in nature, and you will try to answer them about *any* organization you approach. Other questions are very specific, requiring detailed research, and you will have to keep at it, searching, digging, interviewing, until you find out. But the skills you are sharpening up will more than repay you the time spent, a thousandfold. If this whole question of an organization's problems is a difficult concept for you to grasp, just think of five stores you've patronized during the past year, where something went wrong for you as a customer. What was it? You weren't waited on, when it was your proper turn? You weren't told all the information you needed to know, in order to make an intelligent choice? Or what. You will quickly realize, you are more aware of an organization's problems than you thought you were. But if you want some more Basic Training, before you dive in to this phase of your active informational interviewing, there is some reading you can do — if you want. There is *The Handbook of Business Problem Solving,* Kenneth J. Albert, ed., (McGraw-Hill Book Company, 1221 Avenue of the Americas, New York, NY 10020. 1980. $24.95, hardcover.) There is also: *Life in Organizations, Workplaces As People Experience Them,* by Rosabeth Moss Kanter and Barry A. Stein, ed., available from Basic Books, Inc., 10 East 53rd Street, New York, NY 10022. 1979. $17.50, hardcover. Or see your library. And: *Quality is Free: The Art of Making Quality Certain,* by Philip B. Crosby (McGraw Hill Book Company, New York, NY. 1979. $12.50, hardcover). And: *The Briarpatch Book: experiences in right livelihood and simple living,* from the Briarpatch Community. Available from: New Glide Publications, 330 Ellis Street, San Francisco, CA 94102. 1978. $8.00, paper. Some browsing in the above, should be a good crash course in becoming aware of what an organization's problems *might* be.

So much for the general principles. Now, here are some more detailed rules.

**RULES FOR FINDING OUT IN DETAIL
THE NEEDS OR PROBLEMS
OF AN ORGANIZATION**

Rule No. 1: *You don't need to discover the problems of the whole organization (unless it's very small); you only need to discover the problems that are bugging the-person-who-has-the-ultimate-responsibility (or power)-to-hire-you.* The conscientious always bite off more than they can chew. If they're going to try for a job at the Telephone Company, or IBM or the Federal Government, or General Motors or — like that — they assume they've got to find out the problems facing that whole organization. *Forget it!* Your task, fortunately, is much more manageable. Find out what problems are bugging, bothering, concerning, perplexing, gnawing at, the-person-who-has-the-power-to-hire-you. This assumes, of course, that you have first *identified* who that person is. If you did a thorough information-search, of course, you probably have already met that person, in the course of gathering your information. So they are more to you than just a name. If it's a committee (of sorts) that actually has the responsibility (and therefore Power) to hire you, you will need to figure out who that one individual is (or two) who *sways* the others. You know, the one whose judgment the others respect. How do you find that out? By using your contacts, of course. Someone will know someone who knows that whole committee, and can tell you who their *real* leader is. It's not necessarily the one who got elected as Chairperson.

Rule No. 2: *Don't assume the problems have to be huge, complex and hidden. The problems bothering the-person-who-has-the-power-to-hire-you may be small, simple, and obvious.* If the job you are aiming at was previously filled by someone (i.e., the one who, if you get hired, will be referred to as "your predecessor") the problems that are bothering the-person-who-has-the-power-to-hire-you may be uncovered simply by finding out (through those among your contacts, etc. — who know your prospective boss) what bugged them about your predecessor. Samples:

"They were never to work on time, took long lunch breaks, and were out sick too often"; OR

"They were good at typing, but had lousy skills over the telephone"; OR

"They handled older people well, but just couldn't relate to the young"; OR

"I never could get them to keep me informed about what they were doing"; Etc.

Sometimes, it's as simple as that. In your research you may be thinking to yourself, Gosh, this firm has a huge public relations problem; I'll have to show them that I could put together a whole crash P.R. program. That's the huge, complex and hidden problem that you think the-person-who-has-the-power-to-hire-you *ought to be concerned about.* But, in actual fact, what they *are* concerned about is whether (unlike your predecessor) you're going to get to work on time, take assigned lunch breaks, and not be out, sick, too often. Don't overlook the Small, Simple and Obvious Problems which bug almost every employer. (For further boning up, browse through *Management: Tasks, Responsibilities, Practices* by Peter F. Drucker, Harper & Row, 1973; and *Work in America*, Report of a Special Task Force to the Secretary of Health, Education, and Welfare, M.I.T. Press, 1973 — at your local library.)

Rule No. 3: *In most cases, your task is not that of educating your prospective employer, but of trying to read their mind.* Now, to be sure, you may have uncovered — during your information-search — some problem that the-person-who-has-the-power-to-hire-you is absolutely unaware of. And you may be convinced that this problem is *so crucial* that for you even to mention it will instantly win you their undying gratitude. Maybe. But don't bet on it. Our files are filled with sad testimonies like the following:

"I met with the V-P, Marketing in a major local bank on the recommendation of an officer, and discussed with him a program I devised to reach the female segment of his market, which would not require any new services, except education, enlightenment and encouragement. His comment at the end of the discussion was that the bank president had been after him for three years to develop a program for women, and he wasn't about to do it because the only reason, in his mind, for the president's request was reputation enhancement on the president's part . . ."

Inter-office politics, as in this case, or other considerations may prevent your prospective employer from being receptive to

Your Bright Idea. In any event, you're not trying to find out what *might* motivate them to hire you. Your research has got to be devoted rather to finding out what *already does* motivate them *when they decide to hire someone for the position you are interested in.* In other words, you're trying to find out What's Already Going On In Their Mind. In this sense, your task is more akin to a kind of mind-reading than it is to education. (Though *some* people-who-have-the-power-to-hire are *very* open to being educated. You just never know.)

Rule No. 4: *There are various ways of finding out what's going on in their mind: don't try just one way.* We will give a kind of outline, here, of the various ways. (You can use this as a checklist.)

A Analyzing the Organization at a Distance and Making Some Educated Guesses.

1. If the organization is expanding, then they need:
   a. More of what they already have; OR
   b. More of what they already have, but with different style, added skills, or other pluses *that are needed;* OR
   c. Something they don't presently have: a new kind of person, with new skills doing a new function or service

2. If the organization is continuing as is, then they need:
   a. To replace people who were fired (find out why; what was lacking?); OR
   b. To replace people who quit (find out what was prized about them); OR
   c. To create a new position (yes, this happens even in organizations that are not expanding — due to
      1) Old needs which weren't provided for, earlier, but now must be, even if they have to cut out some other function or position.
      2) Revamping assignments within their present staff)

3. If the organization is reducing its size, staff or product/service, then they
   a. Have not yet decided which staff to terminate, i.e., which functions to give low priority to (in which case *that* is their problem, and you may be able to help them identify which functions are "core-functions"); OR

b. *Have* decided which functions or staff to terminate (in which case they may need multi-talented people or generalists able to do several jobs, i.e., functions, instead of just one, as formerly).

B   *Analyzing the problems of the-person-who-has-the-power-to-hire-you by talking to them directly, during your preliminary information-interview.*

Why guess at what's going on in their mind, when you can find out directly by including them in your information survey? *(See "The Quick Job-Hunting Map" in Appendix A on page 182.)*

C   *Analyzing the problems of the-person-who-has-the-power-to-hire-you by talking to their "opposite number" in another organization which is similar (not to say, almost identical) to the one that interests you.*

If, for some reason, you cannot approach — at this time — the organization that interests you (it's too far away, or you don't want to tip your hand yet, or whatever), what you can do is pick a similar organization (or individual) where you are — and go find out what kind of problems are on their mind. (If you are interested in working for, say, a senator out West, you can talk to a senator's staff here, where you are, first; the problems are likely to be similar.)

D   *Analyzing the problems of your prospective employer by talking to the person who held the job before you — OR by talking to their "opposite number" in another similar/ identical organization.*

Nobody, absolutely nobody, knows the problems bugging a boss so much as someone who works, or used to work, for them. If they still work for them, they may have a huge investment in being discreet (i.e., not as honest as you need). Ex-employees rarely are any longer under that sort of pressure. Needless to say, if you're trying to get the organization to create a new position, there is no "previous employee." But in some identical or similar organization *which already has this sort of position*, you can find someone to interview.

E *Using your contacts/friends/everyone you meet, in order to find* someone *who*

1. Knows the organization that intersts you, or knows someone who knows;
2. Knows the-person-who-has-the-power-to-hire-you, or knows someone who knows;
3. Knows who their opposite number is in a similar/identical organization;
4. Knows your predecessor, or knows someone who knows;
5. Knows your "opposite number" in another organization, or knows someone who knows.

F *Supplementary Method: Research in the library,* on the organization, or an organization similar to it; on the individual-who-has-the-power-to-hire-you, or on their opposite number in another organization; etc. (ask your friendly librarian or research-librarian for help — tell them what you're trying to find out).

Rule No. 5: *Ultimately, this is a language-translation problem. You're trying to take your language (i.e., a description of your skills), and translate it into their language (i.e., their priorities, their values, their jargon, as these surface within their concerns, problems, etc.).* You should be aware to begin with that most of the-people-who-have-the-power-to-hire-you for the position that you want DO NOT like the word "problems." It reminds them they are mortal, have hangups, haven't solved something yet, or that they overlooked something, etc. "Smartass" is the word normally reserved for someone who comes in *and shows them up.* (This isn't true of everybody, but it's true of altogether too many.) Since you're trying to use *their* language, speak of "an area you probably are planning to move into" or "a concern of yours" or "a challenge currently facing you" or *anything* except: "By the way, I've uncovered a problem you have." Use the word *problems* in your own head, but don't blurt it out with your prospective employer, unless you hear them use it first.

Beyond this, your goal is to be able to speak of Your Skills in terms of *The Language* of Their Problems. We will close with some examples, in order to bring this all home:

The person who has the power to hire you, was bugged by or concerned about:	You therefore use language which emphasizes that you:
Your predecessor had all the skills, but was too serious about *everything*.	have all the skills (name them) *plus* you have a sense of humor.
This place is expanding, and now needs a training program for its employees.	have the skills to do training, and in the area they are concerned about.
All the picayune details they have to attend to, which they would like to shovel off on someone else.	are very good with details and follow up. (That had better be true.)
This magazine probably isn't covering all the subjects that it should, but that's just a gnawing feeling, and they've never had time to document it, and decide what areas to move into.	have done a complete survey of its table of contents for the last ten years, can show what they've missed, and have outlined sample articles in those missing areas.

So much for the kinds of questions. Now, what resources are there in your local library, that can help you find answers?

WRITTEN RESOURCES

Some tools for helping to identify organizations' problems, are listed below. They are available from your local library, a brokerage office, bank or the organization itself.

American Men and Women of Science.

American Society of Training and Development Directory.
   Who's Who In Training and Development. P.O. Box 5307,
   Madison, WI 53705.

Better Business Bureau report on the organization (call your BBB in the
   city where the organization is located).

Chamber of Commerce data on the organization (visit the Chamber there).

College library (especially *business school* library) if there is one in your
   chosen area.

Company/college/association/agency/foundation *Annual Reports.*
   Get directly from company, etc., or from Chamber or library.

Contacts Influential.

Directory of Corporate Affiliations. (National Register Publishing Co., Inc.)

Dun & Bradstreet's Million Dollar Directory.

Dun & Bradstreet's Middle Market Directory.

Encyclopedia of Associations, Vol. 1, National Organizations,
    Gale Research Company.
Encyclopedia of Business Information Sources (2 volumes).
Fitch Corporation Manuals.
F and S Indexes (recent articles on firms).
F & S Index of Corporations and Industries. Lists "published articles"
    by Industry and by Company name. Updated weekly.
Fortune Magazine's 500.
Fortune's Plant and Product Directory.
The Foundation Directory.
Industrial Research Laboratories of the United States,
    Bowker Publishing, a Division of Xerox Publishing, 1180 Avenue
    of the Americas, New York, NY 10036. (212) 764-5100.
    1977. $65.
Investor, Banker, Broker Almanac
Levine, Michael, How to Reach Anyone Who's Anyone, Price/Stern/Sloan
    Publishers, Inc., 410 N. La Cienega Boulevard, Los Angeles, CA
    90048. 1980. $4.95, paper.
MacRae's Blue Book.
Moody's Industrial Manual (and other manuals).
Greenfield, Stanley R., National Directory of Addresses and Telephone
    Numbers. Bantam Books, Inc., 666 Fifth Avenue, New York,
    NY 10019. 1977. $15.95, paper.
NTPA '80: National Trade & Professional Associations of the U.S. and
    Canada and Labor Unions. Columbia Books, Inc., Suite 1336,
    777 Fourteenth Street, N.W., Washington, DC 20005
    (202) 737-3777. 1980. $30.
Plan Purchasing Directory.
Poor's Register of Corporations, Directors and Executives (may be
    indexed under "Standard and Poor's"). Key executives in 32,000
    leading companies, plus 75,000 directors.
Research Centers Directory.
Register of Manufacturers for your state or area (e.g., California
    Manufacturers Register).
Standard Register of Advertisers.
Standard and Poor's Corporation Records.
Standard and Poor's Industrial Index.
Standard and Poor's Listed Stock Reports (at some broker's office).
Statistical Abstract of the United States (U.S. Department of Commerce).
Thomas' Register of American Manufacturers.
Value Line Investment Survey, from Arnold Bernhard and Co.,
    5 East 44th Street, New York, NY 10017. (Most libraries have a set.)
Walker's Manual of Far Western Corporations and Securities.

If all of this seems like an embarrassment of riches to you, and you don't know where to begin, there's even a guide to all these directories: If you don't know which directory to consult, see

Klein's *Guide to American Directories,*
or
your friendly neighborhood librarian.

Besides all of these directories, some other resources may also be worth perusing: Periodicals: *Business Week, Dun's Review, Forbes, Fortune,* and the *Wall Street Journal;*

Trade Associations and their periodicals; Trade journals.

There are also excellent surveys of key companies, e.g., Moskowitz, Milton; Katz, Michael; and Levering, Robert, ed., *Everybody's Business, An Almanac: The irreverent guide to corporate america.* Harper and Row Publishers, Inc., 10 East 53rd Street, New York, NY 10022. 1980. $9.95, paper.

You will want to note, also, that some libraries — particularly in large cities — have special sections devoted to careers. In Chicago, for example, there is a Business Information Center at The Chicago Public Library, 425 North Michigan Avenue, 11th floor, which publishes a list of its "Career Information Sources," and of the resources available from its "Business/ Science Technology Division," — including computer assisted searches for information. If you are timid about exploring your library's resources, walk up to the reference librarian and ask for help. The point of all this is, libraries are not just for scholars. Libraries are also for job-hunters, and career-changers. What you want to know, in many cases, is there.

Of course, despite this wealth of material, you cannot simply hide yourself away in the libraries all the time. This information out of books *must* be supplemented with talks with *insiders* — brokers, college alumni, friends, anyone you know who has friends within the particular organizations you are interested in, who can give you helpful insights. Use every contact you know.

No matter how thorough your research, remember when you are finally into the interview at a place that interests you, to listen carefully to the employer you are talking to. The greatest problem every employer faces is to find people who will listen and take them seriously. If you listen, you may find the employer discusses their problems — giving you firmer ground to thereafter relate your skills to.

CHECKLIST FOR
YOUR INFORMATION-INTERVIEWING

You say that you've tried informational interviewing, and while it seems like a wonderful idea in theory, it just isn't working for You? Here is a checklist to see if you are doing it right:

☐ Did you do your homework regarding Your Self, so that you know exactly what your skills are? *If not, go to Appendix A, and do the Quick Job-Hunting Map. If you set aside a full weekend, undisturbed, you can get it done.*

☐ Are you following the pattern for informational interviewing, that is outlined on pages 214–216 in the Map? *If not, that may explain your problem. In which case, You Know What You Must Do.*

☐ Are you sending letters asking for appointments? *Unless your interviewees are in a faraway city, don't. Use the phone instead; or, in some cases, it pays to just stop by, without an appointment, and try "pot-luck."*

☐ Are you clear in your own head that you are in a Pre-Job-hunt phase, when you are doing informational interviewing; or do you *really* feel that informational interviewing is just an extra-clever, extra devious way of hoodwinking the employer into thinking you are not a job-hunter, when in reality you are? *If the latter is the case, then you have utterly failed to understand the purpose of informational interviewing. In which case, you had better re-read pages 213–216 five times. For, if you*

secretly think you are job-hunting at this point, then you have become the screenee; when, with genuine informational interviewing, you are in an earlier pre-job-hunt phase, where you are the screener.

☐ If you're having trouble getting in, are you making it clear to the person you want to interview (or their receptionist), that you *only need fifteen (or, at the most, twenty) minutes* of their time? And are you sticking to that self-imposed limit, religiously? *If not, no wonder you can't get in. Every employer or information-source dreads becoming the semi-captive of a two-hour talker; and unless you have reassured them that You Are Brief, you are under suspicion of being a Possible THT.*

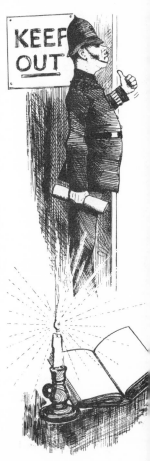

☐ If you're having trouble getting in, are you using your contacts to "get by" whoever it is that is screening you out? *If not, why not? Contacts are not merely to be saved for the final job-hunt phase. You can use them during the informational interviewing phase, as well. If you're trying to get information out of a certain place, and that place is guarded like Fort Knox, try this: for a week, ask EVERYONE you meet: "Do you know someone who works at (and here name the place you are trying to get in, to interview for information)? Or do you know anyone who does?" See what happens. (Of course, it doesn't always work; but you'd be surprised how many times it* does.*)*

☐ If after you get in, you are tongue-tied as to what to say, then obviously you're not clear as to what information you're looking for. *In which case, refer back to question #2 above, or read Billingsley's book* (listed at the end of The Quick Job-Hunting Map).

P.S. A Brief Footnote for Employers, Regarding Informational Interviewing: There are 14 million employing-organizations in this country, and heaven-only-knows how many managers or People-Who-Are-Information-Sources, within those 14 million. So, most of you have not run into Informational Interviewing, and where you have, you have been delighted to find someone who shares your enthusiasm for a particular field or job, and are more than willing to give a helping hand to someone who is up-and-coming, even as someone once gave you a helping hand. However, as we mentioned in the last chapter, a few of you are in highly-obvious organizations, or positions, where people who want information are going to be given your name, again and again. And so, you few will be receiving (over the years) more calls or drop-ins, looking for information, than you can bear. For you, a suggestion: why not schedule one hour a week, or every two weeks, or once a month, when you are willing to sit down and talk with anyone and everyone who wants some information from you about your career field, or your organization, or your particular job? That way, when anyone calls for an informational interview, you can give them an appointment for this particular time you have set aside on your schedule; and thus take care of everyone at once, because you will be doing group interviewing, instead of individual interviewing.

THAT OLD DEBBIL: THE RÉSUMÉ

As you do your survey, through interviewing and research, it should become clearer and clearer to you what kind of a position, and at what kind of a place, you are aiming. You are then in a position to write that most formidable of all personal documents: the resume — if you want one. (Some people prefer to go about this process without one, using themselves instead as "walking resumes.") But, if you want one, there are any number of books that offer samples and suggestions, which you can find in your local book store or library. The best guide, by

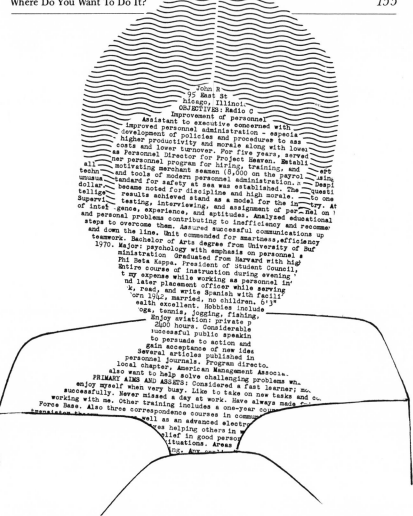

John R
95 East St
hicago, Illinoi.
OBJECTIVES: Radio C
Improvement of personnel
Assistant to executive concerned with
improved personnel administration - especia
development of policies and procedures to ass
higher productivity and morale along with lowe
costs and lower turnover. For five years, served
as Personnel Director for Project Heaven. Establi
ner personnel program for hiring, training, and ert
all motivating merchant seamen (8,000 on the payrol usin,
techn and tools of modern personnel administration. K Despi
unusua tandard for safety at sea was established. The questi
dollar. became noted for discipline and high morale. to one
tellige results achieved stand as a model for the in try. At
Supervi testing, interviewing, and assignment of per nel on
of intel -gence, experience, and aptitudes. Analyzed educational
and personal problems contributing to inefficiency and recomme
steps to overcome them. Assured successful communications up
and down the line. Unit commended for smartness,efficiency
teamwork. Bachelor of Arts degree from University of Buf
1970. Major: psychology with emphasis on personnel a
ministration Graduated from Harvard with hig
Phi Beta Kappa. President of Student Council,
Entire course of instruction during evening
t my expense while working as personnel in'
nd later placement officer while serving
k, read, and write Spanish with facili
'orn 1942, married, no children. 6'3"
ealth excellent. Hobbies include
'oga, tennis, jogging, fishing,
Enjoy aviation: private p
2400 hours. Considerable
uccessful public speakin
to persuade to action and
gain acceptance of new idea
Several articles published in
personnel journals. Program directo.
local chapter, American Management Associa.
also want to help solve challenging problems wh.
PRIMARY AIMS AND ASSETS: Considered a fast learner; mo.
enjoy myself when very busy. Like to take on new tasks and co.
successfully. Never missed a day at work. Have always made
working with me. Other training includes a one-year cou
Force Base. Also three correspondence courses in commu
well as an advanced electro
es helping others in
lief in good perso
ituations. Areas
ng. Any

far, is *Who's Hiring Who*, by Richard Lathrop (Ten Speed Press). [1]

The key to an effective and useful resume is very simple: you must know why you are writing it (to open doors for you, to help people remember you after you've interviewed them, or both), to whom you are writing it (the people who have the power to hire), what you want them to know about you, how you can help them and their organization, and how you can

1. There are also these recently published helps:
Williams, Eugene, *Increase Your Employment Opportunities with the Audiovisual Portfolio*. Competent Associates, Box 6745, Washington, DC 20020. 1980. Paper.
Parker, Yana, *Damn Good Resume Guidelines*. P.O. Box 5446, Berkeley, CA 94705. 1980. $2.00, paper.
Resume Service, *Resumes That Work*. Coles Publishing Co. Ltd., Toronto, Canada. 1979. $4.95, paper.

support this claim so as to convince them to reach a favorable decision about you.

You must know your primary *functional* goal (your strongest *skill*), plus your primary *organization* goal (*where* you can do it best).

If you have followed faithfully the techniques suggested by the creative minority (as outlined in these chapters), your resume will show it. Don't, whatever you do, just copy and adapt someone else's resume. It will be self-evident to the reader, that you didn't go through the processes in these chapters.

FINAL HINTS

Never put in *anything negative that would cause your resume to be screened out.* Save confessions and excruciating honesty for the confessional. E.g., omit "divorced," if that be your case, because it may imply "quitter" about your future in that organization. (Say "three dependents" or "single" and leave it at that.)

Never lie; but do select your truths carefully, as Bernard Haldane says. Don't volunteer something negative. Confessions are for the confessional, not for the resume.

And do figure out just exactly *why* you want a resume in the first place. You got A in Creative Writing? and are dying to use that skill? You should be out seeing people directly instead of inserting a piece of paper between you and them.

Thanks

Hopefully you will remember each night to sit down and write a brief note to each person you saw that *day*. This is *one of the most essential steps in the whole job-seeking process — and the one most overlooked by job-seekers.* Every professional counsels this step, and yet people overlook it continually. *It should be regarded as basic to courtesy, not to mention kindness, that we thank people who help us along the way.* Call them "bread and butter notes." Or whatever. We all ought to be most serious about this business of saying Thank You. Letters along the way also serve secondary purposes, such as underlining things we said, adding or correcting impressions we left behind us, and confirming our understanding of things the people we talked to said.

Don't forget secretaries, either. Get their names. Thank them for their help. They will appreciate you, and remember you. If you go to see their boss again, greet them by name (you did jot it down, didn't you?).

After all, you are presenting yourself as one who has one of the most sought-after skills in the world today: Knowing how to treat people as persons. Prove it, please — day by day. You'll get pleasure from it. And, what's more:

It just may get you the job. (According to one survey, job-hunting success was more related to this "thank you note" process than any other factor.) Indeed, we know of one woman who was actually told that she was hired because she was the only interviewee who sent a thank-you note after the interview.

*Y*ou're a bunch of jackasses.
You work your rear ends off in
a trivial course that no one will
ever care about again. You're not
willing to spend time researching
a company that you're interested in
working for. Why don't you
decide who you want to work for
and go after them?

Professor Albert Shapero
(again) to his students

CHAPTER SEVEN

You must identify the person who has the power to hire you and show them how your skills can help them with their problems.

THE FOURTH KEY TO
CAREER-PLANNING AND JOB-HUNTING

As you have gone through all this intensive research concerning the particular places that you have selected as the places you would like to work, you have achieved two deliberate results:

1. *Your list is probably smaller yet,* as you discovered some of the places that interested you (even after visiting them) *did not have the kind of problems or difficulties that your strongest skills could* a) solve; and b) let you enjoy doing so, during the process.

2. You know *a great deal* about the remaining organizations, including — most specifically — *their problems, and what you can do to help solve them.*

You are going to be a very rare bird when you walk in that front door. Organizations love to be loved (including hospitals, colleges, and everything else). *You know far more than you are ever going to have to use* in the hiring process anyway. But the depth of your knowledge will show, anyway, in your quiet sense of competence. You know they have problems, and you know you can help solve them.

This fact will be of great interest — most of the time — to the person you go to see, provided you have taken the trouble to identify, learn about, and ask to see *the top executive whose responsibility it is to solve the particular problems that you have zeroed in on.*

That is the person you are going to approach, by name, by appointment: the person who has the interest, the responsibility and the motivation for hiring *this problem solver: y · o · u . . .*

You are going to ask to see that person only, and you are going to stay *far away* from

THAT ORGANIZATION'S PERSONNEL DEPARTMENT

This advice is given by just about every book or counselor that you can turn to: Albee, Crystal, Haldane, Harper, Kent, Miller, Miner, Shapero, Snelling, Townsend, and Uris — to name just a few.
The advice is stated strongly by them all:

> the personnel department in most companies,
> they say, is at the bottom of the social and
> executive totem pole; it rarely hears of middle-

> high level vacancies even within its own
> company; when it does know of the vacancies,
> it rarely has power to hire except for entry level;
> in almost all other cases it can only
> screen out applicants, and refer those who
> survive, on up to higher executives; therefore,
> in general, avoid this department like the plague.

Professors in some graduate business schools are predicting that personnel departments, at least as hirers, are either on the way out or on the way to drastic restructuring.

In the meantime, men and women aspiring to jobs above entry-level are advised to go nowhere near these departments. Even executive secretaries would be well-advised to steer clear of the personnel department, and follow the techniques described here.

Instead, you are going to have to do enough research — using *Poor's Register, Who's Who in Commerce and Industry, Who's Who in America, Who's Who in the East,* and any other resources — such as periodicals — that your friendly neighborhood Librarian can suggest, so that in each organization you know who is the *top person responsible for solving the problem that you can help solve,* at that organization. *When in doubt, go higher, rather than lower.*

And it will help greatly if you know something about that person too, so you don't step on their *known prejudices,* if you can help it. (After all they are as entitled to their *tropisms — the things we instinctively go toward, or away from —* as you and I are.) If you were referred to them by someone else that someone else may be able to give you some helpful background at this point.

WELL, YOU WANT TO
SEE THEM, BUT DO
THEY WANT TO SEE YOU?

This is the question that bothers almost everyone new to the job-hunt. We sort of just assume the answer is no. But, on the contrary,

Ten to one the answer is yes. Young or older; male or female.

First of all, you may have already met, during the process of your own personal survey of your chosen geographical area and field.

They may have liked you.

They may even have offered you a job (this happens many times) during your informational interviewing process. And, as indicated earlier, you said at that time the Absolute Truth: you were flattered, you would certainly keep it in mind, but at this point you weren't ready to say yet just exactly where it was that you wanted to work. But now you *are* ready, and you call to tell them so.

On the other hand, maybe the two of you didn't meet before.

Even so, they are interested. The odds are ten to one you've figured out someone who'll refer you, and act as your link to this person; but even lacking that referral you still can tell them that *you want to talk to them about some of the problems of the organization, and what you've discovered that might be helpful to them.*

That's a switch!

Most of the time, when they do interviewing (for hiring, or otherwise) people are there to ask what the employer can do for the would-be employee.

Now, you offer to come in and tell them what *you* can do for *them.*

Are they interested?

Odds are ten to one they are.

(If they are not, maybe you'd better re-evaluate whether you really want to work for this kind of person. And if you decide you still do, maybe you're going to have to convince them that they should hire you — even if they have to establish a new function or position, at a senior level, just for you.

THIS PERSON YOU ARE GOING TO SEE IS
JUST LIKE YOU, BUT UNDER REAL STRESS

The creative minority in this field have correctly pointed out that one of the reasons the hiring process in America today (at the above-$12,000 level) is so difficult, is because of the great stress involved.

Let's look at some of those sources of stress:

1. The odds are very great that the executive who does the interviewing was hired because of what they could contribute to the company, and not because they were such a great interviewer. In fact, their gifts in this field may be rather miserable.

2. They can't entrust the process to someone else, because they have to live with whoever gets hired afterwards. So, hiring-interviews for above-entry-level positions have a heavy accent of "I wish I could get someone else to do this for me, but I just can't."

3. If the person-with-the-power-to-hire makes a mistake, they are going to rub shoulders with that mistake, day by day. They don't usually hire someone, and then never see that new employee again. An executive who has the responsibility of hiring for this position is given (or takes) that responsibility away from the personnel department *because this position is directly under them and they're going to have to live with whoever is hired, day by day.*

4. If they hire a mistake, it's going to make them look very bad with their superiors, board of directors, stockholders, or whoever it is that they report to.

5. If they hire a mistake and they aren't the chief executive yet, this could cost them a promotion personally — since they have proved they have bad judgment; and maybe their department is getting botched up — to boot.

6. If they hire a mistake, it's going to cost money. $64,000 for a top manager, $19-30,000 for a middle manager, $6,800 for a lower-middle manager (according to a study done by one research outfit, anyway.) That's what it costs in "orientation time" for the new exec and those around them. And all wasted, if the new employee doesn't pan out; and having to be spent all over again on whoever is hired next.

Not bad. In one twenty-minute interview (or even several of same), this hapless interviewer can botch up part of the organization, cost the organization a great deal of money, lose their own promotion, be called to account, and acquire a whole new set of ulcers. No wonder hiring is such a stressful situation.

A person could be forgiven for wanting never to do it. But hiring is unavoidable. Experts estimate good presidents spend 25% of their time (of necessity) in looking for new talent within the ranks, and outside.

Failing to get rid of the responsibility entirely, a president (or whoever) could be forgiven for praying at least for a new way to do it — *one with much less stress built in.*

YOU OFFER A PLEASANT LOW STRESS INTERVIEW

This is where you come in.

You are following the suggestions of the creative minority, who all are united in this: *create a situation where you and the-person-with-the-power-to-hire-you for a position you want, can get a look at each other — without having to make a big decision.*

If this person met you during your personal survey of the economic picture in the area, or while you were developing "remembrance and referral" contacts, or now — in your role of problem-solver — they had a chance to see you in a low stress situation. It is a form of talent *window shopping.*

You come into their office on one mission — Mr. or Ms. Researcher, or Surveyor or whatever; but the interviewer has a chance to look at you surreptitiously as Mr. or Ms. Possible-Human-Resource-for-My-Organization.

All the creative minority who have studied the career transition process and the job-hunt are agreed in this: any way you can let an executive windowshop you, without your putting them on the spot, will create a very favorable situation for you.

With this clue firmly in your hand, you may be able to think up an even more inventive approach to the-person-with-the-power-to-hire, in each organization. If so, more power to you.

But let's be very clear about one thing: you are going to show this person how your skills can help them with their problems *as they perceive them.* We cannot stress this strongly enough. You may think you perceive a problem that they are absolutely blind to, in that organization; but if so, you are going to have to delicately and very skillfully explore how they perceive that

Reproduced by Special Permission of PLAYBOY Magazine; copyright © 1979 by Playboy

"I'll tell you why I want
this job. I thrive on challenges.
I like being stretched to my full capacity.
I like solving problems. Also, my car
is about to be repossessed."

particular problem area, before you hit them over the head with your brilliant insight into it all.

We ourselves have had would-be job-hunters approach *us* for a job and confidently tell us that we desperately needed a person with such and such skills (which they just happened to possess) in order to accomplish — and then they proceeded to lay out some goals and priorities for our organization (the National Career Development Project) which we had already intentionally rejected as part of our plan. But they didn't know that, because they hadn't done their homework. So be aware, when you sit across the table from the person you'd most like to work for, that it is crucial you relate your skills to what's going on in *their* head, not merely to what's going on in *yours*. If I'm dying for lack of a creative artist in my organization, and you walk in and show me you have genuine skills in that area, you are interpreting your skills in terms of my problems. But if I have long since decided I don't need any more help with art work, and you try to sell me on the idea that I need one (namely, you), you are falling into the pitfall of interpreting your skills in terms of *your* problems, not mine. I, as employer, will lose interest in you thereafter, at an accelerating rate.

DOES THIS WHOLE PROCESS ALWAYS WORK?

Of course not. This is job-hunting, not magic. As Nathan Azrin has well said, job-hunting is more like choosing a mate, than like buying a car.

No one can absolutely guarantee you a job exactly where you want it, doing exactly what you want, at the salary you want. But most people who follow the method set forth in these last three chapters get very close — with perhaps some compromises — and some succeed in virtually every particular.

This method is, in any event, so far superior to the traditional form of the job-hunt, that it ought to be taught to every job-hunter in this country, and especially to those above the most menial level.

With the traditional numbers game, as you will recall, a man had to send out 300-500 resumes, in order to get 3-5 interviews, and one or two job offers — assuming he was lucky.

On the other hand, with this method, you might have the same experience as did one man (among many we could cite): 107 places that looked interesting in the geographical area he chose, 297 letters sent to them (and 126 phone calls) followed by a visit to the area where he had 45 low-stress interviews as part of his personal economic survey, resulting in 35 job offers — including exactly the job he wanted.

For job-hunters in the process of career transition, this method is infinitely superior to any other — particularly if you are trying to avoid not merely un-employment but the even greater danger of under-employment.

INTERVIEWS, RESUMES, SALARY NEGOTIATIONS

Books on the job-hunt often devote the bulk of their contents to these three topics. We have practically ignored them. There are reasons.

First of all, it is perfectly possible for you to get a job without ever being trained in interview techniques, ever getting together a resume, or knowing the art of salary negotiations . . . provided you follow the techniques in these last four chapters faithfully, step by step.

Secondly, by following those techniques, you get constant practice in the art of talking with high level management — which is, after all what we mean by that dreadful word *interviewing.* Your self-confidence improves, which is — after all — the key to successful interviews, for you. You get this practice in low stress situations.

Thirdly, if you pick up some of the materials we have recommended on pages 220-231 in Appendix B, particularly Lathrop's book, you will find some helpful instructions about the interview, the resume, and salary negotiations for the reader who feels he or she needs more guidance in these areas. It would be folly for us to duplicate here the very things that it explains most carefully.

We will however, give an interview check list here, to be sure you are "up" on what all the books say, as you think through these three special hurdles in the job hunt.

INTERVIEW CHECK LIST

In preparing yourself for an interview, when it comes, you can of course be *really* thorough and try to figure out what is going on in the mind of that person sitting on the other side of the desk, by reading their own training manuals (like, *The Interviewer's Manual* by Henry H. Morgan and John W. Cogger — available at your local library or from The Psychological Corporation, 757 Third Avenue, New York, NY 10017. $7.50). This is, of course, taking the optimistic view, and assuming that your interviewer has had time to read a manual about interviewing.

If you want to take the more realistic view you will assume that every interviewer is a complete individual in his or her own right, and that you don't know anything about that interviewer except that a) they have *enthusiasms.* If you've done your homework thoroughly you have some idea what these are. If you haven't done your homework, use the interview to try to discover what they are; b) they have *problems.* Again, if you have done your homework, you have some idea what they are. Again, if you didn't do your homework, try to use the interview to discover what they think those problems are; c) they have certain questions they are dying to ask you. These latter kinds of curiosities are crucial to you, and — as the most expert career counselor in the country, John Crystal, points out — they tend to fall into three major categories:

1. WHY ARE YOU HERE? Why have you chosen this particular place to come to? If you've done all the research recommended earlier in this book, and followed the steps in funneling (p. 125) you'll *know* the answer. If you haven't, you won't.

2. PRECISELY WHAT CAN YOU DO FOR ME? You will talk about their problems to the degree that you have been able to guess at them, and also listen very carefully to what they have to say. If new factors are revealed, field them as best you can; all the while showing how your skills can help with those problems. Within this category of questions, be prepared also

---

Study Shows Neatness Pays Off In Job Hunt

STANFORD, Calif. (UPI)—Neat, well-dressed college graduates have a better chance to land a job than those who appear in jeans or refuse to wear a bra, according to a Stanford University study.

The wearing of jeans, shorts, sandals, or dispensing with bras creates an impression ranging from "mildly" to "strongly negative," the survey shows.

Applicants who use jargon, have dirty fingernails or fiddle with objects on the desk also earned negative ratings, according to the study by two Stanford students who received doctoral degrees in educational counseling and guidance.

The researchers, Jane Anton and Michael Russell, questioned more than 100 recruiting officers from 17 different industry groups, ranging from accounting and aerospace to government and utilities.

They found that a male creates a mildly positive impression if he wears a sport coat, shirt, tie and slacks. But he creates a stronger impression if he wears a suit.

And the shorter, more neatly trimmed the hair and beard on males, the better the impression on recruiters.

Applicants considered "assertive, intelligent, independent and inquisitive" registered only a mildly positive influence in job interviews.

—Cincinnati Enquirer, 10/23/75

for the particular form of: after you got this job, if you did, how would you start out?

3. HOW MUCH IS IT GOING TO COST ME? They probably have a range in mind (with a two to three thousand dollar variation), if you're seeking a job above the lowest level. If you have done your research thoroughly, you probably have some idea at least of what that range is. Therefore, you will need to quote it at this point, adding that money isn't everything and you are interested in the opportunity and challenge as well.

As can be seen, the research we have exhorted you to do in these chapters previously, is absolutely key to your successful conduct of an interview, and the fielding of these categories of questions. *You will be at a disadvantage precisely to the degree that you have tried to cut corners or short-circuit the whole process described in these chapters (4-7).*

Do remember to look professional. Have a good-looking suit (or dress) on, a decent haircut (or coiffure), clean fingernails, dentally cleaned teeth, deodorant, shined shoes, no smoking or pre-drinking — clean breath. It may seem like a silly game to you, but it's a game with very high stakes, in which you want to be the winner. (Check chart on page 175.)

If you are a male, and want to take a hard look at your appearance to see how it can influence the interview for better or for worse, you may find John T. Molloy's famous *Dress for Success* helpful. (Warner Books, 75 Rockefeller Plaza, New York, NY 10019. 1975. $3.95, paper). He has a similar (but more controversial) book out for women: *The Women's Dress for Success Book* (same publisher, same price).

In any event, his books are representative of a whole fast-growing field called Personal Image Consultancy. How many are in this field may be gauged from the fact that the *1979 Directory of Personal Image Consultants* (Editorial Services Co., 1140 Avenue of the Americas, New York, NY 10036. $10.95) lists 85 such firms, in 20 states and 38 cities.

There are certain questions no employer is any longer allowed to ask you — unless they are BFOQ's — "bona fide occupational qualifications."

Here are some interview guidelines that one major California company has drawn up for its managers and supervisors:

SUBJECT	CAN DO OR ASK	CAN NOT DO OR ASK
Your sex—	Notice your appearance.	Make comments or take notes, unless sex is a BFOQ.
Marital status—	Status after hiring, for insurance purposes.	Are you married? Single? Divorced? Engaged? Living with anyone? Do you see your ex-spouse?
Children—	Numbers and ages of children after hiring, for insurance purposes.	Do you have children at home? How old? Who cares for them? Do you plan more children?
Physical data—	Explain manual labor, lifting, other requirements of the job. Show how it is performed. Require physical examination.	How tall are you? How much do you weigh?
Criminal record—	If security clearance is necessary, can be done prior to employment.	Have you ever been arrested, convicted or spent time in jail?
Military—	Are you a veteran? Why not? Any job-related experience?	What type of discharge do you have? What branch did you serve in?
Age—	Age after hiring. "Are you over 18?"	How old are you? Estimate age.
Housing—	If you have no phone, how can we reach you?	Do you own your home? Do you rent? Do you live in an apartment or a house?

As a job applicant, what can you do if you are asked one of these illegal questions? The Wall Street Journal pointed out you have three courses of action:

"1. Answer the question and ignore the fact that it is not legal.

"2. Answer the question with the statement: 'I think that is not relevant to the requirements of the position.'

"3. Contact the nearest Equal Employment Opportunity Commission office.

"Unless the violation is persistent, is demeaning, or you can prove it resulted in your not being employed, number three should probably be avoided. The whole area is too new; many interviewers are just not totally conversant with the code requirements.

"Answer number two is probably, in most circumstances, the best to give. There are times when it may cost you the job, but are you that interested in working for someone who is all that concerned about your personal life?"

Whatever the interviewer may ask about your past, (like, why did you leave your last job?) remember the only thing they can possibly be really interested in is the future (under what circumstances might you leave me?).

Never volunteer negative information about yourself.

And now for some final thoughts about this whole matter.

Never accept a job on the spot, or reject one. And, unless you are talking with a very "liberated" employer, do not say, I need to talk with my mate (it implies you are not a decision maker on your own). Just say, "I need some time to weigh this."

SALARY NEGOTIATION

A woman was once describing her very first job to me. It was at a soda fountain. I asked her what her biggest surprise at that job was. "My first paycheck," she said. "I know it sounds incredible, but I was so green at all this, that during the whole interview for the job it never occurred to me to ask what my salary would be. I just took it for granted that it would be a fair and just salary, for the work that I would be doing. Did I ever get a shock, when my first paycheck came! It was so small, I could hardly believe it. Did I ever learn a lesson from that!" Yes, and so may we all.

AT ITS SIMPLEST LEVEL

To speak of salary negotiation is to speak of a matter which can be conducted on several levels. The simplest kind — as the above story reminds us — involves remembering to ask during the job-hiring interview what the salary will be. And then stating whether, for you, that amount is satisfactory or not. *That* much negotiation, everyone who is hunting for a job must be prepared to do.

It is well to recognize that you — or the students or clients that you are trying to teach about job-hunting, if you are a career counselor — are at a disadvantage if salary negotiation is approached on this simplest level, however. A figure may be named, and you are totally unprepared to say whether this is a fair salary for that particular job, or not. You just don't know.

AT ITS NEXT HIGHEST LEVEL

Hence, you may prefer to do a little research *ahead* of time. Before you ever get in there, for that interview. This is taking

salary negotiation to its next highest level. Visiting the library in
your community, before you interview for hiring. There's a
smashing new book out, that gives an overview of the whole
subject of salaries. I love it! It's: David Harrop's *Paychecks:
Who Makes What? The Book That Tells You What Everybody
Earns.* Harper and Row, Publishers, 10 East 53rd Street, New
York, NY 10022. 1980. $5.95, paper. Beyond this sort of
survey, there are other resources you can turn to.

If it's a non-supervisory job, you can find out what a 'ball-
park figure' for a particular industry might be by having the
reference librarian, or general librarian, find this sort of table
for you. (See chart at right.) Just add approximately 7% for each
year that has elapsed.

If it's a supervisory job, or one at a higher level than non-
supervisory, you will find that the College Placement Council,
with some frequency publishes reports on salaries being offered
in various industries to college graduates. While this is of primary interest to such graduates, the "Salary Surveys" of the
Council do give some guidance, at least, to other job-hunters.
See your library, or the career counseling and placement office
of a nearby college — rather than buying this Survey, as it is
available only to members of the Council and/or to subscribers
to their Journal Publications Group. (Average cost: $30-35.)

"Let's talk salary. How does 'astronomical' sound to you?"

© Copyright, 1980. *Saturday Review*, April 12, 1980. Used by special permission.

SPENDABLE AVERAGE WEEKLY EARNINGS
IN CURRENT DOLLARS, BY INDUSTRY DIVISION:
ANNUAL AVERAGES, 1947–77

Spendable average weekly earnings, married worker with three dependents*

Year	Total private	Mining	Contract construction	Manufacturing	Transportation and public utilities	Wholesale and retail trade	Finance, insurance, real estate	Services
				In Current Dollars				
1947	$44.64	$56.42	$55.53	$47.58		$37.69	$42.70	
1948	48.51	62.85	62.60	52.31		40.39	45.03	
1949	49.74	60.10	64.55	52.95		42.50	47.15	
1950	52.04	63.81	65.94	56.36		43.88	49.76	
1951	55.79	68.88	71.21	60.18		47.07	53.23	
1952	57.87	71.30	75.51	62.98		48.46	55.07	
1953	60.31	75.65	78.36	65.60		50.57	57.02	
1954	60.85	75.58	80.76	65.65		51.89	58.86	
1955	63.41	81.04	82.16	69.79		53.36	60.37	
1956	65.82	85.57	86.65	72.25		55.21	61.77	
1957	67.71	88.30	89.63	74.31		56.76	63.09	
1958	69.11	86.20	92.51	75.23		58.48	65.15	
1959	71.86	91.94	95.82	79.40		60.44	67.06	
1960	72.96	92.92	99.15	80.11		61.38	68.59	
1961	74.48	94.13	103.29	82.18		62.48	70.15	
1962	76.99	96.90	106.78	85.53		64.37	73.07	
1963	78.56	99.69	110.18	87.58		65.67	75.36	
1964	82.57	104.40	116.40	92.18	$104.92	68.93	78.14	$65.36
1965	86.30	110.27	122.83	96.78	111.64	71.12	81.20	68.71
1966	88.66	113.98	127.38	99.45	112.20	72.70	83.29	71.10
1967	90.86	118.52	134.33	101.26	114.56	74.75	85.79	73.64
1968	95.28	122.52	139.98	106.75	119.54	78.49	90.66	76.53
1969	99.99	131.44	152.80	111.44	125.78	81.66	95.50	81.49
1970	104.61	140.50	166.05	115.90	133.52	85.86	99.76	86.66
1971	112.41	148.45	181.44	124.24	146.02	91.12	107.19	93.43
1972	121.09	161.82	191.23	135.56	162.23	96.91	113.78	100.49
1973	127.41	170.46	199.14	143.20	173.26	100.49	117.04	105.71
1974	134.37	185.96	207.93	151.25	183.93	106.26	123.36	113.41
1975	145.93	211.11	223.10	165.33	199.27	119.34	136.08	126.86
1976	156.50	231.39	239.07	180.03	218.22	125.22	143.64	133.88
1977 ᵖ	170.32	255.32	250.15	198.43	237.04	133.54	154.15	145.32

* Spendable earnings are calculated by taking the average weekly earnings for all production or non-supervisory jobs, both full-time and part-time, and then deducting social security and Federal income taxes applicable to a married worker with three dependents who earned the average amount.

If the job you're looking for information about is not in either of the above sorts of places, there is always the *Occupational Outlook Handbook* in your local library, which has the best available information on earnings in the most popular occupations. You will discover that the only trouble with such information is that it covers all geographic regions in the U.S., all industries, and all periods of economic fluctuations. In other words, the figures are very general.

Your library may have more detailed information for your particular region, regarding the occupation that you are interested in. Witness the following example:

**AVERAGE WEEKLY EARNINGS
OF LEAD DRAFTSMEN**

		REGION	
$ 295.00	Detroit, Michigan		
226.00	Dayton, Ohio	$213.50	North Central
215.50	Chicago, Illinois	202.00	Northeast
206.00	Houston, Texas	199.00	West
193.00	Seattle, Washington	192.00	South
189.50	Columbus, Ohio	204.00	United States
175.00	Salt Lake City, Utah		
173.00	Scranton, Pennsylvania	These figures are now outdated	
172.50	Raleigh, North Carolina	but they show *comparative*	
162.50	Little Rock, Arkansas	differences at least.	

The figures show the fluctuation from region to region may be quite wide. Though it is important to remember that this depends on the particular occupation that you are interested in. For lead draftspersons, Detroit may pay more than any other city. With regard to other occupations, however, Detroit may be at the bottom of the list.

Such regional differences in salary reflect, of course, a variety of factors, such as differences in cost of living, differences in supply and demand, etc. Supply and demand has exercised a big influence on salaries particularly in Alaska, among the various "trades" — as a result of the building of the Alaskan pipe-line or gas-line. So short a preparation as an "oil field technology" course at the Alaska Skill Center in Seward, Alaska, has resulted in relatively easy placement at Prudhoe Bay and Cook Inlet there. This situation may continue in the early 1980s. But similar regional differences in supply and demand, if not as dramatic, occur in other regions, and with other professions.

If your librarian simply cannot find for you, or help you find, the salary information that you want, remember that almost every occupation has its own association or professional group, whose business it is to keep tabs on what is happening salary-wise within that occupation or field. For people interested, by way of example, in the guidance and counseling field, there is the American Personnel and Guidance Association. And it has published a modest volume entitled, "Compen$ation *(sic)* in the Guidance and Counseling Field, 1979." Other associations have similar data (in most cases) at their fingertips. To learn the association or professional group for the field or occupation you are interested in, consult the *Encyclopedia of Associations, Vol. 1,* at your library.

MORE SOPHISTICATED YET

Some job-hunters — you, perhaps, or the clients/students you are helping — may want to get beyond these "ball-park figures" into more detailed salary negotiation. They — or you — may want to walk in on an interview knowing exactly what That Place pays for a job. Why? Well, for one thing, it may be too low for you — and thus you are saved the necessity of wasting your precious time on that particular place. Secondly, and more importantly, many places have — as John Crystal has so insistently pointed out — a *range* in mind. And if you know what that range is, you can negotiate for a salary that is nearer the top of the range, than the bottom.

By permission, from *The Missionary*, Episcopal Diocese of Northern California

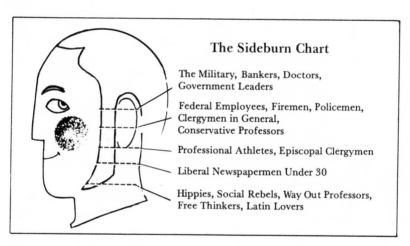

The Sideburn Chart

The Military, Bankers, Doctors, Government Leaders

Federal Employees, Firemen, Policemen, Clergymen in General, Conservative Professors

Professional Athletes, Episcopal Clergymen

Liberal Newspapermen Under 30

Hippies, Social Rebels, Way Out Professors, Free Thinkers, Latin Lovers

So, let us say that you have done some extensive homework — such as is represented by *The Quick Job-Hunting Map* or by the process described in *Where Do I Go From Here With My Life?* And you have gotten it down, by means of the Information Survey, to three or five places that really interest you. You know in general what sort of position you are aiming at, in those particular places — and you are ready to go back and visit them in The Interview for Hiring — *as soon as you know what the salary range is, that they probably have in mind for the position that interests you* (whether that position already exists, or is one you are going to ask them to create). How do you find out what the salary is, or should be, by way of range?

It's relatively easy to Define, as — again — John Crystal has taught us all. The rule of thumb is that you will, generally speaking, be paid more than the person who is below you on the organizational chart, and less than the person who is above you. There are—needless to say—exceptions to this rule: people who don't quite fit in the organizational chart, such as researchers financed by a grant, or consultants. Consequently they may be paid much more than the people who are theoretically above them. But In General, the Rule of Thumb is true.

This makes the matter of salary *research* (which precedes salary negotiation) relatively (I said "relatively") simple. If through your own information search you could discover who is (or would be) above you on the organizational chart, and who is (or would be) below you, and what they are paid, you would know what your salary range is, or would be.

It works out like this:

IF THE PERSON BELOW YOU MAKES:
    a) $6240 or b) $10,000   or c) $22,000
AND THE PERSON ABOVE YOU MAKES:
    a) $7800 or b) $13,500   or c) $27,000
YOUR RANGE WILL BE SOMETHING LIKE:
  a) $6400– or b) $10,500– or c) $23,000–
      7600   12,500   26,000

So, how do you find this information out?

For openers, you do all the kinds of library research that I alluded to, above. Then you go to work on your contacts: you know, everybody who knows you well enough even to misspell your name. And, you pick up a copy of the annual report and any other literature available on that company or organization. Your goal, of course (to go into Overkill) is to discover:

The Names of the people above and below you, if you were to be hired at that organization. And:

What they make.

You will be surprised at how much of this information is in the annual report, or in books available at your library. When those sources produce all they can for you, and you are still short of what you want to know, go to your contacts. You are looking for Someone Who Knows Someone who either is working, or has worked, at that particular place or organization that interests you.

If you absolutely run into a blank wall on that particular organization (you know, everyone who works there is pledged

© Copyright, 1980, Universal Press Syndicate. All rights reserved. Used by special permission

to secrecy, and they have shipped all their ex-employees to Siberia), then seek out information on their nearest *competitor* in the same geographic area (e.g., if Wells Fargo is inscrutable, try Bank of America as your research base; or vice-versa).

But you will be surprised at how well perseverance and legwork pay off, in this. And if your enthusiasm flags along the way, just picture yourself sitting in the interview for hiring, and now you're at the end of the interview (the only proper place for discussion of salary to take place, anyway). The prospective employer likes you, you like them, and then they say: "How much salary were you expecting?" (Employers *love* to toss the

ball to you.) Because you have done your homework, and you know the range, you can name a figure near or at the top of the range — based on your anticipated performance in that job: i.e., "Superior."

But suppose you *didn't* do your research. Then you're Shadow-Boxing in the Dark — as they say. If you name a figure way too high, you're out of the running — and you can't back track, in most cases (Sorry, we'd like to hire you, but we just can't afford you.") If you name a figure way too low, you're also out of the running, in many cases ("Sorry, but we were hoping for someone a little more, ah, professional.") And if you're in the right range, but at the bottom of it, you've just gotten the job — *and lost as much as $2,000 a year that could have been yours.*

So, salary research/salary negotiation — no matter how much time it takes — pays off handsomely. Let's say it takes you a week to ten days to run down this sort of information on the organizations that interest you (three to five). And let us say that because you've done this research, when you go in for an interview for hiring, finally, you are able to ask for and obtain a salary that is $2,000 higher in the range, than you would otherwise have known enough to ask for. In just three years, you'll have earned $6,000 extra, because of that research. Not bad pay, for ten days' work!

AT ITS MOST SOPHISTICATED LEVEL

Job-hunters with incredibly-developed bargaining needs, always ask how salary negotiation is conducted at its most sophisticated level. It is my personal conviction that Most Job-hunters will not operate at this level, and therefore do not need this sort of information. But in case you do, or in case you are simply dying out of curiosity, it is completely described in *Where Do I Go From Here With My Life?* pages 140–142. As honed to a fine point by John Crystal, the most sophisticated salary negotiation goes like this:

You do all the steps described immediately above: i.e., you discover what the range would be. Let us say it turns out that the range is one that varies two thousand dollars. You then "invent" a new range, for yourself, that "hooks" on the old one, in the following fashion:

$$\begin{array}{ll} & \rceil\ \$15,500 \\ \$14,000 \quad \rceil & \\ & \rfloor\ \$13,500 \\ \$12,000 \quad \rfloor & \end{array}$$

And when the employer says, "What kind of a salary did you have in mind?" you respond, "I believe my productivity is such that it would command a salary in the range of $13,500 to $15,500." This keeps you, at a minimum, near the top of their range; and, at a maximum, challenges them to go beyond the top that they had in mind, either immediately — or in terms of *promised* raises. (Don't be afraid, even as Elwood P. Dowd was not, to ask "When?")

FRINGES

In all your research, and ultimate negotiation, do not forget to pay attention to so-called "fringe benefits." In a recent year, it was calculated that such 'fringes' as life insurance, health benefits or plans, vacation or holiday plans, and retirement programs, added up to 25% of manufacturing workers salary, e.g., if an employee received $800 salary per month, the fringe benefits were worth another $200 per month. So, if the employee who is beneath you on the organizational chart gets $700 plus benefits, and the employee who is above you gets $1100 plus benefits, while you during the hiring interview are offered $800 *and no benefits,* you will need to negotiate for more than $1000 salary, in order to make up for that lack of benefits.

Of course, if you don't need that extra money — or you couldn't care less that the person below you makes more than you do, — great! But just in case you do, keep this in mind.

FINALLY, THE MATTER OF THOSE RAISES

Salary negotiation, during the hiring interview, ultimately is more than just a matter of negotiation for your Starting Salary. It is ultimately a matter of negotiating for your Yearly or Semi-yearly Raises, as well. "When, and under what circumstances, can I expect to have my salary raised?" needs not only to be asked, but to be put in writing — if there is a letter of agreement, or any kind of contract forthcoming from your would-be employer. The Road to Hell is paved with Promises that are unwritten, and which employers *conveniently* forget once you are hired. Moreover, employers Leave, and their successor or their own boss may disown unwritten promises ("I don't know what caused them to say that to you, but they clearly exceeded their authority, and we can't be held to that.")

Against That Day, it will pay you to keep a diary, weekly, of your achievements at work, so that when time for discussing raises comes around, you can document — with a one or two page summary — just exactly what you have accomplished there, and why you deserve that raise . . . as Bernard Haldane explains in his classic *How To Make A Habit of Success*

(Acropolis Books, Ltd., 2400 17th Street, N.W., Washington, DC 20009. $3.50).

PROMOTION

We hope *promotion* is not for you a distasteful concept. After all, it means wider responsibility (hopefully), and not just more prestige. It means a widening scope for your desire to be truly helpful to people, and not just (hopefully) an illustration of *The Peter Principle.* Women, in particular, should remember that they are generally much more underpaid than men, that the average woman would require a 71% pay raise, to bring her up to the level of a similarly qualified man.

Do not forget also, that in only twenty-five of the last one hundred years has the cost of living declined and the U.S. dollar gained in buying power. The annual rate of inflation lately has been from 5-15% annually. During the period 1973-1978, inflation totaled 47%, in actual fact. Were it to continue at the same rate for the next five years, a person who made $11,804 in 1978 (incidentally, the median earning that year for the nation's 69.4 million full-time workers) would *have* to earn $17,352 in 1983, just in order to have the very same purchasing power.

So you see, what our society calls "promotion" is necessary *just in order to stand still.* Lack of promotion automatically means going backward — in terms of purchasing power for you and your loved ones.

And this says nothing of opportunities for you to operate in increasing spheres of influence and helpfulness.

The end of the matter is this: if you negotiate only for your initial position and salary, you are likely to lose a great deal.

When and only when you're sure they want you, and they have made a firm offer, negotiate. And when (and if) it's resolved to your satisfaction, (again) *get it in writing, please. Please. Please.*

FOR THOSE WHO LOVE TO
COVER EVERY BASE

If you are by any chance uncomfortable with putting all your eggs in one basket, i.e., with committing yourself to the approach described in chapters 4—7 here, and only to that approach; if you feel there might be some merit to answering classified ads, visiting agencies, etc., you may perhaps be interested in the advice of the agency set up by Bernard Haldane, which recommends that no more than 20% of one's time be allocated to these other methods, in view of the fact that barely 20% (but only 20%) of the jobs above entry level are filled through these other methods. *Many going through the job-hunt prefer, however, to give all their time to the method set forth in these pages — and have done so with great success; so you may want to take this into account in planning your own strategy.*

Remember, in going about all this, you have a tremendous advantage over other job-hunters — and this whole process is, sad to say, at the present time a very competitive business.

You know how to get hired.

In Candide's world, it may be otherwise. But, in this world it remains true:

> The person who gets hired is not
> necessarily the one who can do that
> job best; but, the one who *knows*
> *the most about how to get hired.*

Appendix A

The Quick Job-Hunting Map

A fast way to help

ADVANCED VERSION*

*For the undecided college student
or the housewife going back to work,
or the mid-career changer, or the man or
woman whose job has been terminated,
or anyone else facing obstacles in the job hunt*

---

*Those entering the job-market for the first time, and desiring a simpler skill-list than we have provided here, are referred to *The Three Boxes of Life*, in which the Beginning Version of the Quick Job-Hunting Map may be found. Or that version may be ordered separately, by writing directly to Ten Speed Press, P.O. Box 7123, Berkeley, CA 94707. $1.25 + $.50 for postage and handling.

Introduction:
What You Need To Know
Before You Go Job-Hunting

You need to know, basically, that there are two methods of job-hunting. The first, or traditional, method is the one everybody knows about: want-ads, employment agencies, recruiters, resumés, etc. This method works very well for *some job-hunters.* In case you want to know what the odds are, before you start, a survey of ten million job-seekers by the Bureau of the Census[1] revealed that for every 100 who use:

a) classified-ads in the daily or weekly papers, 24 find a job thereby; 76 out of the 100 don't.

b) private employment agencies, 24 (again) find a job thereby; 76 out of the 100 don't.

c) the Federal/State Employment Service, 14 find a job thereby; 86 out of the 100 don't.

d) their school or college placement office, 22 find a job thereby; 78 out of the 100 don't.

e) Civil Service examinations, 13 find a job thereby; 87 out of the 100 don't.

f) friends, relatives, teachers, etc., 22 find a job thereby; 78 out of the 100 don't.

In a separate study, of those who send out resumés,[2] it was found that employers made one job-offer to a job-hunter for every 1470 resumés they received, on an average. That means that 1469 out of every 1470 resumés do not result in a job.

Fortunately, there is a second method of job-hunting. Which is *dreadfully* important for you to know, if the first method doesn't work for you. In fact, many many job-hunters prefer to begin with this second method, without even waiting to see whether or not they are successful using the first or traditional method. The success rate of this second method, in records kept for over 13 years,[3] is that 86 out of every 100 job-hunters who use it find a job thereby; only 14 out of every 100 don't.

In order to go about your job-hunt using this second method, you are going to have to do a bit of homework on yourself before setting out to pound the pavements. This homework has three parts, which we have symbolized throughout this MAP under the figures of a cart, a horse, and a road:

---

1. Published in the *Occupational Outlook Quarterly,* Winter, 1976.
2. Summarized in "Tea Leaves: A New Look at Resumés," Ten Speed Press, Box 7123, Berkeley, Calif. 94707.
3. By John C. Crystal, author of *Where Do I Go from Here with My Life?,* Ten Speed Press.

a ● **THE CART** is the symbol of pages 185 through 207 in this MAP. These pages are to help you identify:

What skills you have and most enjoy using.
Skills are the basic building-blocks of jobs. You have picked up a lot of marketable skills regardless of how young you are, and regardless of whether you have worked a lot outside your home, or not. But you need to identify *what* skills you have, and—more importantly—which of these you *enjoy.*

b ● **THE HORSE** is the symbol of pages 208 through 212. These pages are to help you identify:

Where you want to use your skills.
Your skills, by themselves, are like a cart sitting in the middle of a road. The cart needs to be hooked up to something. Your skills need to be hooked up with the *kinds* of places you would most like to use those skills. Only you can say *where* you want to use your skills. For example, if you are good at (and enjoy) welding, do you want to weld a wheel, or the casing of a nuclear bomb? You must decide.

c ● **THE ROAD** is the symbol of pages 213 through 217. These pages are to help you put it all together, and are to show you:

How to identify the kind of job you want,
once you've decided the *What* and the *Where.*
How to identify the kind of organizations which have that sort of job,
in your chosen geographical area.
How to get hired there.

We have chosen the road as the symbol of this third part of your homework, because if you don't know how to identify the job, and the organization, and get hired there, it's like leaving the cart and the horse simply standing in the middle of the road.

This Job-Hunting MAP,* then, is devoted to helping you do this homework, in three steps, in order to go about job-hunting *the second way*—using the Method that works for 86 out of every 100 persons who use it. How long will it take? Who can say? If you devote a whole weekend to the task, you should be able to work through the whole MAP to page 212. After that, you will need to go see people. Some people, using this MAP, have found a job in a week. Others have taken nine months. One thing for sure: used conscientiously, this MAP will greatly *shorten* the time your job-hunt (or career-change) takes. If your job-hunt isn't Quick, it will at least be Quicker than it would be, otherwise.

---

*Using the excellent insights of John Crystal, John Holland, and Bernard Haldane (see Bibliography, **p. 217**), to whom we are all indebted.

What Skills You Have and
Most Enjoy Using

Generally speaking, all skills divide into six clusters or families. To see which ones you are *attracted to,* try this exercise:

Below is an aerial view of a room in which a two-day (!) party is taking place. At this party, people with the same or similar interests have (for some reason) all gathered in the same corner of the room—as described below:

A

People who have athletic or mechanical ability, prefer to work with objects, machines, tools, plants, or animals, or to be outdoors.

F

People who like to observe, learn, investigate, analyze, evaluate, or solve problems.

B

People who like to work with data, have clerical or numerical ability, carrying things out in detail or following through on other's instructions.

The Party

E

People who have artistic, innovating or intuitional abilities, and like to work in unstructured situations, using their imagination or creativity.

C

People who like to work with people— influencing, persuading or performing or leading or managing for organizational goals or for economic gain.

D

People who like to work with people—to inform, enlighten, help, train, develop, or cure them, or are skilled with words.

(1) Which corner of the room would you instinctively be drawn to, as the group of people you would most *enjoy* being with for the longest time? (leave aside any question of shyness, or whether you would have to talk with them.) Write the *letter* for that corner here:

(2) After fifteen minutes, everyone in the corner you have chosen, leaves for another party crosstown, except you. Of the groups *that still remain* now, which corner or group would you be drawn to the most, as the people you would most *enjoy* being with for the longest time? Write the letter for that corner here:

(3) After fifteen minutes, this group too leaves for another party, except you. Of the corners, and groups, which remain now, which one would you most enjoy being with for the longest time? Write the letter for that corner here:

_____   _____   _____

(4) Now, underline the skills in each corner that you like best.

If you don't like parties, think of this as a library, or bookstore, with different book-sections: which one would you be most attracted to, etc.? Or think of it as a job-fair, with the employers grouped into different sections, etc.

However you think of it—party, library, job-fair—it should end up giving you a GENERAL idea about what skills you have—for it is based on the theories of Dr. John L. Holland about skill groupings, and on the idea that we are attracted to People, Books, Jobs which use the skills we *already have* and most enjoy.

GETTING DETAILED

But now you must have MORE DETAILED ideas about your skills. We can find these out by looking at different things you have ALREADY done—and, for the next exercise, you are going to need SEVEN.

So, please take

SEVEN BLANK PIECES OF PAPER
(lined or unlined, any size)

You have a choice as to what you write on these seven sheets. Here are three ways you can go:

First Choice: You can describe the seven *most satisfying accomplishments or achievements* you have ever done—in different periods of your life, and in your leisure or learning times or working times. Just be sure each accomplishment is one where you were *the active 'agent' who did the thing,* rather than just someone to whom something was done. (Being given a prize, etc. *won't do,* unless you say what you DID to earn the prize.) Put one accomplishment on each piece of paper, and give each one a brief title.

Alternative Choice #2: If the word "accomplishment" or "achievement" just makes you *freeze* ("Achievement? Who—little ol' me?"), then here is an alternative. Describe seven *jobs* you have had, paid or unpaid, full or part-time. Describe the seven you most ENJOYED doing. One on each piece of paper. And: give each a brief title.

Alternative Choice #3: If you haven't had seven jobs yet, or if you had seven or more, but hated every one of them, try instead describing seven *roles* you have (or have had) in your life. For example, if all your working experience so far has been in the home, and you are a married woman with children let us say, your seven roles might be: wife, mother, cook, homemaker, volunteer worker, student, citizen, etc. One role on each piece of paper; a brief title above each.

TALK, TALK, TALK

Now, go back over each sheet of paper, and be SURE you have described each achievement/job/role in enough detail, so that you can see what it is you really did.

How much detail? Well, let's take an example. This WON'T DO: "The Halloween Experience. I won a prize on Halloween for dressing up as a horse."

This WILL DO:

SAMPLE

"My Halloween Experience When I Was Seven Years Old. Details: When I was seven, I decided I wanted to go out on Halloween dressed as a horse. I wanted to be the front end of the horse, and I talked a friend of mine into being the back end of the horse. But, at the last moment he backed out, and I was faced with the prospect of not being able to go out on Halloween. At this point I decided to figure out some way of getting dressed up as the whole horse, myself. I took a fruit basket, and tied some string to both sides of the basket's rim, so that I could tie the basket around my rear end. This filled me out enough so that the costume fit me, by myself. I then fixed some strong thread to the tail so that I could make it wag by moving my hands. When Halloween came I not only went out and had a ball, but I won a prize as well."

SORT OF MEMORIZING

When you have finished writing out ALL SEVEN accomplishments/jobs/roles in detail, and each has a title, turn to page 188 and write the seven titles in, at the top of the SKILLS INVENTORY. Then, read over the seven sheets of paper two or three times, to be sure each story is very clear in your mind. So much so, that the title alone will recall the whole story to you.

ONE BY ONE

● MANY PEOPLE, incidentally, have found all of this is much easier for them, *if they don't write all seven accomplishments/jobs/roles at the same time,* but WRITE ONLY ONE, "run it through" the SKILL INVENTORY (pages 188–206). THEN write the next one, run it through the Inventory, THEN write the next one, etc. People who do it this way say they have a better idea of *which* accomplishments to choose, and *how* to write them up, as a result.

Your Functional/Transferable Skills Inventory

Webster's dictionary says: "**function**: *one of a group of related actions contributing to a larger action.*" And, "**transferable**: *usable in any occupational field.*" You are now about to take each experience of your own (your accomplishment/job/role), by title, and do an Inventory of it.

DIRECTIONS. This Skills Inventory is essentially a Coloring Book.

- Let's try it out with the sample we just saw on the previous page. We write the title in at the top: "The Halloween Experience". Then we start down the grid. (The letters, such as A^1, correspond to the letters of the Party exercise which you did on page 185. A^1 and A^2 correspond to the A-corner of the Party, etc.)

- The first "paragraph" or "box" of skill words has: "Designing_____; Molding_____; Shaping_____;" etc. So we ask ourselves, did we — in doing the Halloween Experience — use ANY or ALL of those skills? The answer is: "Yes". So, we do two things:
  (a) We *color in* the square (sort-of) next to that paragraph, to indicate "this experience used one or more of these skills in this paragraph; AND THEN
  (b) We *underline*, within the paragraph, the skill(s) used. In the case of the Halloween Experience, it was "designing" — so, we underline it. (We have put it in italics here, so as not to confuse you when you come to your own underlining.)

- Then we go on to the next "paragraph", which begins with "Preparing_____; Clearing_____;" etc. We ask ourselves, did we use ANY or ALL of these skills, in doing the Halloween Experience? The answer is "No" so we leave it blank and go on to the next. The answer there is "No" also.

- We go on to the paragraph which begins with "Handling/fingering/feeling_____;" etc. We ask ourselves the same question again, and here the answer is "Yes". So: (a) We *color in* the square.
  (b) We *underline*, within the paragraph, the skills used in the Halloween Experience. Several here appear relevant: "Handline, Manual dexterity, and Manipulating". We underline, therefore, these words (we have italicized them, again, so as not to confuse you). And so on to the end of page 206.

Sample: The Halloween Experience

Skill Paragraphs

A¹

Machine or Manual Skills

I can do because I did do:

Skill	sample	1	2	3	4	5	6	7	Additional experiences
Designing____ ; Molding____ ; Shaping; *Developing____* ; Composing____ (e.g., type)	▨								
Preparing____ ; Clearing____ ; Building____ ; Con- structing____ ; Assembling____ ; Setting Up____ ; Installing____ ; Installation of____ ; Laying____									
Lifting/Pushing/Pulling/Balancing____ ; Carrying____ ; Unloading/Moving/Shipping____ ; Delivering____ ; Collecting									
Handling/fingering/feeling____ ; Keen sense of touch; Keen sensations; Finger dexterity (as in typing, etc.); *Manual*/hand *dexterity* (as in typing, etc.); *Manual*/hand *dexterity*; Handling____ ; *Manipulating____* ; Weaving/Knitting; Handicraft- ing/craft skills; Making models	▨								
Precision-working; Punching____ ; Drilling____ ; Tweezer dexterity; Showing dexterity or speed									
Washing; Cooking/culinary skills									
Feeding____ ; Tending____									
Controlling/Operating____ ; Blasting____ ; Grinding____ ; Forging____ ; Cutting____ ; Filling____ ; Applying____ ; Pressing____ ; Binding____ ; Projecting____									
Operating tools; operating machinery (e.g. radios); operating vehicles/equipment; Driving____ ; Switching____									
Fitting____ ; Adjusting____ ; Tuning____ ; Maintain- ing____ ; Fixing/Repairing____ ; Masters machinery against its will; Trouble-shooting____									
Producing____									
Other skills which you think belong in this family but are not listed above:									

Machine or Manual Skills continued

and I used the above skills with:

	sample	1	2	3	4	5	6	7	Additional experiences
Tools (specify kinds):									
Work aids (what kinds?):									
Trees/stones/metals/other:									
Machines/equipment/vehicles:									
Processed materials (kinds?):									
Products being made (kinds?):									
Other:									

A2

Athletic/ Outdoor/ Traveling Skills

I can do because I have proven:

	sample	1	2	3	4	5	6	7	Additional experiences
Motor/Physical coordination & agility; *Eye-Hand-Foot coordination*; Walking/Climbing/Running									
Skilled at general sports: Skilled in small competitive games; Skilled at ____ (a particular game)									
Swimming: Skiing/ Recreation; Playing. Hiking/ Backpacking/Camping/Mountaineering; Outdoor survival skills; Creating, planning, organizing outdoor activities; Traveling									
Drawing samples from the earth; Keen oceanic interests; Navigating									
Horticultural skills; Cultivating growing things; Skillful at planting/nurturing plants; Landscaping and groundskeeping									
Farming; Ranching; Working with animals									
Other skills which you think belong in this family, but are not listed above:									

B¹

Detail/Follow-through Skills

I can do because I did do:

	sample	1	2	3	4	5	6	7	Additional experiences
Following-through; Executing _____; Ability to follow detailed instructions; *Expert at getting things done*; Implementing decisions; Enforcing regulations; Rendering support services; Applying what others have developed; Directing production of _____ (kind of thing)									
Precise attainment of set limits, tolerances or standards; Brings projects in on time, and within budget; Skilled at making arrangements for events, processes; Responsible; Delivering on promises, on time.									
Expediting _____; Dispatching _____; Consistently tackles tasks ahead of time; Adept at finding ways to speed up a job; Able to handle a great variety of tasks and responsibilities simultaneously and efficiently: *Able to work well under stress, and still improvise*; Good at responding to emergencies									
Resource expert; Resource broker; Making and using contacts effectively; Good at getting materials; Collecting things; Purchasing _____; Compiling _____									
Approving _____; Validation of information; Keeping confidences or confidential information.									
A detail man or woman; Keen and accurate memory for detail; Showing careful attention to, and keeping track of, details; Focusing on minutiae; High tolerance of repetition and/or monotony; Retentive memory for rules and procedures (e.g. protocol); *Persevering* _____									
Checking _____									
Explicit, ordered, systematic manipulation of data; Good at the processing of information; Collates data accurately, comparing with previous data; Tabulation of data; Keeping records (time, etc.); Recording _____ (kinds of data)									
Facilitating/Simplifying other people's finding things; Orderly organizing of data or records									

B2

Numerical/ Financial/ Accounting/ Financial (Money) Management Skills

I can do because I did do:

	sample	1	2	3	4	5	6	7	Additional experiences
Organizing written and numerical data according to a prescribed plan; Classification skills; Classifying materials expertly; Filing; Filing materials; Retrieving data									
Clerical ability; Typing; Operating business machines and data processing machines to attain organizational and economic goals; Copying; Reproducing materials									
Other skills which you think belong in this family, but are not listed above:									
Numerical ability; Expert at learning and remembering numbers; number memory; Remembering statistics accurately, for a long period of time									
Counting; Taking inventory; Calculating; Computing; Arithmetical skills; High accuracy in computing /counting; Rapid manipulation of numbers; Rapid computations performed in head or on paper									
Managing money; Financial planning and management; Keeping financial records; Accountability									
Appraising _____ ; Economic research and analysis; Doing cost analysis; Effective Cost Analyses, Estimates, Projections, and Comparisons; Financial/Fiscal Analysis and Planning/Programming									
Developing a budget; Budget Planning, Preparation, Justification, Administration, Analysis and Review									
Extremely economical; Skilled at Allocating Scarce Financial Resources									
Preparing financial reports; Bookkeeping; Doing accounting; Fiscal Cost Audits, Controls, and Reductions									
Using numbers as a reasoning tool; Very sophisticated mathematical abilities; Effective at solving statistical problems									
Others which you think belong in this family of skills, but are not listed above:									

C1

Influencing/ Persuading Skills

I can because I did:

	sample	1	2	3	4	5	6	7	Additional experiences
Develop rapport / trust; Inspiring trust in the minds and hearts of others; Encouraging people									
Helping people identify their own intelligent self-interest									
Persuading_____ ; Expert in reasoning persuasively / developing a thought; Debating, Influencing the attitudes or ideas of others									
Promoting_____ ; (Face to face) Selling of tangibles/ intangibles; Selling ideas or products without tearing down competing ideas or products; Selling an idea, program or course of action to decision-makers; Developing targets/building markets for ideas or products; Fund-raising/money-raising									
Recruiting talent or leadership; Attracts skilled, competent creative people; *Enlisting;* Motivating others; Mobilizing_____ ; Stimulating people to effective action									
Getting diverse groups to work together; Wins friends easily from among diverse or even opposing groups or factions; Adept at conflict management									
Arbitrating/mediating between contending parties or groups; Negotiating to come jointly to decisions; Bargaining; Crisis intervention; reconciling_____									
Renegotiating_____ ; Obtaining agreement on policies, after the fact									
Charting mergers; Manipulating_____ to achieve_____ ; Arranging financing									
Other skills which you think belong in this family, but are not listed above:									

and I used the above skills with:

	sample	1	2	3	4	5	6	7	Additional experiences
Opinions									
Attitudes									
Judgments, Decisions									
Products									
Money									
Other:									

	sample	1	2	3	4	5	6	7	Additional experiences

C2 Performing Skills

I can do because I did do:

Getting up before a group; Very responsive to audiences' moods or ideas; Diverting; Contributes to others pleasure consciously; Performing

Demonstrating ____ (products, etc.); *Modelling* ____ ; Artistic (visual) presentations

Showmanship; A strong theatrical sense; Poise in public appearances

Addressing large or small groups; (Exceptional) speaking ability/articulateness; Public address/public speaking/oral presentations; Lecturing; Stimulating people/stimulating enthusiasm; Poetry reading

Playing music; Making musical presentations; Singing; Dancing

Making people laugh; Understands the value of the ridiculous in illuminating reality

Acting; Making radio and TV presentations/films

Public sports

Conducting and directing public affairs and ceremonies; Conducting musical groups

Other skills which you think belong in this family, but are not listed above:

C3 Leadership Skills

I can do because I did do:

Initiating ____ ; Able to move into totally new situations on one's own; Able to take the initiative or first move in developing relationships; Skilled at striking up conversations with strangers

Driving initiative; Continually searches for more responsibility; Persevering in acquiring things (like ____)

Excellent at organizing one's time; *Unusual ability to work self-directedly, without supervision;* (Very) self-directed at work

	sample	1	2	3	4	5	6	7	Additional experiences
Unwillingness to automatically accept the status quo; Keen perceptions of things as they could be, rather than passively accepting them as they are; Promoting and bringing about major changes, as change agent; Planning for/and effecting/initiating change; *Sees and seizes opportunities*	▨								
Sees a problem and acts immediately to solve it; Deals well with the unexpected or critical; Very decisive in emergencies; Adept at confronting others with touchy or difficult personal matters	▨								
Showing courage; No fear of taking manageable risks; Able to make hard decisions; Adept at policy making; Able to terminate projects/people/ processes when necessary	▨								
Leading others; guiding _____ ; Inspiring, motivating and leading organized groups; Impresses others with enthusiasm and charisma; Repeatedly elected to senior posts; Skilled at chairing meetings									
Deft in directing creative talent; Skilled leadership in perceptive human relations techniques									
Other skills which you think belong in this family, but are not listed above:									
Planning _____ ; Planning and development _____ ; Planning on basis of lessons from past experience; A systematic approach to goal-setting									
Prioritizing tasks; Establishing effective priorities among competing requirements; Setting criteria or standards; Policy-making; Policy formulation or interpretation									
Designing projects; Program development/Pro- gramming; Skilled at planning and carrying out well-run meetings, seminars or workshops	▨								
Organizing _____ ; Organizational development; Organizational analysis, planning and building; adept at organizing, bringing order out of chaos with masses of (physical) things									

C4

Developing/ Planning/ Organizing/ Executing/ Supervising/ Management Skills

	Developing/Planning/Organizing/Executing/ Supervising/Management Skills, continued	sample	1	2	3	4	5	6	7	Additional experiences
I can do because I did do:	Organizing others, bringing people together in cooperative efforts; Selecting resources; Hiring; *Able to call in other experts/helpers as needed*; Team-building; Recognizing and utilizing the skills of others; Contracting/Delegating ___									
	Scheduling ___ ; Assigning ___ ; Setting up and maintaining on-time work-schedules; Coordinating operations/details; Arranging/Installing ___									
	Directing others; Making decisions about others; Supervising others in their work; Supervising and administering ___									
	Managing/Being responsible for others' output; Management___; Humanly-oriented technical management; Real property, plant and facility, management; R & D Program and Project Management; Controlling___									
	Producing___ ; Achieving___ ; Attaining___									
	Maintaining___ ; Trouble-shooting___ ; Recommending___									
	Reviewing___ ; Makes good use of feed-back; Evaluating___ ; Recognizes intergroup communication gaps; Judging people's effectiveness									
	Other skills which you think belong in this family, but are not included above:									
and I used those skills with:	*Individuals*									
	Personnel									
	Groups									
	Organizations									
	Management systems									
	Office procedures									
	Meetings									
	Projects / Programs									
	Educational events									
	Other:									

D¹

Language/ Reading/ Writing/ Speaking/ Communications Skills

I can do because I did do:

	sample	1	2	3	4	5	6	7	Additional experiences
Reading; Love of reading voraciously or rapidly; Love of printed things; Relentlessly curious									
Comparing____; Proofreading____; Editing effectively____; Publishing imaginatively____									
Composing____ (kinds of words)									
Communicating effectively; Expresses self very well; Communicates with clarity; Making a point and cogently expressing a position; Thinking quickly on one's feet; Talking/Speaking; Encouraging communication									
Defining____; Explaining concepts; Interpreting____; Ability to explain difficult or complex concepts, ideas and problems									
Translating____; Verbal/linguistic skills in foreign languages; Linguistics; Teaching of languages; Adept at translating jargon into relevant and meaningful terms, to diverse audiences or readers									
Summarizing____; Reporting accurately; Very explicit and concise writing; Keeping superior minutes of meetings									
Outstanding writing skills; Ability to vividly describe people or scenes so that others can visualize; Writes with humor, fun and flair (related to *Diverting*, below); Employs humor in describing experiences, to give people courage to embrace them									
Uncommonly warm letter composition; Flair for writing reports; Skilled speech-writing									
Promotional writing; Highly successful proposal writing for funding purposes; Imaginative advertising and publicity programs									
Other skills which you think belong in this family, but are not listed above:									

Language/Reading/Writing/Speaking Communications Skills continued	sample	1	2	3	4	5	6	7	Additional experiences
Ideas									
Feelings									
Facts									
Articles									
Reports/Newsletters									
Brochures/catalogs/journals									
Books									
Other:									

and I used those skills with:

D2

Instructing/ Interpreting/ Guiding/ Educational Skills

I can because I have:

Proven myself to be very knowledgeable; Having a commitment to learning as a life-long process

Briefing ____; Informing ____; Enlightening ____; Explaining ____; Instructing ____; Teaching ____; In-Service training

(Unusually) skillful teaching; Fosters a stimulating learning environment; Creating an atmosphere of acceptance; Patient teaching; Adept at inventing illustrations for principles or ideas; Down to earth; Adept at using visual communications (charts, slides, chalkboards, etc.); Instills love of the subject; Conveys tremendous enthusiasm

Coaching about ____ (finances, etc.); Advising/aiding people in making decisions; Giving advice about ____; Giving insight concerning ____

Encouraging ____; (cf. Influencing/Persuading Family of Skills, above)

Adept at two-way dialogue; Communicates effectively; Ability to hear and answer questions perceptively; Acceptance of differing opinions; (Keen) ability to help others express their views; Consulting

and I used those skills with:		sample	1	2	3	4	5	6	7	Additional experiences
	Enabling/Facilitating personal growth and development; Helping people make their own discoveries in knowledge; Helping people to develop their own ideas or insights; Clarifying goals and values of others; Counseling; Putting things in perspective; Brings out creativity in others; Shows others how to take advantage of a resource									
	Group-facilitating; Discussion group leadership; Group dynamics; Behavioral modification									
	Empowering____; Training and Development____; Training someone in something; Designing educational events; Organization and administration of inhouse training programs									
	Other skills which you think belong in this family, but are not listed above:									
	Information									
	Ideas / Generalizations									
	Values / standards									
	Goals / decisions									
	Other									
D3 *Serving/ Helping/ Human Relations Skills*	Relates well in dealing with the public/public relations									
	Servicing____; Customer relations and services; Attending____; Adjusting____ (e.g. bills); Referring (people)____									
	Rendering services to____; Being of service; Helping and serving									
	Sensitivity to others; Interested in/manifesting keen ability to relate to people; Intense curiosity about other people—who they are, what they do; Remembers people and their preferences; Adept at treating									

I can because I did:

Serving/Helping *Human Relations Skills continued*	sample	1	2	3	4	5	6	7	Additional experiences
people fairly; Listening intently and accurately; A good trained effective listener; Good at listening and conveying awareness; Consistently communicates warmth to people; Conveying understanding, patience and fairness; Readily establishes warm, mutual rapport with ___ ; Able to develop warmth over the telephone									
Interpersonal competencies; (Unusual) perception in human relations; Expertise in interpersonal contact; Keen ability to put self in someone else's shoes; Empathy: instinctively understanding how someone else feels; Understanding; Tact, Diplomacy and Discretion; Effective in dealing with many different kinds of people / Talks easily with all kinds of people									
Caring for/Nursing children or the handicapped; Watching over ___ ; Love of children; Guiding ___									
Administering a household; Hostessing; Shaping and influencing the atmosphere of a particular place; Providing comfortable, natural and pleasant surroundings; Warmly sensitive and responsive to people's feelings and needs in social or other situations; Anticipating people's needs									
Works well on a teamwork basis; Has fun while working, and makes it fun for others; Collaborates with colleagues skillfully; Treats others as equals, without regard to education, authority, or position; Refuses to put people into slots or categories; Ability to relate to people with different value systems; Motivates fellow workers; Expresses appreciation faithfully; Ready willingness to share credit with others									
Takes human failings/limitations into account; Able to ignore undesirable qualities in others; Deals patiently and sympathetically with difficult people; Handles super-difficult people in situations, without stress; Handles prima donnas tactfully and effectively; Works well in a hostile environment									

	sample	1	2	3	4	5	6	7	Additional experiences

Serving / Helping
Human Relations Skills continued

Nursing_____; Skillful therapeutic abilities; Curing_____; Gifted at helping people with their personal problems; Raises people's self-esteem; (Thorough) understanding of human motivations; Understands family relationships and problems; Aware of people's need for supportive community; Adept at aiding people with their total life adjustment/Mentoring

Unusual ability to represent others; Expert in liaison roles; Ombudsmanship

Other skills which you think belong in this family, but are not included above:

and I used those skills with:

Children

The young

Adolescents

Adults or *Peers*

The aging

All age groups

Other:

E1

Intuitional and Innovating Skills

Imagining_____; Highly imaginative; *Possessed of great imagination, and the courage to use it*

Ideaphoria/Continually conceiving, developing and generating ideas; Conceptual ability of the highest order; Being an idea man or woman; Inventing; *Inventive: Ability to improvise on the spur of the moment*

Innovating; Having many innovative and creative ideas; Creative, perceptive effective innovator; *Willing to experiment with new approaches*; Experimental with ideas, procedures, and programs; Strongly committed to experimental approaches; Demonstrating continual originality; Love of exercising the mind-muscle

Intuitional and Innovating Skills continued

I can do because I did do:

Intuitional and Innovating Skills	sample	1	2	3	4	5	6	7	Additional experiences
Synthesizing perceptions, etc.; Seeing relationships between apparently unrelated factors; Integrating diverse elements into a clear coherent whole; Effective dissolution of barriers between ideas or fields; Ability to relate abstract ideas; Balancing factors /Judging/Showing good judgement									
Deriving things from others' ideas; Improving ____; Updating ____; *Adapting* ____; Reflection upon ____; Sees the theoretical base in a practical situation; Significant theoretical modeling; *Model developing*; Developing ____; Formulating ____; Developing innovative program ideas									
Generating ideas with commercial possibilities; Able to see the commercial possibilities of abstract ideas or concepts; Applying ____; Applying theory; Applied research; Creating products; Entreprenurial									
Form perception; Perception of patterns and structures; *Visualizing shapes*; Graphing and reading graphs; Visualizing in the third-dimension; Able to read blueprints									
Spatial memory; Memory for design; Able to notice quickly (and/or remember later) most of the contents of a room; Remembering ____; Memory for faces									
Showing foresight; Recognizing obsolescence before compelling data is yet at hand; Instinctively gathering resources even before the need for them becomes clear; Forecasting									
Perceiving intuitively; Color-discrimination (of a very high order)									
Other skills which you think belong in this family, but are not listed above:									

E2

Artistic Skills

I can because I did:

	sample	1	2	3	4	5	6	7	Additional experiences
Shows strong sensitivity to, and need for, beauty in the environment; Adept at coloring things; instinctively excellent taste									
Expressive; Exceptionally good at facial expressions used to express or convey thoughts, without (or, in addition to) words; Ability to use the body to express feelings eloquently; Uses voice tone and rhythm as unusually effective tool of communication; Skilled in telephone-voice; Can accurately reproduce sounds (e.g., foreign languages spoken without accent); Mastery of all forms of communication									
Good sense of humor/playfulness									
Creative imagining/Creating original ____; Operates well in a free, unstructured, unsupervised environment; Bringing new life to traditional (art) forms; Translating ____; Restoring ____									
Aware of the value of symbolism, and deft in its use; Skilled at symbol formation (words, pictures, and concepts); Visualizing concepts; Creating poetry, or poetic images; Designing and/or using audio-visual aids; Photographing									
Visual & spatial designing; Artistic talent (drawing, etc.); Illustrating; Mapping; Drafting/Mechanical drawing									
Fashioning/Shaping things; *Making* ____; Designing in wood or other media; Redesigning structures; Styling ____; Decorating ____									
Writing; Playwriting; Assisting in/directing the planning, organizing and staging of theatrical productions									
Musical knowledge and taste; Tonal memory; Uncommon sense of rhythm, Exceedingly accurate melody recognition; Composing									
Other skills which you think belong in this family, but are not listed above:									

	sample	1	2	3	4	5	6	7	Additional experiences
Artistic Skills continued *and I used those skills with:* Colors Spaces *Shapes, faces* Handicrafts Arts, drawing, paints Fashion, jewelry, clothing, furs, furniture Music Other:									
F¹ *Observational/ Learning Skills* *I can do because I did do:* Observing ____; (Highly) observant of people/data/things; (Keen) awareness of surroundings									
Reading ____ (e.g., dials); Adept at scanning radar or other sophisticated observational systems; Estimating ____ (e.g., speed)									
Listening skillfully; Hearing accurately; Keen sense of smell; (Tremendously) sensitive sense of tasting									
Perceptive: Perceiving ____; Detecting ____; Discovering ____; A person of perpetual curiosity/discovery, delighting in new knowledge; Continually seeking to expose oneself to new experiences; Highly committed to continual personal growth and learning; Learns from the example of others; Learns quickly									
Alert in observing human behavior; Studying other people's behavior perceptively; Perceptive in identifying and assessing the potential of others; Recognizes and appreciates the skills of others									
Appraising ____; Assessing ____; Screening applicants; Realistically assessing people's needs; Accurately assessing public moods; *Quickly sizes up situations and instinctively understands political realities*									

	sample	1	2	3	4	5	6	7	Additional experiences
Exceptional intelligence, tempered by common sense									
Other skills which you think belong in this family, but are not listed above:									
Data (what kinds?)									
People (any special kinds?)									
Ideas									
Behavior									
Procedures									
Operations									
Phenomena									
Instruments									
Other									

and I used those skills with:

F2

Research/ Investigating/ Analyzing/ Systematiz- ing/ Evaluating Skills

Anticipates problems before they become problems; Recognizing need for more information before a decision can be made intelligently; Skilled at clarifying problems or situations

Surveying____; Interviewing____; Adept at gathering information from people by talking to them; Researching resources, ways and means; Researching personally, through investigation and interviewing; Inquiring

Inspecting____; Examining____; Surveying organizational needs; Researching exhaustively; Collecting information/Information gathering; Academic research and writing

Analyzing____; Dissecting____; *Breaking down principles into parts*; Adept at atomizing/breaking down into parts; Analyzing community needs, values, and resources; Analyzes communication situations; Analyzes manpower requirements; Analyzing performance specifications

Research / Investigating / Analyzing / Systematizing / Evaluating Skills continued

	sample	1	2	3	4	5	6	7	Additional experiences
Diagnosing____; Organizing/Classifying____; Identifies elements, relationships, structures, and organizing principles of organizations to be analyzed; Isolating elements; *Able to separate 'wheat from chaff'*; Reviewing large amounts of material, and extracting essence; Perceiving and Defining Cause & Effect relationships; Ability to trace problems, ideas, etc. to their source	▨								
Grouping____; Perceiving common denominators; Systematizing/Organizing material/information in a systematic way									
*Testing*____ (e.g. an idea, or hypothesis)									
Determining/Figuring out____; Solving____; Problem-solving; Trouble-shooting									
Reviewing/Evaluating____; Screening____ (e.g., fund proposals); Critiquing____; Evaluating by measurable or subjective criteria; Accurately evaluating____ (e.g., programs administered by others; experiments; loan applications; papers; quizzes; work; records; staff; program bids; evidence; options; qualifications; etc.)									
Decision-making skills; Re-evaluating									
Other skills which you think belong in this family, but are not listed above:									
People (what kinds?)									
Data (what kinds?)									
Things (what kinds?)									
Ideas (theoretical, abstract, symbolic, systematic?)									
Articles, artifacts, or processes									
Matter (inert or moving) or Energy									
Phenomena (physical, biological, scientific, mathematical, or cultural?)									
Other:									

I can because I did:

and I used those skills with:

PATTERNS AND PRIORITIES

When you've finished this whole Inventory, for all seven of your accomplishments/achievements/jobs/roles or whatever, you want to look for PATTERNS and PRIORITIES.

a) For Patterns, because it isn't a matter of whether you used a skill once only, but rather whether you used it repeatedly, or not. "Once" proves nothing; "repeatedly" is very convincing.

b) For Priorities, because the job you eventually choose may not be able to use all of your skills. You need to know *what you are willing to trade off, and what you are not.* This requires you to know what your priorities are: i.e., which skills, or family of skills, are most important to you.

PHOTO-COPY, DOUBLE-COLOR, PRIORITIZE

We therefore suggest you tear out the preceding pages of the Skills Inventory, *arrange to photo-copy the opposite side of each page,* and then spread them all out on a table or on the floor.

Now you have a complete "aerial view" of all the skills you have. At this point, we suggest you use a second color (like red) and go back over all the "squares" you colored in. Ask yourself, do I enjoy this skill/these skills still today? If the answer is "Yes" DOUBLE-COLOR that particular square. And DOUBLE-UNDERLINE, in red, the particular skills you ENJOY, in each corresponding Skill Paragraph.

When you are all done, look at the total "aerial view" of your skills, to see which family of skills has the most DOUBLE-COLOR (say, red); put it up at the top of the table or floor lay-out. Which family of skills has the next most DOUBLE-COLOR? Put it next. Thus, you will quickly see which skills are most important to you.

Enter the results on the diagram on page 212.

Now it is time to go on to the second part of your homework, and consider:

Where You Would Most Enjoy Using These Skills

Where You Would Most Enjoy Using These Skills

It is, of course, nice to 'stay loose' and be willing to use your skills any place that there is a vacancy. Unfortunately, experts say that 80% of all the vacancies which occur in this country, above entry level, are never advertised through any of the channels or avenues that job-hunters traditionally turn to.

So, you're going to have to approach any place and every place that looks attractive to you.

So, you can't rule out any place that looks interesting to you, because it's just possible they have a vacancy that you don't know about. Or will develop one *while you're there.* Or will decide (since they may be expanding) to create a job just for you.

You can't, of course, go visit EVERY place that looks interesting. Hence, the importance of this part of your homework. You've GOT to "cut the territory down" to some manageable size, by using:

SIX PRINCIPLES OF EXCLUSION, FOR NARROWING DOWN THE AREA YOU NEED TO FOCUS ON

1. *First Principle for Narrowing Down the Organizations You Will Need to Visit:* WHAT STATE, CITY OR AREA DO YOU MOST WANT TO WORK IN? If it's where you presently live, get a city (or county) street map, decide the longest time or distance you are willing to commute, and then cut a piece of string *that length,* stick a pencil through one end, a pin at the other, put the pin at the place where you presently live, and swing an arc with the pencil. That gives you the area where you will go job-hunting. If it's not where you presently live, decide on the name of the city or place you'd most like to work, followed by two alternatives (in case). Enter your answer on page 212.

2. *Second Principle for Narrowing Down the Organizations You Will Need to Visit:* WHERE, WITHIN THAT GEOGRAPHICAL AREA, DO YOU WANT TO WORK, IN TERMS OF SPECIAL KNOWLEDGES? Consider all the subjects you know quite a bit about, knowledges you picked up in the home, in your leisure, in school, or on the job. On a blank sheet of paper, list them all. Then prioritize them, using the grid on the next page.

PRIORITIZING GRID

LIST, COMPARE

Here is a method for taking (say) ten items, and figuring out which one is most important to you, which is next most important, etc.

1 2   Make a list of the items and number them. *In the case of Specific Knowledges, make a list of ten subjects you know quite a bit*
1 3   2 3   *about, then number them 1 thru 10.* Now, look at the first line of this grid. You see a 1 and a 2 there. So, compare
1 4   2 4   3 4   items one and two on your list. Which one is more important to you? *State the question any way*
1 5   2 5   3 5   4 5   *you want to: in the case of Specific Knowl-*
1 6   2 6   3 6   4 6   5 6   *edges, you might ask yourself: if I was being offered two jobs, one which*
1 7   2 7   3 7   4 7   5 7   6 7   *used knowledge # 1, and one which used #2, other things*
1 8   2 8   3 8   4 8   5 8   6 8   7 8   *being equal, which would I prefer?* Circle it.
1 9   2 9   3 9   4 9   5 9   6 9   7 9   8 9   Then go on to the next pair,
1 10   2 10   3 10   4 10   5 10   6 10   7 10   8 10   9 10   etc.

CIRCLE, COUNT

Total Times Each Number Got Circled:

1____ 2____ 3____ 4____ 5____ 6____ 7____ 8____ 9____ 10____

When you are all done, count up the number of times each number got circled, all told. Enter these totals in the spaces just above.

RECOPY

Finally, recopy your list, beginning with the item that got the most circles. This is your *new #1.* Then the item that got the next most circles. This is your *new #2.*

In case of a tie (two numbers got the same number of circles), look back on the grid to see when you were comparing those two numbers there, which one got circled. That means you prefer That One over the other; thus you break the tie.

P.S. If you need to compare any list that has more than ten items to it, just keep adding new rows to the bottom of the grid. Thus:
1 *11*   2 *11,*   etc.   Until you have all the numbers compared.

You will need to use the above grid several times, in the course of completing this map. Just copy it on a separate piece of paper each new time you need to use it.

Once you have listed, in the order of their priority, the special
knowledges you most enjoy using, list them in the appropriate place
on page 212. Also, get together with two or three of your friends and
have them suggest the kinds of places where such special knowledges
might be useful on the job.

3. *Third Principle for Narrowing Down the Organizations You Will Need
to Visit:* WITHIN THE ORGANIZATIONS WHICH USE THE
SPECIAL KNOWLEDGES YOU CARE THE MOST ABOUT,
WHAT KINDS OF PEOPLE WOULD YOU LIKE TO BE SUR-
ROUNDED BY—
    a) Defined, first of all, in terms of skills? *(Here enter your answers—
spelled out—from The Party Exercise, on page 185. List the three corners
you liked best, in order, plus the words you underlined in each of those
three corners.)*
    b) Defined, secondly, in terms of characteristics: e.g., competent,
friendly, etc. If you have trouble thinking of characteristics, think of
the *kinds* of people who turn you off, then list their opposites, here.
Prioritize this list—using the grid, on page 209. Enter the answers in
the appropriate place on page 212.

4. *Fourth Principle for Narrowing Down the Organizations You Will Need
to Visit:* WITHIN ORGANIZATIONS THAT USE YOUR FAVOR-
ITE SPECIAL KNOWLEDGES, AND HAVE PEOPLE WITH THE
SKILLS AND CHARACTERISTICS YOU LIKE BEST, WHAT
GOALS/PURPOSES/VALUES DO YOU WANT THAT ORGANI-
ZATION TO BE TRYING TO ACHIEVE?
    a) Working primarily on the mind—trying to bring more truth
into the world? OR working primarily with the emotions—trying to
bring more beauty or love into the world? OR working primarily
with the moral will—trying to bring more justice, honesty, perfection,
etc. into the world? OR: what?
    b) Producing a product, making money, offering services,
making better bodies, reducing mortality, or what?
    List all your answers to both a) and b), prioritize them (using the
grid on page 209), then list your answers in order of priority at the
appropriate place on page 212.

5. *Fifth Principle for Narrowing Down the Organizations You Will Need to Visit:* YOU WILL DO YOUR BEST AND MOST EFFECTIVE WORK WITHIN ONE OF THE ABOVE ORGANIZATIONS THAT ALSO HAS WHAT SORT OF WORKING CONDITIONS:

a) Outdoors, indoors, with large windows, indoors anywhere?

b) In an organization with more than 500 employees, 300 or so, 100, less than 50, less than 10, or—what?

c) What sort of dress code, supervision, openness to change, use of authority, and—what else?

d) List distasteful working conditions you have endured in the past on the job/at school/at home, and then state the opposite of these—in more positive form.

List all your answers to a), b), c) and d) above on a separate blank sheet of paper, prioritize them all together (using the grid on page 209), then list your answers at the appropriate place on page 212.

6. *The Sixth, and Final, Principle for Narrowing Down the Organizations You Will Need to Visit:* IN THE ORGANIZATIONS DESCRIBED BY YOUR ANSWERS TO THE ABOVE QUESTIONS, WHAT KIND OF RESPONSIBILITY DO YOU WANT, AND (TO PUT IT ANOTHER WAY) AT WHAT SALARY LEVEL?

a) Do you want to work alone, OR in tandem with one other co-worker, OR as a member of a team, OR as a supervisor, boss or owner, OR—what?

b) How much, and what kinds, of initiative would you like to be able to take on the job?

c) What's the minimum salary you could stand? What's the maximum you hope for/would like to get?

Enter this information at the appropriate place on page 212. together with any other thoughts you have, related to this question.

And Now, To Put It All Together:

All the information gathered so far, on the subject of

WHAT (skills do I have, and most enjoy using); and

WHERE (do I want to use those skills)

must now be summarized, all together, on the diagram on the next page:

The Flower:

A PICTURE OF THE JOB
I AM LOOKING FOR

1.
Where
Geography-wise?
(in order of priority for me)

2.
In organizations
using **these**
special knowledges:
(in order of priority for me)

6.
At **this** level of
responsibility
and salary:

USING
THESE
TRANSFERABLE SKILLS:
(in order of priority for me)

1
2
3
4 5

Listed by Skill Family, with Favorite Skills in Each Family Also Listed

3.
In organizations
having
these people-
environments:
(in order of priority for me)

5.
With **these**
working-
conditions:
(in order of priority for me)

4.
Serving **these**
goals/purposes/values:
(in order of priority for me)

COPY THIS ON
A LARGE SHEET
OF PAPER AND
FILL IT IN

Now, on to the third part of your homework:

How to identify the job you have just drawn a picture of, by name or by title;

How to identify the kind of organizations which have such a job;

How to get hired there.

There are three steps to the HOW part of your homework:

● *The First Step on the Road to Your Job:*

PRACTICE INTERVIEWING

You need to go out and practice talking to people. Just for practice. In a non-job, low-stress, practice interview situation—just for information. You can take someone with you, if you want. If you're shy, maybe you want to take someone with you who is more at ease with people than you are; and watch how he/she does it. Anyway, by yourself, or with someone:

Your task here is to go out and talk with somebody. Somebody at *A Place That Fascinates or Interests You*—like, say, an airport (how does it get run), a toy-store, a television station, or whatever; OR somebody who has *The Same Hobby or Leisure-Activity That You Do*—like, say, skiing, gardening, painting, music, color, or whatever; OR somebody who is working on *Some Issue That Fascinates or Interests You*—like, say, affirmative action, or ecology, or assertiveness, or lower taxes, or whatever. Use your phone book (the Yellow Pages) or friends to find the kind of person you're looking for: e.g., for skiing, try a ski-supply store, or instructor.

When you find him or her, talk about your mutual enthusiasm. If you don't know what else to ask them, here are four suggestions:

1. How did you get into this work? Or: How did you get interested in this?

2. What do you like best about doing this?

3. What do you like least about doing this?

4. Where else could I find people who share this enthusiasm, or interest, or are interested in this issue?

Then go visit the people they suggest, and ask them (if nothing else) the same four questions. Keep at this, practice it as long as you need to, until you feel comfortable talking to people.

Then, on to the next step.

● *The Second Step on the Road to Your Job:*

INFORMATION INTERVIEWING
TO PUT IT ALL TOGETHER

Once you feel comfortable interviewing people, you are ready to go find what kind of job, and organizations, that PICTURE OF THE JOB I AM LOOKING FOR points to.

THE SIMPLER FLOWER

So, begin with that picture (page 212). Take a large piece of blank paper (like, shelf paper or notebook paper 8½ x 11″) and

a) COPY THE OUTLINE of the flower (one centerpiece, six petals around its outside). Then:

b) COPY YOUR TWO most favorite skills onto the centerpiece of this New flower. Copy them off the Flower on page 212.

c) COPY THE TWO most important items on each of the six petals (e.g., your two top special knowledges, your two top people-environments, your two top goals/values, etc.)

d) On this *Simpler Flower* you will now have 12-14 items, all together. Make a list of these on the margin of your diagram, and prioritize them (using a blank copy of the prioritizing grid on page 209; and asking the question in the case of each pair, "If I had two job offers and they were both the same, except that one gave me (here name the first factor you are comparing) and the other gave me (here name the second factor you are comparing), which job would I take?")

e) NOW NUMBER THE 12-14 FACTORS ON THIS Simpler Flower in the order of priority or importance to you.

f) THEN FILL IN THE BLANKS BELOW WITH THE CORRESPONDING ITEM off your "Prioritized Simpler Flower": e.g., each time a 1. occurs below, copy your first—or most important—factor there.

THE INTERVIEWS FOR
INFORMATION ONLY

1 — *On my first information interview(s) I'm going to go see someone whose job uses/is characterized by*

1. _____

and I'm going to ask him/her what kind of jobs they know about which use:

1. _____ *AND*

2. _____

2 On my second information interview(s) I'm going to go see the kind of person suggested to me in my first interview(s) above, namely, someone whose job uses/is characterized by

1. _____ AND

2. _____

and I'm going to ask him/her what kind of jobs they know about which use:

1. _____ AND

2. _____ AND

3. _____

And if they don't know, I'll ask them who they think does.

3 — On my third information interview(s) I'm going to go see the kind of person suggested to me in my second interview(s) above, namely, someone whose job uses/is characterized by

1. _____ AND

2. _____ AND

3. _____

and I'm going to ask him/her what kind of jobs they know about which use:

1. _____ AND

2. _____ AND

3. _____ AND

4. _____

And if they don't know, I'll ask them who they think does.

4 — On my fourth information interview(s), I'm going to go see the kind of person suggested to me in my third interview(s) above, namely, someone whose job uses/is characterized by

1. _____ AND

2. _____ AND

3. _____ AND

4. _____

and I'm going to ask him/her what kind of jobs they know about which use:

1. _____ AND

2. _____ AND

3. _____ AND

4. _____ AND

5. _____

And if they don't know, I'll ask them who they think does.

5 — On my fifth information interview(s), etc.

(You can surely finish this diagram for yourself, on a separate sheet of blank paper.)

If at any time during this informational interviewing, you can't get to see someone who actually holds the job you are interested in holding, ask to talk to his/her superior or boss, rather than to a co-worker or someone under him/her.

Whenever you run into a stone-wall, use your contacts (friends, family, school alumni, former employers, etc.) for suggestions as to where you can turn next.

● *The Third and Last Step on the Road to Your Job:*

In the course of the above interviewing, you will not only discover the kind of job(s) you would most like to have, but you will—in the course of your interviewing—inevitably discover what organizations have such jobs, as you will have to visit those organizations in the course of your informational interviewing.

Now, your task is TO RETURN TO THE TWO OR THREE ORGANIZATIONS YOU LIKED THE BEST and tell them so—together with why (your chance to discuss all the factors on The Flower Picture of the job you are looking for).

You are now, but only now, coming to visit them as Job-hunter. Whether they have a vacancy or not, is immaterial. You are going to seek out in each organization among your top three or so, the person who has the power to hire (not the personnel department); and you are going to tell him or her

a • what impressed you about their organization, during your information survey (stage 2),

b • what sorts of challenges, needs or "problems" (go slow in using this latter word with sensitive employers) your survey suggested exists in this field in general, and with this place in particular—that intrigue you.

c • what skills seem to you to be needed, in order to meet those challenges or needs in his or her organization.
d • the fact that you have these skills (here use the information summarized on the Map, page 212).

They, for their part, will have four basic questions they will want to know the answers to, about YOU:
a • why are you here (i.e., why did you pick out their organization)?
b • what can you do for them (i.e., what are your skills and special knowledges)?
c • what kind of person are you (i.e., what are your goals/values, self-management, etc.)?
d • how much are you going to cost them (your salary *range* — maximum, minimum)?

They may ask you directly about these, or they may try to find them out by just letting the interview happen.

Hopefully, this will lead to your being offered the job. If it does not, go on to the next place you liked the best.

For further information about any part of the above process, see What Color Is Your Parachute?

Good luck, Peace, and Shalom.

IF YOU WANT ADDITIONAL HELP

Where Do I Go From Here With My Life? by John C. Crystal and Richard N. Bolles. 1974. Ten Speed Press, Box 7123, Berkeley, Calif. 94707.
$9.95 + .50 postage and handling.

Career Planning and Job Hunting for Today's Student: The Nonjob Interview Approach, by Edmond Billingsley. 1979. Available from Goodyear Publishing Company, Inc., Santa Monica, Calif. 90401.
$9.50, paperback.

Who's Hiring Who, by Richard C. Lathrop. 1977. At your local bookstore, or order directly from Ten Speed Press, address above.
$5.95 + .50 postage and handling.

Making Vocational Choices: A Theory of Careers, by John L. Holland. 1973. Order directly from Prentice-Hall, Inc., Englewood Cliffs, New Jersey 07632. $4.95, paperback.

Job Power Now! The Young People's Job Finding Guide, by Bernard Haldane, Jean Haldane and Lowell Martin. 1976. At your local bookstore or order directly from Acropolis Books Ltd., 2400 17th Street, N.W., Washington, D.C. 20009. $3.95, paperback.

My son, be admonished:
of making many books there is no end;
and much study is a weariness of the flesh.

Ecclesiastes

Appendix B
Resources Guide:

Books

BOOKS are an inexpensive way of getting information,
advice, coaching, and supervision.

Books are an inexpensive way of transporting *Someone Knowledgeable* into your living room or library for an hour's conversation or two, with you.

On the other hand:

Books are also large blocks of black print, often boring, sometimes filled with mis-information delivered with a pontifical ring — which may, *however unwittingly*, lead the reader down some primrose path.

So, you will have to read with caution and care — except for the first five works we list here, which are recommended absolutely without reservation of any kind:

HIGHLY
RECOMMENDED

Crystal, John, and Bolles, Richard N., *Where Do I Go From Here With My Life? The Crystal Life Planning Manual.* 1974. A more detailed step-by-step explanation of the process described in chapters 5-7 of this book you are now reading. From: Ten Speed Press, Box 7123, Berkeley, CA 94707. $9.95, paper.

Lathrop, Richard, *Who's Hiring Who*. Ten Speed Press, Box 7123, Berkeley, CA 94707. 1977. $5.95, paper. Simply excellent resource. Now back in print, revised and improved.

Holland, John L., *Making Vocational Choices: a theory of careers.* Prentice-Hall, Inc., Englewood Cliffs, NJ. 1973. $4.95, paper. This book is simply excellent, including as it does John Holland's instrument (The Self-Directed Search) for determining the people-environments that you prefer. (We recommend, however, that after you have arrived at your final 'people-environment code,' you do not at that point turn back to the sample Occupations Finder, since this is a very limited classification. Instead, we recommend you use the translation of the Holland 'code' into the 'codes' of the Dictionary of Occupational Titles [p. 136f in Holland's book] in order to find out *clues;* and then we urgently recommend you go on your own information-gathering expeditions around town, as we suggested on page 213ff, asking people who are in the D.O.T. occupations that go with your Holland 'people-environment': "What other occupations are there, that surround you with the same kind of people?" You will begin to discover some very unbelievable ways in which people make their living while at the same time being surrounded by the kinds of people that appeal to *you*. Thus, when you begin to focus down on the kinds of occupations that interest you, you will be doing so from a multitude of possibilities. Confucius say: when you choose a card, be sure it is from a full deck.)

Bolles, Richard N., *The Quick Job-Hunting Map: a fast way to help.* For the undecided college student or the housewife going back to work, or the mid-career changer, or the man or woman whose job has been terminated, or anyone else facing obstacles in the job-hunt. Ten Speed Press, Box 7123, Berkeley, CA 94707. 1979. $1.25. Specify Beginning Version or Advanced Version. See Advanced Version page 182 ff of this book.

Azrin, Nathan H., and Besalel, Victoria A., *Job Club Counselor's Manual.* University Park Press, 233 East Redwood Street, Baltimore, MD 21202. 1980. $14.95, paper.

> *Our Canadian readers will want to note that a number of the previous books — by Bolles, Lathrop, Crystal, etc. — as well as other (Canadian-oriented) publications, may be procured from the* UNIVERSITY AND COLLEGE PLACEMENT ASSOCIATION *(of Canada), 43 Eglinton Avenue East — Suite 1003, Toronto, Ontario M4P 1A2. Just ask for their publication list, related to Career Planning, Placement, Recruitment and Employment.*

THE BEST OF THE REST

Billingsley, Edmond, *Career Planning & Job Hunting for Today's Student: The Nonjob Interview Approach.* Goodyear Publishing Company, Inc., Santa Monica, CA 90401. 1978. $9.50, paper. A first-rate workbook, dealing in great detail, and step-by-step, with the process described in chapters 6 and 7 of the book you are holding in your hands.

Djeddah, Eli, *Moving Up: How to get high-salaried jobs,* (New edition). Ten Speed Press, Box 7123, Berkeley, CA 94707. 1978, 1971. $4.95, paper.

Miller, Arthur F., and Mattson, Ralph T., *The Truth About You: Discover what you should be doing with your life.* Fleming H. Revell Company, Tappan, NJ. 1977. $6.95, hardcover. I like it.

Stanat, Kirby W., with Patrick Reardon, *Job-Hunting Secrets & Tactics.* Published by Westwind Press, A Division of Raintree Publishers Ltd. Distributed by: Follett Publishing Company, 1010 West Washington Street, Chicago, IL 60607. 1977. $4.95, paper. Points out all the strengths and weaknesses of "the numbers game." Excellent tips.

Haldane, Bernard, *How to Make a Habit of Success.* Acropolis Books, Ltd., 2400 17th Street NW, Washington, DC 20009. $3.50, paper. The pioneer book in this field, first published in 1960.

Haldane, Bernard, and Jean, and Martin, Lowell, *Job Power Now! The Young People's Job Finding Guide.* Acropolis Books Ltd., 2400 17th St. NW, Washington, DC 20009. 1976. $3.95, paper. Probably the best book for high school students.

Noer, David, *How to Beat the Employment Game.* Ten Speed Press, Berkeley, CA 94707. 1978. $4.95, paper. He tells the truth about the numbers game. Highly recommended.

Campbell, David P., *If you don't know where you're going, you'll probably end up somewhere else.* Argus Communications, Niles, IL. 1974. $1.95, paper.

Irish, Richard K., *Go Hire Yourself An Employer.* Anchor Press (Doubleday & Co., Inc.), New York, NY. 1978, 1973. $2.95, paper.

Edlund, Sidney and Mary, *Pick Your Job and Land It.* Sandollar Press, Santa Barbara, CA 93101. 1938. $4.95, paper.

FOR SPECIAL REFERENCE
OR BROWSING

Libraries are just filled with books related to the world of work, choosing careers, and the job-hunt process. The worse the economy becomes, at any time, the more publishers dust off old titles, or run to find new ones on this subject. Now: every book, to be sure, has something valuable in it. But in some books (no names) it's like panning for gold. You may strike an ore-vein the first five minutes. In other cases, hours, even days may go by, without your getting much. I hate to tell you, but there are a lot more books in the latter class, than in the former — in my moderately-humble opinion.

But, just so that you'll know what's available, herewith we present just about the most comprehensive and up-to-date resources guide, in this field (job-hunting and career-changing). In order to make this resources guide more digestible, I have broken it down into a number of categories; namely:

1. The World of Work in America Today
2. Vocational or Career Planning
3. General Books on Job-Hunting
4. Job-Hunting Resources Especially for High School Students
5. For College Students
6. For Women
7. For Minorities
8. For Handicapped Job-Hunters
9. For Executives and Those Interested in the Business World
10. For Those Going Out on Their Own
11. Job-Hunting Resources Dealing With Writing and Getting Published
12. Arts and Crafts, and Selling
13. Getting a Government Job
14. Volunteer Opportunities or Social Change
15. Mid-Life or Second Careers
16. Clergy and the Military
17. The Nature of Your Brain, Decision-Making and
    How to Stimulate Creativity
18. Analysis of Skills
19. Interviewing
20. Surviving on the Job, Getting Promoted
21. Concerning Being Fired

In earlier editions of *Parachute*, I have listed the books or resources in the most haphazard order imaginable. But, now I list the books — within each category — in the order of their publishing (or copyright) date, starting with the most recent books at the head of the list, and thence working back, in time.

Since *Parachute* is revised annually, this enables me to add new books at the beginning of each category, and drop the really old and outdated books from the end of each category, yearly.

So, look over these resources to see what you can find that looks as though it might be helpful *to you.* In response to numerous requests — I think we got at least two, this past year — I have begun adding some brief commentary about some of the newer books. It's only one man's opinion, but some may find it helpful. *If you find a recent book listed here and think you might like to buy it, check out the possibility that it has been issued in paperback by the time this falls into your hands. If you are looking for one of the older books — in any category — and you simply cannot find it, it may well be out of print. In which case, see if your local library has a copy of it. If they do not, and you really want to be persistent, ask them to get it for you on inter-library loan. Or write directly to the publisher, whose address we have usually listed after each book, to see if you can still order it directly from them.*

Admittedly, not all readers of this book will have found their way back here into this bibliography. *As almost everyone knows, the only people who usually read bibliographies are:*
• people who want to know what some other good books are in the general field that they have been trained in; or
• people who are knowledgeable in the subject, and want to see what new books have appeared that they may not be aware of; or
• people who question seriously the scholarship and/or orthodoxy of the author, and want to scrutinize the bibliography as a test of his credentials; or
• speed-reading graduates who have run through three libraries already, and are desperate for some new fodder for a long winter's night.

I will offer no comment on any of these prospective users of *this* bibliography, except to say that yours truly is a speed reading dropout.

1. THE WORLD OF WORK
IN AMERICA TODAY

Cluster, Dick, and Rutter, Nancy, *Shrinking Dollars Vanishing Jobs: Why the Economy Isn't Working for You.* Beacon Press, Boston, MA. 1980. $5.95.

Best, Fred, *Flexible Life Scheduling.* Praeger Publishers, 521 Fifth Avenue, New York, NY 10017. 1980. $8.95, paper.

U.S. Department of Labor Employment and Training Administration, *Exchanging Earnings for Leisure: Findings of an Exploratory National Survey on Work Time Preferences.* For sale by the Superintendent of Documents, U.S. Government Printing Office, Washington, DC 20402. Paper.

Edwards, Patsy, B., *Leisure Counseling Techniques.* Constructive Leisure, 511 North La Cienega Blvd., Los Angeles, CA 90048. $11.95 per copy, postpaid (add 6% sales tax in California), paper.

The Task Force on Education and Employment, *Education for Employment:* Knowledge for Action. Acropolis Books Ltd., Colortone Building, 2400 17th Street N.W., Washington, DC 20009. 1979. $14.95, hardcover.

Job Sharing in the Public Sector, New Ways to Work, 149 Ninth Street, San Francisco, CA 94103, (415) 552-1000. A survey of job-sharing programs in various public agencies. 1979.

Lathrop, Richard, *The Job Market.* The National Center for Job-Market Studies, P.O. Box 3651, Washington, DC 20007. 1978. $4.85. What would happen if we decreased the length of the job-hunt in America, and other iconoclastic ideas which are also eminently sensible.

Miller, Jeffery M., *Innovations in Working Patterns.* The Communications Workers of America, 1925 K Street NW, Washington, DC 20036. 1978. A report of the U.S. Trade Union Seminar on Alternative Work Patterns in Europe, such as flexitime, elastic workweek, phased retirement, etc.

Robinson, David, *Alternative Work Patterns: Changing Approaches to Work Scheduling.* Work in America Institute, Inc., 700 White Plains Road, Scarsdale, NY 10583. 1978, 1976. $5.00, paper. Discusses such patterns as flexitime, staggered work hours, job-sharing, permanent part-time, etc. — together with case studies.

Meier, Gretl, *Job-Sharing: A New Pattern for Quality of Work and Life.* W. E. Upjohn Institute for Employment Research, 300 South Westnedge Ave., Kalamazoo, MI 49007. 1978. $4.50, paper.

Working Less But Enjoying It More: A Guide to Splitting or Sharing Your Job. New Ways to Work, 149 Ninth Street, San Francisco, CA 94103, (415) 552-1000. A description of the process involved in negotiating a shared job. $4.25.

Work is for People: Innovative Workplaces of the San Francisco Bay Area. New Ways to Work, 149 Ninth Street, San Francisco, CA 94103, (415) 552-1000. Descriptions and discussions of workplaces experimental in process or product. 1978. $4.75.

Adjusting Work Time: Three New Models. New Ways to Work, 149 Ninth Street, San Francisco, CA 94103, (415) 552-1000. Descriptions of three models of reduced work time: work sharing, job sharing, leave time. 1978. $3.50.

First National Directory on Part-Time and Flexitime Programs. National Council for Alternative Work Patterns, 1925 K Street NW, Suite 308A, Washington, DC 20036. 1978.

Babson, Steve, and Brigham, Nancy, *What's Happening to Our Jobs?* Popular Economics Press, Box 221, Somerville, MA 02143. 1976. $1.45, paper.

Vocations for Social Change, *No Bosses Here: A Manual on Working Collectively.* VSX, P.O. Box 211, Essex Station, Boston, MA 02112. 1976. $3.00, paper. Deals with how to set up and run a collective. Detailed and practical.

Clark, Ann, *New Ways to Work: a gestalt perspective*. Vitalia, Box 27253, San Francisco, CA 94127. 1975. $1.50.

O'Toole, James, "The Reserve Army of the Underemployed. I. The World of Work. II. The Role of Education," a series of articles appearing in *Change Magazine*, May and June 1975.

Terkel, Studs, *Working*. Avon Paperback, New York. 1974. $2.25. A classic.

Herzberg, Frederick, *Work and The Nature of Man*. The New American Library. 1301 Avenue of the Americas, New York, NY 10019. 1973, 1966. $1.50, paper. A classic on motivation.

Work in America. Special Task Force to the Secretary of Health, Education, and Welfare, administered by the W. E. Upjohn Institute for Employment Research. MIT Press (Cambridge, MA). 1973. Or: Available from National Technical Information Service, U.S. Department of Commerce, Springfield, VA 22151. December 1972. PB 214 779. $6.75. Another classic.

2. VOCATIONAL OR CAREER PLANNING

U.S. Department of Labor, Bureau of Labor Statistics, *Exploring Careers*. Superintendent of Documents, Washington, DC 20402. $10.00.

Miller, Donald B., *Careers '80/'81*. Vitality Associates, P.O. Box 154, Saratoga, CA 95070. 1980. $11.95.

Zehring, John William, *Making Your Life Count*. Judson Press, Valley Forge, PA 19481. 1980. $3.95, paper.

Borchard, David D.; Kelly, John J.; and Weaver, Nancy Pat K., *Your Career: Choices Chances Changes*. Kendall/Hunt Publishing Company, Dubuque, IA 52001. 1980. Paper.

Gifford, J. Nebraska; Shestack, Melvin B.; and the editors of Gallery Press, *Secrets of Success: A Plan Book for Making It in the 1980's*. Pocket Books, 1230 Avenue of the Americas, New York, NY 10020. 1980. $7.95, paper.

Guide for Occupational Exploration. Superintendent of Documents, U.S. Government Printing Office, Washington DC 20402. 1979. $11.00. Occupations organized by interest and job title.

Mitchell, Anita M.; Jones, Brian G.; and Krumboltz, John D., ed., *Social Learning and Career Decision Making*. The Carroll Press, 43 Squantum Street, Cranston, RI 02920. 1979.

Mitchell, Joyce Slayton, *The Men's Career Book: Work and Life Planning For a New Age*. Bantam Books, Inc., 666 Fifth Avenue, New York, NY 10019. 1979. $2.25, paper.

Tiedeman, David V., *Career Development: Designing Our Career Machines*. Carroll Press, 43 Squantum Street, Cranston, RI 02920. 1979. $9.95 paper. How to use computers to design a career-decision-and-development system.

Basso, Janice L.; Kendall, Nancy P.; and Miller, Donna S. M., *Creating a Canadian Career Information Centre*. University and College Placement Association, 43 Eglinton Avenue East, Suite 1003, Toronto, Ontario M4P 1A2. 1979.

Montana, Patrick J.; and Higginson, Margaret V., *Career Life Planning for Americans: Agenda for Organizations and Individuals.* Amacom, 135 West 50th Street, New York, NY 10020. 1978. $17.95, hardcover.

Feldman, Beverly Neuer, *Jobs/Careers serving children and youth,* (including Supplement: Appendix C, and Index — inserted into the book, but separate). Till Press, P.O. Box 27816, Los Angeles, CA 90027. 1978. $9.95, paper. Groups the jobs and careers according to how much education the job-hunter has had. For all those who want to work with youth or children.

The Outdoors and Your Career, U.S. Department of Labor pamphlet. Superintendent of Documents, U.S. Government Printing Office, Washington, DC 20402. 1978.

Kotter, John P.; and Fauz, Victor A.; and McArthur, Charles, *Self-Assessment and Career Development.* Prentice-Hall, Inc., Englewood Cliffs, NJ 07632. 1978. Based on a course, using cases and exercises.

Kirn, Arthur G., and Kirn, Marie O'Donahoe, *Life Work Planning.* Fourth Edition. McGraw-Hill Book Company, 1221 Avenue of the Americas, New York, NY 10020. 1978, 1975, 1972, 1971. $13.95, hardcover. This life work planning workbook has been around a long time, but this edition is a quantum leap forward, over its predecessors. Better designed, better exercises, better everything. It's nice to see authors who keep growing. (There are so few of us left.)

Schein, Edgar H., *Career Dynamics: matching individual and organizational needs.* Addison-Wesley Publishing Co., Jacob Way, Reading, MA 01867. 1978.

Bachhuber, Thomas D., and Harwood, Richard K., *Directions: A guide to career planning.* Houghton Mifflin Company, 2 Park Street, Boston, MA 02107. 1978. Career awareness, exploration, and decision-making — employing a career development model that also involves self-awareness and academic awareness. Uses Holland, some government publications, and a brief summary of *Parachute,* along the way.

Hagberg, Janet, and Leider, Richard, *The Inventurers: Excursions in Life and Career Renewal.* Addison-Wesley Publishing Company, Inc., Jacob Way, Reading, MA 01867. 1978. Stories about people who ventured inward, to explore and consider new options, plus exercises to help you do the same.

Gillies, Jerry, *Moneylove: How to Get the Money You Deserve for Whatever You Want.* M. Evans and Company, Inc., 216 East 49th Street, New York, NY 10017. 1978. $7.95, hardcover. From the title, it's hard to tell that this book is about career planning. But it is (among other things). Valuable questions, such as: what did I get the most praise for doing in my life? What do people often compliment me on? What have people suggested I do more of?, etc. Very helpful book.

Zenger, John H.; Miller, Dale E.; Florance, Jeannine; and Harlow, Phoebe, *How to work for a living and like it: a career planning workbook.* Addison-Wesley Publishing Company, Jacob Way, Reading MA 01867. 1977, 1975. $4.50, paper. Perforated tear-out pages, interesting illustrations, beguiling headings (Your Abilities — Tone-deaf bandleaders don't make it.), helpful graphs, and forms for you to fill out. I like it.

Miller, Donald B., *Personal Vitality Workbook: A Personal Inventory and Planning Guide*. Addison-Wesley Publishing Company, Jacob Way, Reading, MA 01867. 1977. $4.50, paper. Deals with a life-career checkup, job and career questions, work environments, inputs, outputs, values review, goals and action plans, etc. Long on data-gathering (about oneself) and reflecting on that data. Short on how you put it all together; but then, that's the Achilles heel of all inventories. Good chapter on "life balance — personal space."

Barkhaus, Robert S., and Bolyard, Charles W., *Threads, A Tapestry of Self and Career Exploration*. Kendall/Hunt Publishing Company, 2460 Kerper Blvd., Dubuque, IA 52001. 1977.

Shepard, Herbert A., *The Career Management System: Life Planning*. Management Decision Systems, Inc., P.O. Box 35, Darien, CT 06820. 1976. Cassettes and workbook.

Loughary, John W., and Ripley, Theresa M., *Career & Life Planning Guide: How to Choose Your Job, How to Change Your Career, How to Manage Your Life*. Follett Publishing Company, attn: T. K. Washburn, 1010 W. Washington Blvd., Chicago, IL 60657. 1976. $5.95, paper.

Ford, George A., and Lippitt, Gordon L., *Planning Your Future: A workbook for personal goal setting*. University Associates, Inc., 7596 Eads Avenue, La Jolla, CA 92037. 1972, 1976.

Nash, Katherine, *Get the Best of Yourself! How to find your "career success pattern."* Grossett & Dunlap, 51 Madison Avenue, New York, NY 10010. 1976. $4.95, paper.

McClure, Larry, *Career Education Survival Manual: A Guidebook for Career Educators and Their Friends*. Olympus Publishing Company, 1670 East Thirteenth South, Salt Lake City, UT 84105. 1975. An absolutely superb little handbook for everyone who wants to understand more about how to relate education to the world of work (and vice versa). Imaginatively laid out, and written by one of the experts in this field.

Career Education: What It Is and How to Do It. Kenneth Hoyt and others. Second Edition. Olympus Publishing Company, 1670 E. Thirteenth South, Salt Lake City, UT 84105. 1974. $6.95.

Cosgrave, Gerald, *Career Planning: Search for a Future*. Guidance Centre/Faculty of Education/University of Toronto. 1973. Available from Customer Service, Teacher's College Press, 1234 Amsterdam Ave., New York, NY 10027. $4.45; or from Consulting Psychologist's Press, 577 College Ave., Palo Alto, CA 94306. Unusual in that it relates to John L. Holland's six people-environments.

Crites, John O., *Vocational Psychology*. McGraw Hill Book Company, New York, NY. 1969. Very comprehensive.

Fine, Sidney A., *Use of the Dictionary of Occupational Titles to Estimate Educational Investment*. The W. E. Upjohn Institute for Employment Research, Inc., Kalamazoo, MI. 1968.

Hoppock, Robert, *Occupational Information: Where to Get It and How to Use It in Counseling and in Teaching*. 3rd Edition. McGraw Hill, New York, NY. 1967. A pioneer in this field.

Super, Donald E., et. al., *Career Development: Self-Concept Theory. Essays in Vocational Development.* College Board Publication Orders, Box 2815, Princeton, NJ 08540. 1963. $4.50, paper.

3. GENERAL BOOKS ON JOB-HUNTING

The number of books coming out on job-hunting, to (hopefully) aid the job-hunter, increases each year. We are listing here and in the following sections as many of them as we have heard of, purchased, and read. Many — if not most of them — simply tell you all about "the numbers game." Why are we listing them here? Well, first of all, we know of no such extensive list anywhere else. For sure, someone somewhere out there is looking for a list like this, for some purpose or other (to cure insomnia?) and now at last, the search is over.

Secondly, since we digested most of these books either before writing *Parachute* or since (in which case any exceptionally worthwhile ideas they had were incorporated into subsequent revisions of this book), you will now be reassured that we digested *a lot. Parachute* is partly a compendium, you see, of all that has come out to date, in addition to its own hopefully original ideas.

Well, all of this is but a preamble to the $64,000 question: should you buy and/or read any of these books, to supplement what you have learned from this book you presently hold in your hands? Well, sure, under either of two conditions:

(1) You have some spare time for further reading on the job-hunt, and you see a title, an author, or a glimmer, below that intrigues you. Go buy. Go read. You will find something helpful in any of these books, to supplement what you have already read. *Parachute* is not after all, a compendium of *all* wisdom about the job-hunt. It would have to have been 2000 pages long, and cost you $45 if it were to be that. In other words, for most of you, this sort of supplementary reading is Optional — depending on how much time and curiosity you have.

(2) If however, after reading all of *Parachute,* you thought the most fascinating chapter — and the only one you want to follow — was chapter 2, then reading some of the following books is absolutely Obligatory. You'll need all the help you can get.

Klingner, Donald E., and Davis, Anthony J., *The Job-Seeker's Guide: A Workbook For Improving Your Career Situation.* Human Sciences Press, 72 Fifth Avenue, New York, NY 10011. 1980. $9.95, paper.

Boros, James M., and Parkinson, J. Robert, *How to Get a Fast Start in Today's Job Market.* Prentice Hall, Inc., Englewood Cliffs, NJ 07632. 1980. $3.99, paper.

Michelozzi, Betty Neville, *Coming Alive From Nine To Five: The Career Search Handbook.* Mayfield Publishing Company, 285 Hamilton Avenue, Palo Alto, CA 94301. 1980. $5.95, paper.

Figler, Howard E., *The Complete Job Search Handbook: Presenting the Skills You Need to Get Any Job, And Have A Good Time Doing It.* Holt, Rinehart and Winston, 383 Madison Avenue, New York, NY 10017. 1979.

$5.95, paper. Tries to identify twenty skills the job-hunter needs in order to pull off a job hunt *successfully.*

Cohen, Leonard, *Choosing to Work: An Action-Orientated Job Finding Book.* Reston Publishing Co. Inc., 11480 Sunset Hills Rd., Reston, VA 22090. 1979. $8.95, paper.

Moran, Pamela J., *Seek And You Will Find: A Practical Job-Hunting Guide.* The Word of God, P.O. Box 7087, Ann Arbor, MI 48107. 1978. A job-seeking handbook for Christians.

Jackson, Tom, *Guerrilla Tactics In The Job Market.* Bantam Books, Inc., 666 Fifth Avenue, New York, NY 10019. 1978. $2.50, paper.

_____ , *28 Days to a Better Job.* Hawthorn Books, Inc., New York, NY. 1977. $6.95, paper. "A day-by-day action approach that has helped thousands to find jobs they want."

Biegeleisen, J. I., *Job Resumes: How to Write Them, How to Present Them, Preparing for Interviews.* Revised/enlarged. Grosset & Dunlap, Publishers, 51 Madison Avenue, New York, NY 10010. 1976, 1969. If you believe in resumes (salvation by mail), this is the historic book in the field — a very thorough sampler of all kinds of resumes, together with helpful rationale.

Jackson, Tom, and Mayleas, Davidyne, *The Hidden Job Market, A System to Beat the System.* Quadrangle/The New York Times Book Co., 10 East 53 St., New York, NY 10022. 1976. $12.00, hardcover.

Moore, Charles G., *The Career Game.* Ballantine Books, 201 E. 50th St., New York, NY 10022. 1976. $5.95, paper. Written by an economist, from an economist's point of view.

Sheppard, Harold L., and Belitsky, A. Harvey, *Promoting Job Finding Success for the Unemployed.* (Summarizing part of the authors' book: *The Job Hunt: Job-Seeking Behavior of Unemployed Workers in a Local Economy.* The John Hopkins Press, Baltimore, MD. 1966.) The W. E. Upjohn Institute, Kalamazoo, MI. 1968. An excellent pioneer research study.

4. JOB-HUNTING RESOURCES ESPECIALLY FOR HIGH SCHOOL STUDENTS

Hardigree, Peggy, *Working Outside: A Career and Self-Employment Handbook.* Harmony Books, A Division of Crown Publishers, Inc., One Park Avenue, New York, NY 10016. 1980. $7.95, paper.

O'Brien, Barbara, ed., *1981 Summer Employment Directory of the United States.* Writer's Digest Books, 9933 Alliance Road, Cincinnati, OH 45242. 1980. $6.95, paper. This book comes out each year. It lists 50,000 summer job openings at resorts, campuses, amusement parks, hotels, conferences and training centers, ranches, restaurants, national parks, etc. 1000 places, in all.

Douglas, Martha C., *Go For It.* Chronicle Books, 879 Market St., Suite 915, San Francisco, CA 94102. Based on Ms. Douglas' experience as coordinator of an industry training program for teenagers, at the *Contra Costa Times* newspaper in Walnut Creek, California.

Morton, Alexander Clark, *The Official 1979-1980 Guide to Airline Careers.* International Publishing Co., 665 La Villa Dr., Miami Springs, FL 33166. 1979. $6.95, paper.

Moldafsky, Annie, *Welcome to the Real World.* Doubleday and Company, Inc., 245 Park Avenue, New York, NY 10017. 1979. $4.95, paper.

Berliner, Don, *Want a Job? Get Some Experience. Want Experience? Get a Job.* Amacom, a division of American Management Associations, 135 West 50th Street, New York, NY 10020. 1978. $5.95, paper.

Blanchard, Nina, *How to Break Into Motion Pictures, Television, Commercials and Modeling.* Doubleday & Co., Inc., Garden City, NY. 1978. $8.95, hardcover.

Shedd, Charlie, ed., *You Are Somebody Special.* McGraw-Hill Book Co., 1221 Avenue of the Americas, New York, NY 10020. Chapters are written by various authors including Bill Cosby, Irene Kassorla, Rick Little (who created the idea for the book), Eugene Nida, and Ye Olde Author — among others. 1978. $2.25, paper. Written particularly for seniors in high school.

Mitchell, Joyce Slayton, *The Work Book — A Guide to Skilled Jobs.* Bantam Books, Inc., 666 Fifth Avenue, New York, NY 10019. 1978. $2.25, paper. Skilled jobs, by definition, require 2 weeks to 2 years of schooling or training, beyond high school. This book is largely based on the *Occupational Outlook Handbook,* and reviews in the *Vocational Guidance Quarterly.* Interesting chapter on "work talk — a new language" for the graduating high school student.

Career World — The Continuing Guide to Careers (a periodical), Joyce Lain Kennedy, Executive Editor. From $3.25 up, per subscription. Curriculum Innovations, Inc., 501 Lake Forest Avenue, Highwood, IL 60040.

Lieberoff, Allen J., *good jobs, High Paying Opportunities, working for yourself or for others.* Prentice-Hall, Inc., Englewood Cliffs, NJ 07632. 1978. $5.95, paper. Essentially for the high school graduate, discussing career options that (allegedly) pay well.

Garrison, Clifford B., et al., *Finding a job you feel good about.* Argus Communications, 7440 Natchez Avenue, Niles, IL 60648. 1977. $2.50, paper. Good for high school students, especially.

Stevens, Laurence, *Your Career in Travel and Tourism.* Merton House Publishing Company, Inc., 8 South Michigan Avenue, Chicago, IL 60603. 1977. $6.00, paper.

Boesch, Mark, *Careers In The Outdoors*. E. P. Dutton & Co., Inc., 2 Park Ave., New York, NY 10016. 1975. $4.95, paper.

Carkhuff, Robert, *The Art of Developing a Career*. Human Resource Development Press, Box 863, Dept. M-18, Amherst, MA 01002. 1974. $6.95 for students' guide; $9.95 for helper's guide. For grades 10-16.

Flanagan, John C., et al., *The Career Data Book: Results from Project TALENT's Five-Year Follow-Up Study*. American Institutes for Research, Box 1113, Palo Alto, CA 94302. 1973. $5.50; student's booklet $3.00 for 25 copies, $10.00 for 100 copies.

5. FOR COLLEGE STUDENTS

Figler, Howard E., *Path: A Career Workbook for Liberal Arts Students*. The Carroll Press Publishers, 43 Squantum Street, Cranston, RI 02920. 1979, 1975. Second Edition, Completely Revised. Good stuff.

Thain, Richard J., *The Managers: Career Alternatives For The College Educated*. The College Placement Council, Inc., P.O. Box 2263, Bethlehem, PA 18001. $4.95, paper.

Mitchell, Joyce Slayton, *Stopout! Working Ways To Learn*. Avon Books, 959 Eighth Avenue, New York, NY 10019. 1978. Using learning in order to work, using working in order to learn. $2.95, paper.

Liberal Arts and Your Career, U.S. Department of Labor pamphlet. Superintendent of Documents, U.S. Government Printing Office, Washington DC 20402. 1978.

Fox, Marcia R., *Put Your Degree to Work: A Career Planning and Job Hunting Guide for the New Professional*. W. W. Norton Co., 500 Fifth Ave., New York, NY 10036. 1979. Advice for the new professional with a graduate degree. $4.95, paper.

Shingleton, John, and Bao, Robert, *College to Career: Finding Yourself in the Job Market*. McGraw-Hill Book Company, 1221 Avenue of the Americas, New York, NY 10020. 1977. $5.95, paper.

Cartter, Alan M., *Ph.D.s and the Academic Labor Market*. McGraw-Hill, New York, NY. 1976. $12.50. Actual and projected data relating to the employment outlook for Ph.D.s. (Read before enrolling in graduate school.)

Malnig, Lawrence R., and Morrow, Sandra L., *What Can I Do with a Major in. . . ?* Saint Peter's College Press, 2641 Kennedy Blvd., Jersey City, NJ 07306. 1975. Describes how 10,000 alumni (based on a 76 per cent sample) actually used their college training and what fields various majors went into. The answer to 'what can I do with a major in. . . ?' ultimately proves to be the same as the answer to 'what does a 2000 pound gorilla do on his birthday?' — namely, Anything he wants to.

Loughary, John W., and Ripley, Theresa M., *This Isn't Quite What I Had in Mind: A Career Planning Program for College Students*. United Learning Corporation, 3255 Olive Street, Eugene, OR 97405. 1974. Very entertaining.

Our Canadian readers will want to know that their University and College Placement Association (43 Eglinton Avenue East, 10th Floor, Toronto, Ontario, M4P 1A2) puts out a number of publications for those related to the college scene. These include:

McClure, Ross M., *Destiny: Career Planning Manual.* 1980. Paper.

Gartley, Wayne, ed., *Your Future After High School.* 1980. Paper.

_____, ed., *1980-1981 Annuaire D'Orientation Professionnelle.* Association de placement universitaire et collegial, 1980. Paper.

Carney, T.F., *Teaching Effective Letter Writing.* 1980. Paper.

_____, *Teaching Effective Resume Writing.* 1980. Paper.

University of Toronto Career Counselling and Placement Centre, *Guide to Resume Writing.* 1978. Paper.

Dunlop, Elizabeth, *et. al., Career Opportunities for Liberal Arts Graduates.* 1979. Paper.

6. FOR WOMEN

Now, just a (perhaps unnecessary) word of common sense — uncommon common sense, sad to say — about this whole business of job-hunting publications for women. There is a difference between *form* and *content.* In these days of liberated consciousness (or conscious liberation?) there is a great preoccupation with *form:* i.e., does this book use non-sexist language? But let us not forget *content,* please. A book that does little more than outline the old numbers game (see chapter 2) is not going to do you much good, no matter how superb (i.e., non-sexist) its form may be. On the other hand, a book with helpful *content* (i.e., the creative minority's prescription) is going to help you, no matter how chauvinistic its language might be (just shut your eyes, and grit your teeth). The best of all possible worlds, of course, is to have both: a book whose form *and* content are both superb: that's the ideal women's book. But don't get hypnotized just by *form,* please.

Shields, Laurie, *Displaced Homemakers: Organizing for a New Life.* McGraw-Hill Book Company, 1221 Avenue of the Americas, New York, NY 10020. 1981. $5.95, paper.

The Catalyst Staff, *Marketing Yourself, The catalyst women's guide to successful resumes and interviews.* G. P. Putnam's Sons, 200 Madison Avenue, New York, NY 10016. 1980. $9.95, hardcover.

Since we're on the subject of CATALYST, let me also mention that this organization provides a host of other self-guidance career materials for women: for the college student, a series of booklets on Career Options; and for the "returning woman," a self-guidance series, a career-opportunities series, and an education–opportunities series. Write them (address above) for a complete Order Form. You may also wish to know that they maintain a clearinghouse (library) of information on all aspects of women and work — and in case you have specific questions, you can call, visit or write them.

Lee, Nancy, *Targeting the Top: Everything a Woman Needs to Know to Develop a Successful Career in Business, Year after Year.* Doubleday and Company, Inc., 245 Park Avenue, New York, NY 10017. 1980. $11.95, hardcover.

Burack, Albrecht and Seitler, *Growing: A Woman's Guide to Career Satisfaction.* Lifetime Learning Publications, Ten Davis Drive, Belmont, CA 94002. 1980. $6.95, paper. I like it.

Kleiman, Carol, *Women's Networks.* Lippincott and Crowell, Publishers, 521 Fifth Avenue, New York, NY 10017. 1980. $5.95, paper.

Welch, Mary Scott, *Networking.* Harcourt Brace Jovanovich, Inc., 757 Third Avenue, New York, NY 10017. 1980. $9.95, hardcover.

Catalyst, *What to Do with the Rest of Your Life: the Catalyst Career Guide for Women in the '80s.* Simon and Schuster, 1230 Avenue of the Americas, New York, NY 10020. 1980. $16.95, hardcover.

Chambers, Marjorie Bell, President, *Job Hunter's Kit.* American Association of University Women, 2401 Virginia Avenue, NW, Washington, DC 20037.

Business & Professional Women's Foundation, "Where The Jobs Are: An Annotated Selected Bibliography." B&PWF, 2012 Massachusetts Avenue NW, Washington DC 20036. 1979. This foundation publishes a number of other booklets which may be of interest to women job-hunters or career-changers, including "Financial Aid: Where to Get It, How to Use It" (1978); "The Status of Clerical Workers" (1979) and some research not yet published. The foundation also runs workshops, conferences and seminars on career planning, at various places around the country, from time to time. If you are interested, you can ask them about these, when you write.

Mouat, Lucia, *Back to Business: A Woman's Guide to Reentering the Job Market.* Sovereign Books, Simon & Schuster Building, 1230 Avenue of the Americas, New York, NY 10020. 1979. $7.95, hardcover.

Hall, Francine S.; and Hall, Douglas T., *The Two-Career Couple.* Addison-Wesley Publishing Co., Inc., Jacob Way, Reading, MA 01867. 1979. $5.95, paper.

Lederer, Muriel, *Blue-Collar Jobs For Women.* A Sunrise Book. E. P. Dutton, 2 Park Avenue, New York, NY 10016. 1979. $7.95, paper.

Farley, Jennie, *Affirmative Action and the Woman Worker: Guidelines for Personnel Management.* Amacom, 135 West 50th Street, New York, NY 10020. 1979. $14.95, hardcover.

Bird, Caroline, *The Two-Paycheck Marriage.* Rawson, Wade Publishers, Inc., New York, NY. 1979. $8.95, hardcover.

Mitchell, Joyce Slayton, *I Can Be Anything: Careers and Colleges for Young Women.* Bantam Books, Inc., 666 Fifth Avenue, New York, NY 10019. 1978. $2.25, paper.

Harragan, Betty Lehan, *Games Mother Never Taught You: Corporate Gamesmanship for Women.* Warner Books, Inc., 75 Rockefeller Plaza, New York, NY 10019. 1978, 1977. $2.50, paper. Detailing corporate politics as practiced by males, and how upwardly-mobile female executives can map their own game plan.

Trahey, Jane, *Jane Trahey on Women & Power.* Avon Books, A Division of The Hearst Corporation, 959 Eighth Avenue, New York, NY 10019. 1978, 1977. $2.25, paper. A book about who's got power, and how women can get power.

© Copyright, 1980, King Features Syndicate, Inc. Reprinted by special permission.

Scholz, Nelle Tumlin; Prince, Judith Sosebee; and Miller, Gordon Porter, *How To Decide, A Workbook for Women*. Avon Books, A Division of The Hearst Corporation, 959 Eighth Avenue, New York, NY 10019. 1978, 1975. $4.95, paper. Where are you as a woman, who are you, what do you need to know, and how do you take action?

Elkstrom, Ruth B.; Harris, Abigail M.; and Lockheed, Marlaine E., *How To Get College Credit for What You Have Learned As A Homemaker and Volunteer*. Educational Testing Service, Princeton, NJ 08540. 1977. Even for those not interested in college credit, but only in assessing the skills they picked up or sharpened up as a volunteer or homemaker, this is an excellent resource. Classifies the skills under the various roles: administrator/manager, financial manager, personnel manager, trainer, advocate/change agent, public relations/communicator, problem surveyor, researcher, fund raiser, counselor, youth group leader, group leader for a serving organization, museum staff assistant (docent), tutor/teacher's aide, manager of home finances, home nutritionist, home child caretaker, home designer and maintainer, home clothing and textile specialist, and home horticulturist.

Catalyst, *Resume Preparation Manual: A Step-by-Step Guide for Women*. Catalyst, 14 East 60th Street, New York, NY 10022. 1976. $4.95, paper. Rumor hath it that Catalyst, one of the leading women's advocacy groups in the country, had this written by a man — which mildly amuses me (but not everyone shares my sense of the ironic — probably just as well). In any event, this is a very well-written step-by-step resume workbook for women. And for men too, I would guess. *If* you believe in resumes, that is. Most job-hunters do — no matter what some folks say.

Ross, Susan C., *The Rights of Women: An American Civil Liberties Union Handbook*. Avon Books, New York, NY. $1.75.

Pettman, Barrie O., *Equal Pay for Women: Progress and Problems in Seven Countries*. Hemisphere Publishing Corporation, McGraw-Hill Book Company, Washington/London.

A Guide for Affirmative Action. Equal Employment Opportunity in State and Local Governments. U.S. Office of Personnel Management (formerly the Civil Service Commission), Washington, DC. They also publish a wealth of other material on Equal Opportunity for those who want to pursue the legal route, *while at the same time* using the principles in this book as their alternative route. (Court cases in some places are alleged to have a backlog equivalent to a two-year waiting period, and you don't want to wait *that* long for a job, do you?) Materials available from: U.S. Office of Personnel Management, Bureau of Intergovernmental Personnel Programs, Washington, DC 20415.

7. FOR MINORITIES

Wiseberg, Laurie S., ed., and Scoble, Harry M., ed., *North American Human Rights Directory.* Garrett Park Press, Garrett Park, MD 20766. 1980. Prepaid, $11.00; billed, $12.00.

Cole, Katherine W. ed., *Minority Organizations: A National Directory.* Garrett Park Press, P.O. Box 4265, Garrett Park, MD 20766. $16.00. An annotated directory of 2,700 Black, Hispanic, Native, and Asian American organizations.

"Career Planning Needs of Unemployed Minority Persons," Special Issue of the *Journal of Employment Counseling*, Vol. 15, No. 4, December

1978. $2.50 per copy, from Publication Sales, 1607 New Hampshire Ave. NW, Washington, DC 20009.

Johnson, Willis L., ed., *Directory of Special Programs for Minority Group Members: Career Information, Services, Employment Skills Banks, Financial Aid Sources — Third Edition.* Garrett Park Press, Garrett Park, MD 20766. 1980. $19.00 if payment is enclosed with order.

A Study of Successful Persons from Seriously Disadvantaged Back-grounds. Human Interaction Research Institute, Los Angeles, CA. PB 199 438 NTIS. March 31, 1970.

8. FOR HANDICAPPED JOB-HUNTERS

Mitchell, Joyce Slayton, with a special section by Wallach, Ellen J., *See Me More Clearly.* Harcourt Brace Jovanovich, Inc., 757 Third Avenue, New York, NY 10017. 1980. $8.95, hardcover.

Benjamin, Libby, ed., and Walz, Garry R., *Counseling Exceptional People.* Publications, ERIC/CAPS, 2108 School of Education, University of Michigan, Ann Arbor, MI 48109. 1980. $8.50.

Cook, Paul F.; Dahl, Peter R.; and Gale, Margaret Ann, *Vocational Opportunities: Vocational Training and Placement of the Severely Handi-capped.* The American Institutes for Research in the Behavioral Sciences. Published by: Olympus Publishing Company, 1670 East Thirteenth South, Salt Lake City, UT 84105. 1978. $7.95, paper. *Sensational* book. Lists barriers (such as "low self-esteem," "impaired ability to read," "lack of independent living skills," etc.) then occupational clusters/divisions, jobs held by handicapped workers, and which handicaps are able to do which tasks/jobs in each division.

Appleby, Judith A., et al., *Training Programs and Placement Services: Vocational Training and Placement of the Severely Handicapped.* The American Institutes for Research in the Behavioral Sciences. Published by: Olympus Publishing Company, 1670 East Thirteenth South, Salt Lake City, UT 84105. 1978. $16.95, hardcover. Lists, by region/state *effective* programs for helping the handicapped — one hundred fifty-two, in all. Describes each facility/program in detail. Very helpful.

Dahl, Peter R.; Appleby, Judith A.; and Lipe, Dewey, *Mainstreaming Guidebook for Vocational Educators: Teaching the Handicapped.* The American Institutes for Research in the Behavioral Sciences. Published by: Olympus Publishing Company, 1670 East Thirteenth South, Salt Lake City, UT 84105. 1978. $16.95, hardcover. Designed for counselors/teachers helping the handicapped — whether it be developing positive atti-tudes, modifying curricula, placing handicapped students in jobs, or what-ever. Very useful, as are the other two books in this series, previously mentioned.

Bruck, Lilly, *Access: The Guide to A Better Life for Disabled Ameri-cans.* David Obst Books, Random House, Inc., 201 East 50th St., New York, NY 10022. 1978. $5.95, paper. Deals with jobs, health-care, travel, shopping without leaving home, special products, special technologies, etc. as these relate to disabled Americans. *Very* thorough.

"The So-Called 'Handicapped' Job-Hunter: Strategies for Helping Him or Her in Today's Job-Market," The November-December 1978 issue of the _Newsletter about life/work planning._ Single copies free if you send a self-addressed, stamped envelope (9+" x 4") to: Newsletter, National Career Development Project, P.O. Box 379, Walnut Creek, CA 94596.

Robison, David, _Training and Jobs Programs in Action: Case Studies in Private-Sector Initiatives for the Hard-to-Employ._ Committee for Economic Development, Work in America Institute, Inc., 700 White Plains Road, Scarsdale, NY 10583. 1978. $5.00, paper. Describes programs that work with youth, ex-offenders, drop-outs, the aged, minorities, veterans, the handicapped, and the hardest-to-employ.

Phillips, Linda, _Barriers and Bridges: An Overview of Vocational Services Available for Handicapped Californians._ California Advisory Council on Vocational Education, 708 Tenth Street, Sacramento, CA 95184. Copies may be obtained from: California State Department of General Services, Office of Procurement, Publications Section, P.O. Box 1015, North Highlands, CA 95660. 1977. $3.00, paper. Discusses the "state of the art" in California, vis-a-vis helping the handicapped. Lists and describes information services, educational activities, guidance-related activities, pre-service and in-service educational programs, etc., as well as publications, organizations, etc.

American Coalition of Citizens with Disabilities: Has a new program, designed to help _employers_ who are looking for qualified disabled applicants for various jobs. ACCD gives assistance regarding employment, recruitment, interviewing, awareness training, architectural accessibility, etc. Write: Ted Brosnan, ACCD, 1346 Connecticut Avenue NW, No. 817, Washington, DC 20036.

9. FOR EXECUTIVES AND THOSE INTERESTED IN THE BUSINESS WORLD

Boll, Carl R., Executive Jobs Unlimited. Updated Edition. Macmillan Publishing Co., Inc., 866 Third Avenue, New York, NY 10022. 1979, 1965. $8.95, hardcover. The classic in the executive job-hunting field.

Campbell, David, _If I'm in Charge Here Why is Everybody Laughing?_ Argus Communications, 7440 Natchez Avenue, Niles, IL 60648. 1980. $2.50, paper.

Ferguson, Stewart, and Ferguson, Sherry Devereaux, _Intercom: Readings in Organizational Communication._ Hayden Book Company, Inc., 50 Essex Street, Rochelle Park, NJ 10016. 1980. Paper.

Garry, William, ed., _et. al., A Checklist for Technical Skills & Other Training._ American Society for Training and Development, P.O. Box 5307, Madison, WI 53705.

Rust, H. Lee, _Jobsearch: A Complete Guide to Successful Job Changing._ Amacom. A guide for the experienced manager or professional on self-marketing. 1979. $12.95.

Traxel, Robert G. _Managers's Guide to Successful Job Hunting._ McGraw-Hill Book Company, Inc., New York, NY. 1978. $8.95, hardcover.

Now, how could I say anything bad about a book that begins its Chapter Two with: "I'd like to recommend that you do yourself a favor. Put this book down, go directly to the nearest bookstore or library, and buy or check out a copy of *What Color Is Your Parachute?* by Richard N. Bolles. That's right, do it now. Then read the book, and read it thoroughly." *Obviously* an author of rare intelligence, perception, and grace.

Cohen, William A., *The Executive's Guide to Finding a Superior Job.* Amacom. 135 West 50th Street, New York, NY 10020. 1978. $12.05, hardcover.

Cohen, Barbara S., *Career Development in Industry: A Study of Selected Programs and Recommendations for Program Planning.* Educational Testing Service, Princeton, NJ 08540. 1978. Discusses the programs in twenty-four corporations.

Jameson, Robert J., *The Professional Job Changing System: World's Fastest Way to Get a Better Job.* 1978 edition. Performance Dynamics, 300 Lanidex Plaza, Parsippany, NJ 07054. $9.95, hardcover.

Kanter, Rosabeth Moss, *Men and Women of the Corporation.* Basic Books, Inc., Publishers, New York, NY. 1977. $12.00, hardcover. A thoroughgoing study of how a corporation works, and how it affects the lives of the women and men in it.

Haldane, Bernard, *Career Satisfaction and Success: A Guide to Job Freedom.* Amacom Executive Books, 135 West 50th Street, New York, NY 10020. 1974. $3.95, paper. For executives and professionals seeking in-house career advancement that starts with identification of strengths.

Drucker, Peter, *Management: Tasks, Responsibilities, Practices.* Harper & Row, Publishers, 10 East 53rd Street, New York, NY 10022. 1973. $15.00. Should be absolutely required reading for anyone contemplating entering, changing to, or becoming a professional within the business world, or any organization.

Townsend, Robert, *Up the Organization: How to Stop the Corporation from Stifling People and Strangling Profits.* Alfred A. Knopf, New York, NY. 1970. Classic in the field.

Drucker, Peter F., *Technology, Management and Society.* Harper and Row, New York, NY. 1970.

Peter, Laurence F., and Hull, Raymond, *The Peter Principle: Why Things Always Go Wrong.* William Morrow & Company, Inc., New York, NY. 1969. $4.95, hardback. Another classic.

10. FOR THOSE GOING OUT ON THEIR OWN

Stickney, John, *Self-Made: Braving an Independent Career in a Corporate Age.* G. P. Putnam's Sons, New York, NY. 1980. $10.95.

Fox, Philip J., and Mancuso, Joseph R., *402 Things You Must Know Before Starting a New Business.* Prentice-Hall, Inc., Englewood Cliffs, NJ 07632. 1980. $5.95, paper.

Schepps, Solomon J., ed., *The Concise Guide to Patents: Trademarks and Copyrights.* Bell Publishing Company, A Division of Crown Publishers, Inc., One Park Avenue, New York, NY 10016. 1980. $2.98, hardcover.

Levinson, Jay Conrad, *Earning Money Without A Job: The Economics of Freedom*. Holt, Rinehart, and Winston, 383 Madison Avenue, New York, NY 10017. 1979.

Rosenthal, Ed, and Lichty, Ron, *132 Ways To Earn A Living Without Working (For Someone Else)*. St. Martin's Press, 175 Fifth Avenue, New York, NY 10010. 1978. $5.95, paper.

Hallock, Robert Lay, *Inventing for Fun and Profit*. Harmony Books, A Division of Crown Publishers, Inc., One Park Avenue, New York, NY 10016. 1978. $3.95, paper.

Clark, Leta W., *How To Open Your Own Shop or Gallery*, St. Martin's Press, 175 Fifth Avenue, New York, NY 10010. 1978. $8.95, hardcover.

Lefferts, Robert, *Getting A Grant: How To Write Successful Grant Proposals*. Prentice-Hall, Inc., Englewood Cliffs, NJ 07632. 1978. $4.95, paper.

Baranov, Alvin B., *Incorporation Made Easy. Form Your Own Corporation With a Minimum of Expense*. Legal Publications, Inc., P.O. Box 3723, Van Nuys, CA 91407. 1978. $8.50, paper.

Mancuso, Anthony, *How To Form Your Own California Corporation*. Nolo Press, P.O. Box 544, Occidental, CA 95465. 1977. $9.95.

Hoge, Cecil C., Sr., *Mail Order Moonlighting*. Ten Speed Press, P.O. Box 7123, Berkeley, CA 94707. 1976. $7.95, paper.

Weaver, Peter, *You, Inc. A detailed escape route to being your own boss*. Doubleday & Company, Inc., Garden City, NY. 1973. $7.95.

Nicholas, Ted, *How to Form Your Own Corporation Without a Lawyer for Under $50.00. Complete with tear-out Forms, Certificate of Incorporation, Minutes, By-Laws*. Enterprise Publishing Co., Inc., 1000 Oakfield Lane, Wilmington, DE 19810. 1973. $7.95 plus 45¢ for postage and handling.

11. JOB-HUNTING RESOURCES DEALING WITH WRITING AND GETTING PUBLISHED

I used to live in an apartment-complex, and as I walked through the courtyard each day, I could hear typewriters going incessantly, out of every open window. They can't *all* be part-time secretaries, working at home. Obviously, there are a lot of budding authors and authoresses, in the land. For them: some helps.

Brohaugh, William, and Beraha, Judith Ann, assisted by Kuroff, Barbara *1981 Writer's Market: where to sell what you write*. Writer's Digest Books, 9933 Alliance Road, Cincinnati, OH 45242. 1980. $15.95, hardcover.

Directory of Publishing Opportunities in Journals and Periodicals, 4th Edition, Marquis Academic Media, 200 East Ohio Street, Chicago, IL 60611. 1979. $44.50. (See your library, *please!*)

Appelbaum, Judith, and Evans, Nancy, *How To Get Happily Published: A Complete and Candid Guide.* Harper & Row, Publishers, Inc., 10 East 53rd Street, New York, NY 10022. 1978. $9.95, hardcover. Judy is managing editor of Publishers Weekly, and Nancy is no slouch at the publishing business, either. As one reviewer put it, it has "sage advice and tricks of the publishing trade that will be news even to the most experienced authors."

Polking, Kirk, and Meranus, Leonard S., ed., *Law and the Writer,* Writer's Digest Books, Div. F & W Publishing Corporation, 9933 Alliance Road, Cincinnati, OH 45242. 1978. $9.95, hardcover. Deals with such *minor* little matters as: libel, invasion of privacy suits, the new copyright law, your first book contract, subsidiary rights, how to get paid if a publisher defaults, federal taxes and the writer, etc.

Greenfeld, Howard, *Books: From Writer to Reader.* Crown Publishers, Inc., One Park Avenue, New York, NY 10016. 1976. $4.95, paper. Describes the role of the literary agent, publishing house, editor, illustrator, copy editor, designer, production supervisor, compositor, proofreader, indexer, printer, binder, etc. Fascinating.

12. ARTS AND CRAFTS, SELLING

If your creativity is not out of the left-hemisphere of your brain (words, words, words), but out of the right-hemisphere (pictures, pictures, crafts, and so forth), there are books for you, too:

Lapin, Lynne, ed., *1981 Artist's Market.* Writer's Digest Books, 9933 Alliance Road, Cincinnati, OH 45242. 1980. $11.95, hardcover.

_____, ed., *1981 Craftworker's Market.* Writer's Digest Books, 9933 Alliance Road, Cincinnati, OH 45242. 1980. $12.95, hardcover.

Brohaugh, William, *1981 Songwriter's Market.* Writer's Digest Books, 9933 Alliance Road, Cincinnati, OH 45242. 1980. $11.95, hardcover.

Connaughton, Howard W., *Craftsmen in Business: A Guide to Financial Management & Taxes.* Rev. ed. American Crafts Council, 22 W. 55th St., New York, NY 10019. 1979. $6.50. Concise and useful.

Dooling, D. M., ed., *A Way of Working.* Anchor Books, Doubleday, Garden City, NY. 1979. $3.50, paper. Looking at craftsmanship from a philosophical point of view.

Berlye, Milton K., *How To Sell Your Artwork: A Complete Guide For Commercial and Fine Artists.* Prentice-Hall, Inc., Englewood Cliffs, NJ 07632. 1978. $7.95, paper.

Money Business: Grants and Awards for Creative Artists. The Artists Foundation, Inc., 100 Boylston Street, Boston, MA 02116. 1978. $7.00, paper.

Cochrane, Diane, *This Business of Art.* Watson-Guptill Publications, A Division of Billboard Publications, Inc., 1515 Broadway, New York, NY 10036. 1978. $12.50, hardcover. Deals with copyrighting your creation, contracts with dealers, insurance, selling, renting, exhibiting, commissions, consignment, dealing with museums, cooperative galleries, income taxes, etc. Written by the editor of *American Artist Business Letter.*

Goodman, Calvin J. and Florence J., eds., *Art Marketing Handbook.* Published by: gee tee bee, 11901 Sunset Boulevard, 102, Los Angeles, CA 90049. 1978. Deals with planning, sales, promotion, sales aids, pricing, marketing works of art. Calvin also appears in the aforementioned *American Artist Business Letter* — and other places.

13. GETTING A GOVERNMENT JOB

Zehring, John William, *Careers in State and Local Government.* Garrett Park Press, Garrett Park, MD 20766. 1980. Prepaid, $9.95 per copy; billed, $10.95.

Rashad, Hohari M., *Federal Job-Hunting Simplified.* James H. McFadden Publications, P.O. Box 56252, Washington, D.C. 20011. 1979. $2.95, plus $.50 postage and handling.

Moore, Donna J., *Take Charge of Your Own Career.* Donna J. Moore, P.O. Box 723, Baidbridge Island, WA 98110. 1979. $6.95, paper, plus $.80 for postage and handling. A guide for federal employees, or would-be federal employees.

Hawkins, James E., *The Uncle Sam Connection: An Insider's Guide to Federal Employment, Revised and Updated.* Follett Publishing Company, attn: T. K. Washburn, 1010 W. Washington Blvd., Chicago, IL 60607. 1978. $4.95, paper. The author, at one time Deputy Assistant Secretary in the Department of Commerce, knows the federal hiring system inside and out. A helpful book, for those seeking a government job.

14. VOLUNTEER OPPORTUNITIES OR SOCIAL CHANGE

Aptakin, Karen, ed., *Good Works: A Guide to Social Change Careers.* Study of Responsive Law, Washington, DC 20036. 1980. $22.50, paper.

Brennan, David, ed., *et al., Boston People's Yellow Pages.* Vocations for Social Change, P.O. Box 211, Essex Station, Boston, MA 02112. 1980. $4.95, paper.

Gartner, Alan, and Riessman, Frank, *Help: A Working Guide to Self-Help Groups.* New Viewpoints / Vision Books, A Division of Franklin Watts, 730 Fifth Avenue, New York, NY 10019. 1980. $9.95, paper.

Edited by Communities, Journal of Cooperative Living, *A Guide to Cooperative Alternatives.* Community Publications Cooperative, P.O. Box 426, Louisa, VA 23093. 1979. $5.95, paper.

Barkas, J. L., *The Help Book.* Charles Scribner's Sons, 597 Fifth Avenue, New York, NY 10017. 1979. $9.95, paper.

Invest Yourself, published by LAOS/ASF. Order from: Invest Yourself, Circulation Department, 418 Peltoma Road, Haddonfield, NJ 08033. $2.25, first class mail. Check payable to Invest Yourself *must* accompany order. Lists 26,000 openings.

Mitchell, Joyce Slayton, *Stopout! Working Ways to Learn: Internships and Volunteer Programs.* Garrett Park Press, Garrett Park, MD 20766. 1978. For high school and college students, listing internships and volunteer programs by occupational clusters, by geographical area, and alphabetically.

15. MID-LIFE OR SECOND CAREERS

Weaver, Peter, *Strategies for the Second Half of Life.* Franklin Watts, 730 Fifth Avenue, New York, NY 10019. 1980. $12.95, hardcover.

Aslanian, Carol B., and Schmelter, Harvey B., *Adult Access to Education and New Careers: A Handbook for Action.* College Entrance Examination Board, Box 2815, Princeton, NJ 08541. 1980. $9.75, paper.

Olson, Richard P., *Mid-Life a Time to Discover, A Time to Decide: A Christian Perspective on Middle Age.* Judson Press, Valley Forge, PA 19481. 1980. $5.95, paper.

Swenson, Allan A., *Starting Over: How to Recharge Your Lifestyle and Career.* A & W Publishers, Inc., 95 Madison Avenue, New York, NY 10016. 1978. $8.95, hardcover.

McCoy, Vivian Rogers; Nalbandian, Carol; and Ryan, Colleen, *Create: A New Model for Career Change.* Independent Study, Division of Continuing Education, University of Kansas, Lawrence, KS 66044. 1979. $10.00, paper.

Levinson, Daniel J., with Darrow, Charlotte N.; Klein, Edward B.; Levinson, Maria H.; and McKee, Braxton, *The Seasons of A Man's Life.* Alfred A. Knopf, Inc., 201 East 50th Street, New York, NY 10022. 1978. $10.95, hardcover. The theory of developmental periods or stages, based on long-term interviewing of 40 selected men.

Gould, Roger L., *Transformations, Growth and Change in Adult Life.* Simon and Schuster, A Division of Gulf & Western Corporation, Simon and Schuster Building, Rockefeller Center, 1230 Avenue of the Americas, New York, NY 10020. 1978. $9.95, hardcover. The developmental stages theory of life again, this time as a consequence of a study of almost a thousand subjects. Thesis: most problems of adult crisis and change are age-related.

Vaillant, George E., *Adaptation to Life.* Little, Brown and Company, 34 Beacon Street, Boston, MA 02106. 1977. $9.95, hardcover. A longitudinal (long-range) study of 268 subjects, in order to find out how — over forty years — these people coped, and how they found (or did not find) happiness. Adaptive mechanisms — methods of coping — are illustrated over various periods or stages.

Sheehy, Gail, *Passages, Predictable Crises of Adult Life.* Bantam Books, Inc., 666 Fifth Avenue, New York, NY 10019. 1977, 1976. $2.50, paper. Gail acknowledges "a primary professional debt" to the three authors above.

Robbins, Paula I., *Successful Midlife Career Change: Self-Understanding and Strategies for Action.* Amacom, A Division of the American Management Associations, 135 West 50th Street, New York, NY 10020. 1978. $12.95, hardcover. Very up-to-date, very thorough, very helpful. Probably the best book dealing with this problem.

Chew, Peter, *The Inner World of the Middle-Aged Man*. Macmillan Publishing Company, Inc., 866 Third Avenue, New York, NY 10022. 1976. $8.95, hardcover. Discusses all the various problems and crises of middle-age, including the career crisis. Extended section on John Crystal's work.

Koyl, Leon F., M.D., *Employing The Older Worker; Matching The Employee to the Job*. The National Council on the Aging, Inc., 1828 L Street NW, Washington, DC 20036. 1974. Job and man/woman are rated according to seven categories: general, upper, lower, hearing, eyesight, mentality and personality.

LeShan, Eda J., *The Wonderful Crisis of Middle Age: Some Personal Reflections*. David McKay Company, Inc., New York, NY. 1973. $7.95.

Albee, Lou, *Job Hunting After Forty*. Arco Publishing Company, Inc., New York, NY. 1971. $1.45. (Former title: Over Forty—Out of Work? 1970.)

16. CLERGY AND THE MILITARY

Rightor, Henry, *Pastoral Counseling in Work Crises*. Judson Press, Valley Forge, PA 19481. 1979. $2.95, paper.

Harris, John C., *The Minister Looks for a Job, Finding Work as a Parish Minister*. From: The Alban Institute, Inc., Mount St. Alban, Washington, DC 20016. 1974. $1.50.

Richardson, Robert Brooks, *An Examination of the Transferability of Certain Military Skills and Experience to Civilian Occupations*. Distributed by Clearinghouse for Federal Scientific and Technical Information, Springfield, VA 22151. No. PB 177 372. September 1967.

17. THE NATURE OF YOUR BRAIN, DECISION-MAKING AND HOW TO STIMULATE CREATIVITY

Our whole vocational system is oriented toward people with verbal skills, rather than intuitive; and toward achievement, rather than relationship goals. Those who wish to delve further into this realm will find the following books very helpful:

Turner, Charles Hampden, *Maps of the Mind*. Macmillan Publishing Co., Inc., 866 Third Avenue, New York, NY 10022. 1981. $14.95.

LeBoeuf, Michael, *Imagineering: How to Profit From Your Creative Powers*. McGraw-Hill Book Company, 1221 Avenue of the Americas, New York, NY 10020. 1980. $9.95, hardcover.

Goleman, Daniel, and Davidson, Richard J., ed., *Consciousness: Brain, States of Awareness, and Mysticism*. Harper & Row Publishers, Inc., 10 East 53rd Street, New York, NY 10022. 1979.

Russell, Peter, *The Brain Book*. Hawthorne Books, Inc., 260 Madison Avenue, New York, NY 10016. 1979. $12.95, hardcover.

Edwards, Betty, *Drawing on the Right Side of the Brain: A Course in Enhancing Creativity and Artistic Confidence.* J. P. Tarcher, Inc., Publisher, 9110 Sunset Blvd., Los Angeles, CA 90069. 1979. $8.95, paper. Absolutely top-notch. On the surface, a book about drawing. Actually, a book about creativity in all its facets. Splendid.

Weinhold, Barry, and Andresen, Gail, *Threads, Unraveling the Mysteries of Adult Life.* Richard Marek Publishers, 200 Madison Avenue, New York, NY 10016. 1979. $9.95, paper.

de Kay, James T., *The Left-Hander.* M. Evans and Company, Inc., 216 East 49th Street, New York, NY 10017. 1979. $3.95, paper.

Bry, Adelaide, with Bair, Marjorie, *Visualization: Directing the Movies of Your Mind.* Harper and Row, Publishers, Inc., 10 East 53rd Street, New York, NY 10022. 1978. $3.95, paper.

a compilation of feelings by Right Brain People in a Left Brain World, as expressed to Evelyn Virshup through art as therapy. The Guild of Tutors Press, 1019 Gayley Avenue, Los Angeles, CA 90024. 1978. $9.95, paper.

Rainer, Tristine, *The New Diary.* J. P. Tarcher, Inc., 9110 Sunset Blvd., Los Angeles, CA 90069. 1978. $9.95. Ideas for stimulating creativity in writing about the present as well as delving into the past.

Harvey, Bill, *Mind Magic.* Ourobourus Institute, Sundown Press, P.O. Box 6, Sundown, NY 12782. 1978. $7.95, paper.

Leeuwenberg, E. L. J., and Buffart, H. F. J. M., ed., *Formal Theories of Visual Perception.* John Wiley & Sons, Inc., 605 3rd Avenue, New York, NY 10016. 1978.

Pick, Jr., Herbert L., and Saltzman, Elliot, ed., *Modes of Perceiving and Processing Information.* Lawrence Erlbaum Associates, Inc., 62 Maria Drive, Hillsdale, NJ 07642. 1978.

Edwards, David D., *How To Be More Creative.* Occasional Productions, 470 Del Medio Avenue, Mountain View, CA 94040. 1978. $4.95, paper.

Campbell, David, *Take the road to creativity and get off your dead end.* Argus Communications, 7440 Natches Avenue, Niles, IL 60648. 1977. $2.60. Simple, inventive, and helpful.

Hanks, Kurt; Belliston, Larry; and Edwards, Dave, *Design Yourself!* William Kaufmann, Inc., One First Street, Los Altos, CA 94022. 1977. $6.50, paper.

Knowles, Malcolm S., *Self-Directed Learning: A Guide for Learners and Teachers.* Association Press, 291 Broadway, New York, NY 10007. 1975. Fascinating.

Buzan, Tony, *Use Both Sides Of Your Brain.* E. P. Dutton & Co., Inc., 2 Park Avenue, New York, NY 10016. 1974. $4.95.

McClelland, David C., and Steele, Robert S., *Human Motivation, A Book of Readings.* General Learning Press, 250 James Street, Morristown, NJ 07960. 1973. $7.80. Superb.

Ornstein, Robert E., *The Psychology of Consciousness.* Viking Press, New York, NY. 1972. $8.95. Fascinating book about the two sides of the brain; raises acute questions about how much we have oriented our whole culture toward one side of the brain rather than the other.

de Kay, James T., *The Left-Handed Book.* M. Evans and Company, 216 East 49th Street, New York, NY 10017. 1966. $1.95, paper.

18. ANALYSIS OF SKILLS

First of all, there are books or pamphlets dealing with the theory of (and behind) skills analysis. Most of these are from the brilliant brain of Sidney Fine:

McCormick, Ernest J., *Job Analysis: Methods and Applications.* Amacom, 135 West 50th Street, New York, NY 10020. 1979. $25.95, hardcover.

Brickell, Henry M., and Paul, Regina H., *Minimum Competencies and Transferable Skills: What Can Be Learned From The Two Movements.* The National Center for Research in Vocational Education, Ohio State University, 1960 Kenny Road, Columbus, OH 43210. 1978. Paper.

Sjogren, Douglas, *Occupationally-Transferable Skills and Characteristics: Review of Literature and Research.* The Center for Vocational Education, Ohio State University, 1960 Kenny Road, Columbus, OH 43210. 1977.

Miguel, Richard J., *Developing Skills for Occupational Transferability; Insights Gained from Current Practice.* The Center for Vocational Education, Ohio State University, 1960 Kenny Road, Columbus, OH 43210. 1977.

Fine, Sidney A., *Functional Job Analysis Scales: A Desk Aid.* Methods for Manpower Analysis, No. 5. April 1973.

_____ , and Wiley, Wretha W., *An Introduction to Functional Job Analysis: A Scaling of Selected Tasks from the Social Welfare Field.* Methods for Manpower Analysis, No. 4. September 1971.

_____ , *A Systems Approach to New Careers: Two Papers.* Methods for Manpower Analysis, No. 3. November 1969.

_____ , *Guidelines for the Design of New Careers.* September 1967.

The W. E. Upjohn Institute for Employment Research's *Studies on Functional Job Analysis and Career Design.*

The above pamphlets are available from The W. E. Upjohn Institute for Employment Research, 300 South Westnedge Avenue, Kalamazoo, MI 49007.

Fine, Sidney A., *Nature of Skill: Implications for Education and Training.* 1870 Wyoming Ave. N.W., Washington, DC 20009. A superb summary of some recent thinking from the father of skills analysis in the Dictionary of Occupational Titles.

19. INTERVIEWING

American Entrepreneur's Association, Business Research Division, *Simple Methods for Hiring the Best People.* American Entrepreneur Association, Los Angeles, CA 90064. 1980. Paper.

Meyer, John L., and Donaho, Melvin W., *Get the Right Person for the Job.* Prentice-Hall, Inc., Englewood Cliffs, NJ 07632. 1979. $7.50, paper.

Medley, H. Anthony, *Sweaty Palms: The Neglected Art of Being Interviewed.* Lifetime Learning Publications, Ten Davis Drive, Belmont, CA 94002. 1978. $4.95, paper. Very helpful.

Robertson, Jason, *How To Win in a Job Interview.* Prentice-Hall, Inc., Englewood Cliffs, NJ 07632. 1978. $3.95, paper.

Geeting, Baxter, and Geeting, Corinne, *How To Listen Assertively.* Monarch Press, Simon & Schuster Building, 1230 Avenue of the Americas, New York, NY 10020. 1976. $3.95, paper.

Saxenian, Hrand, "To Select a Leader." *Technology Review*, Vol. 72, No. 7, May 1970, pp. 54f. Written to guide both interviewer and interviewee. *Very* helpful. (Ask your local public library for it.)

Alex, Charles, *How to Beat Personality Tests.* Arco Books, 219 Park Avenue South, New York, NY 10003. 1965. $1.95.

20. SURVIVING ON THE JOB,
GETTING PROMOTED

There is not enough said, generally, in job-hunting books about surviving after you get the job. The enemy is both within, and without. From within, the now-familiar problem of burnout. From without, various adversaries — both animate and inanimate. Marilyn Moats Kennedy, a former student of mine, has written the best overall book on this subject. Other resources follow.

Kennedy, Marily Moats, *Career Knockouts: How to Battle Back.* Follett Publishing Company, 1010 W. Washington Blvd., Chicago, IL 60607. 1980. $10.95, hardcover.

Edelwich, Jerry, with Brodsky, Archie, *Burn-Out: Stages of Disillusionment in the Helping Professions.* Human Sciences Press, 72 Fifth Avenue, New York, NY 10011. 1980. Hardcover.

Vash, Carolyn L., *The Burnt-Out Administrator.* Springer Publishing Company, Inc., 200 Park Avenue South, New York, NY 10003. 1980. Hardcover.

You will also find some very helpful words on this subject in *Where Do I Go From Here With My Life?* (Ten Speed Press, Box 7123, Berkeley, CA 94707, 1974), pages 241-245, and 150-160 ("How to Survive After You Get the Job").

Scheele, Adele M., Ph.D., *Skills for Success: A Guide to the Top.* William Morrow and Company, Inc., 105 Madison Avenue, New York, NY 10016. 1979. Discusses and identifies the critical skills needed in order to advance.

Howard, John; Cunningham, David; and Rechnitzer, Peter, *Rusting Out, Burning Out, Bowing Out: Stress and Survival on the Job.* Financial Post Books, 481 University Avenue, Toronto, Ontario M5W 1A7. 1978. Paper.

Drucker, Peter F., "How to Be an Employee," in *Psychology Today,* March 1968 (an issue of "The Great Job Dilemma"). Excellent, as anything from Peter Drucker's pen is.

21. CONCERNING BEING FIRED

Cowle, Jerry, *How To Survive Getting Fired—And Win!* Follett Publishing Company, 1010 W. Washington Blvd., Chicago, IL 60607. 1979. $9.95, hardcover.

Irish, Richard K., *If Things Don't Improve Soon I May Ask You to Fire Me: The Management Book for Everyone Who Works.* Anchor Press/Doubleday, Garden City, NY. 1975. $7.95, hardcover.

Two are better than one;
    for if they fall,
the one will lift up his fellow;

but woe to him that is alone when he falleth,
and hath not another to lift him up.

Ecclesiastes

Appendix C
Resources Guide:

Professional
Help

How To Save A Lot of Money

The listing of an organization, agency, or person in this directory of professional help for the job-hunter does *not necessarily* constitute an endorsement of their program or services. There are some here that we think very highly of. However, you are urged, indeed exhorted, to do comparison shopping, and make up *your* own mind about which places are best. If you don't comparison-shop, you will deserve what you get.

While information concerning the groups listed here is believed to be accurate and reliable, it is not possible to guarantee the accuracy of all information given. We apologize in advance to anyone who is thereby offended. Moreover, be wary. Phone numbers change, staffs change, and places fold up, almost weekly, in this field.

Needless to say, this is not a complete directory in any sense of the word. There are some very good organizations, agencies, and places, which are not listed here. This directory is only *a sampling* of same. If you want help badly, you will need to supplement this directory with your own research in your own city.

Cost for professional help will range from $75 or less (for aptitude testing only) to $3000 or more (for complete guidance throughout the whole job-hunting process).

In this job-hunting and career-counseling field, some counselors have all the right training and credentials, but have a miserable record as 'enabler' of those looking for a job or career. Others with or without credentials have a fabulous rate of success as 'enabler' of men and women in the job-hunt process. The only thing that counts are the results. The credentialing is, so far as a prospective client is concerned, irrelevant. Someday, to be sure, we may see a credentialing process which sets as its principal test the *counselor's* ability to go out and get the job they want, where they want it, and at the proper level — *before* they presume to counsel others in the job hunt . . . even as psychoanalysts must undergo analysis before they presume to analyze others. Until then, you're going to have to be wary. Very wary. The wallet or purse you save may be your own.

SOME BASIC TRUTHS ABOUT
PROFESSIONAL HELP

In the whole big field of The Job Hunt, all professional help divides up (one regrets to say) into the following inevitable categories:

1. Professionals who are sincere and skilled.
2. Professionals who are sincere but inept.
3. Professionals who are insincere and inept.

(One could list a fourth category, but charity must assert itself at some point — and, anyway you have a good imagination.)

Now, the problem we all face when we are thinking of going to a particular professional is, of course, do they fall into category No. 1, or into one of the other two (which of the other two is really irrelevant, from the point of view of the individual job-seeker — ineptness is ineptness whether sincere, or not)?

The various clues which may at first occur to us are, upon more serious examination, not terribly fruitful. Let us tick off some of them, and see why:

★ Clue No. 1: Perhaps we can tell who is sincere and skilled, by the name of the specialist or their agency. Difficulty: names vary greatly from one operation to another, even when the operations are similar. Among the names which some counselors or agencies bear, you will find: executive career counselors, executive career consultants, career management teams, executive consulting counselors, career guidance counselors, executive advisors, executive development specialists, executive job counselors, career advisors, executive recruitment consultants, professional career counselors, management consultants, professional placement specialists, executive search specialists, professional vocational counselors, etc. If, tomorrow, some legitimate counselor who is sincere and skilled takes on a new name, the day after that some counselor who is insincere and inept will copy the name directly. What it all comes down to, is this. Wolves need sheep's clothing. Names are sheep's clothing. Trouble is, hidden in there, are some genuinely helpful people. We need another clue.

★ Clue No. 2: Perhaps we can tell who is sincere and skilled by reading everything that the agency or counselor has written. Difficulty: both good and bad counselors know the areas where the job-hunter feels exceedingly vulnerable. Consequently, there are "turn on" words which occur in almost everybody's advertisements, brochures, and books: we will give you help, say they, with evaluating career, in-depth analysis of your background, establishment of your objective, in-depth analysis of your capabilities, your resume, names of companies, preparing the covering letter, background materials on companies, interview techniques, salary negotiations, filling out forms, tests, answering ads, aptitude tests, special problems — unemployment, age, too broad a background, too narrow a background, too many job changes, too few job changes, poor references, etc. — opening doors for you, and so forth. Both the counselors who are skilled and those who are inept will never get anyone in their doors if they don't mention the areas that have put the job-hunter in Desperation City. So this doesn't separate the sheep from the goats, unfortunately. One further warning: some founders of various agencies have written excellent books which it would appear some of their own employees haven't yet comprehended, sad to say. Next clue?

★ Clue No. 3: Perhaps we can tell who is sincere and skilled by the fee they charge? I mean, they wouldn't charge a high fee, would they, if they weren't skilled? Difficulty: as insiders say, low fees may mean well-intentioned but amateurish help. However, the reverse of this is *not* true. As we have already mentioned, the vacuum created by the chaotic condition of our job-hunting process has attracted both competent people *and* people who are willing to prey upon the acute anxiety that job-hunters are often seized by. And when the latter say "Let us prey" they *really* prey. And they *thrive*. P. T. Barnum knew what he was talking about.* Next.

★ Clue No. 4: Perhaps we can tell which professionals are both sincere and skilled, by talking to satisfied clients — or asking our friends to tell us who was helpful to them. Difficulty: what are they recommending? — the whole nationwide agency (assuming it is nationwide)? or the branch thereof that is in their city? or the particular counselor (or counselors) that they saw at that branch? If you stop to think about it, you will realize this most crucial truth: *all they can possibly speak to you about is the*

---

*A sucker is born every minute. Or as the post office has updated it: "A sucker is shorn every minute."

particular counselor or counselors that they worked with, at that agency, in that particular city. Should you go to the same place, and get a different counselor, you might have a very different experience. One bad counselor in an agency that has say, six good ones, can cost you much money, time, and self-esteem, if *you* get that bad one as *your* counselor. The six good ones might as well be in Timbuktu, for all the good they'll do you. So should any of your friends offer (or should you solicit from them) advice about a place they went to, be sure to find out the counselor (or counselors) they worked with, there, *by name* so you will know who to ask for, if you decide to investigate or follow their lead.

Before we leave this clue, let us also observe that with most professional career counselors, though they will show you letters from satisfied customers, or even give you (in some cases) their names to check out, it is impossible to find out what percentage of their total clientele these satisfied persons represent: 100%? 10? 1? .1? a fluke? If you want a clue, you may make what you will out of the fact that the top officers of the largest executive counseling firm, which allegedly did over 50% of the business in the industry before it declared bankruptcy in the fall of 1974, (namely, Frederick Chusid & Co.) gave testimony during a civil suit in a New York Federal district court which indicated that only three or four out of every ten clients had been successful in getting a new job, during a previous six-month period. Are these figures average for the industry? Better than average? Worse? Nobody knows.

CAVEAT EMPTOR*,
AND AGAIN I SAY

Now that we have seen which clues are not particularly helpful, we are ready to suggest some crucial guidelines for choosing a professional career counselor — *if* you decide you need one — now, or later on in your life:

BEFORE YOU CHOOSE A PROFESSIONAL CAREER COUNSELOR, READ THIS THREE TIMES:

☐ Try to do the four steps toward a successful job hunt (decide you are going to keep at it constantly, decide *what* you want to do, *where* you want to do it, and then research the organizations that interest you exhaustively before approaching *the one person* in each organization who has the power to hire you), by yourself or with the aid of family and friends. *If you bog down, make a list for yourself of exactly where you are bogging down.* What steps in the process are eluding you?

☐ Look over the recommended books (Appendix B) in your libraries, to see if you can get additional help with the particular steps that you made a list of (No. 1 above). Also check out free professional help for those roadblocks.

☐ If you decide you need professional help with the whole process, consult this Appendix and choose *at least three places to check out personally.* How helpful they are going to be *for you* is a judgment *you* must make for yourself, and that is why comparison shopping is a *must.*

In choosing three places, you will probably *not* find it helpful to visit your local Better Business Bureau, since neither their booklet on career counseling nor their evaluation of specific firms in your city is likely to be very enlightening, for your purposes.

☐ Visit *in person* each of the three places you have chosen. These are exploratory visits only. Leave your wallet and your

---

* Let the buyer beware.

checkbook home, please! You are comparison shopping, not decision reaching!!

Make this unmistakably clear, *before* the interview begins. We also recommend *that you take careful, handwritten notes — to refresh your memory — and theirs.* Questions you will be seeking answers to, at each place — and please, write out these questions beforehand, and at each place ask every question (omitting none):

• *What is their program?* When all their gimmicks are set aside (and some have great ones, like rehearsing for interview on closed circuit TV, or using video-tape or cassettes to record your skills or your resume, etc.) what are they offering: is it basically "the numbers game," *or* is it basically some variation of the creative minority's prescription?

• *Who will be doing it?* Do you get the feeling that you must do most of it, with their basically assuming the role of coach? (if so, three cheers); or do you get the feeling that everything (including decision making about what you do, where you do it, etc.) will be done for you (if so, three warning bells should go off in your head)?

• *What guarantee is there that it will work?* If they make it clear that they have had a good success rate, but if you fail to work hard at the whole process, then there is no guarantee you are going to find a job, give them three stars. On the other hand, if they practically guarantee you a job, and say they have never had a client that failed to find a job, no matter what, *watch out.* Pulmoter job-counseling is very suspect; lifeless bodies make poor employees.

• *How many boxes are they building for you, as they talk?* A typical box in the *what-do-I-want-to-do?* area is: "let's face it, you may be unfair to yourself in trying to look for a job only in this particular geographical area — you may have to go where the work is." And so forth. *Press them about these kinds of limits.* The less boxes they build for you, the better; the more they build for you, the more demerits you should give them. The line between realism and pessimism is very thin in the head of an inept counselor; they will press you into a shape they can sell.

• *Are you face-to-face, and talking, with the actual persons who will be working with you, should you decide to become a client?* It might help you to be aware that some job-hunting or career counseling firms have professional salesmen who introduce you to the company, convince you of their 100% integrity and charm, secure your decision, get you to sign the contract — and then you never see them again. You work with someone entirely different (or a whole team). *Ask the person you are talking to, if they are the one (and the only one) you will be working with, should you eventually decide to become a client.* If they say No, ask to meet those who would be actually working with you — even if it's a whole battery of people. When you actually meet them, there are three considerations you should weigh:

(1) *Do you like them?* Bad vibes can cause great difficulties, even if this person is extremely competent. Don't dismiss this factor!

(2) *How long have they been doing this?* Ask them! And what training did they have for it? (Legitimate questions; if they get huffy, politely thank them for their time, and take your leave gently *but firmly.*) Some agencies hire former clients as new staff. Such new staff are sometimes given only "on the job training." Since you're paying for Expertise already acquired, you have a *right* to ask about this before making up your mind.

(3) *How much time will they give you?* Each of them, if it is a team. As a minimum? As a maximum? (There's got to be a maximum, no matter what they may at first claim. Every agency runs into extremely dependent types as clients, who would be there all day every day if the agency didn't have some kind of policy about maximum. *Press* to find out what it is, just so you'll know.) Over how long a period can you use their services? And, *will they put this in writing?* (That's the question that separates the men from the boys, and the women from the girls.)

• *What is the cost of these services? Are there any additional costs for additional services (like printing and sending out resumes)? If so, what are those services, and how much do they cost? Also, do you have to buy the whole program or will they sell you their help for just parts of it, in those areas where you feel you need help the most? What provisions are there about payment?* These are essential questions to ask while you are still doing comparison shopping, before your mind is closed and your wallet or purse is open. Clues: fees will range from $200 on up to $3000 if you're talking to some of the large career counseling agencies out there in Secularland. Whether you choose *any* of these places or not, will probably depend upon whether you're a high school or college student, say, looking for your first job (in which case, forget it!) or a professional in mid-career crisis, looking for top-flight help (in which case, *maybe*).

• *What does the contract state? What does it bind them to? What does it bind you to? What provision is there for a refund of part of the fee if you become unhappy with their help? After what point will no refund be given? (Crucial.)* Ask to see the contract (a legitimate request on your part). Study your notes to see what they promised that is important to you: are these all included in the contract? If not, ask if they can be. If the answer is no, ask Why?

With some firms the promises that attract the client to choose that particular firm, turn out — upon inspection — to be all verbal, none of them spelled out in the actual contract of promised services and hence it's your word against theirs, in the event you are subsequently dissatisfied. Hello, sucker.

Having gotten the information *you* want, and therefore having accomplished *your* purpose for this particular visit, you politely thank them for their time and trouble, and depart. You then go on to two other places, and ask the very same questions, please! There ought to be no charges involved for such comparison-shopping visits as this, and if they subsequently bill you, inquire politely whether or not a mistake has been made by their accounting department (good thinking). If they persist in billing you, pay a visit to your local friendly Better Business Bureau, and lodge a nice unfriendly complaint against the firm in question. You'd be surprised at how many firms experience *instant repentance* when the Better Business Bureau phones them. They don't want a complaint on their BBB record.

☐   Back home now, after visiting the three places you chose for your comparison shopping, you have to decide: a) whether you want none of the three, or b) one of the three and if so, which one.

Time for thought, maybe using some other people as a sounding board (wife, husband, professor, placement center, friend, buddy, business friend, consultant friend, or whoever) and time for some thoughtful meditation. What's at stake is a lot of *bread*, as they say, and you ought not to spend it casually – even if you have managed some savings, and are feeling rather desperate.

Look over your notes on all three places. Compare those places. Study your notes. Choose the career counselor you like best, go back, get their contract if they use a contract, *take it to a lawyer* and if the lawyer sees nothing wrong with it, sign it.

You haven't gotten a job yet, but hopefully you've gotten what *you* wanted: *expert coaching.*

HELP

I. FOR ANYONE

Crystal Management Services, Inc. of McLean, Virginia. Our good friend John C. Crystal has dissolved his Crystal Management Services, Inc. and is now founder and director of

The John C. Crystal Center, Inc., 390 Plandome Road, Manhasset, NY 11030. John Crystal devotes himself exclusively now to the work of this Center. The Center offers public lectures, one day-workshops, one week intensive courses and a twelve-week course, either in New York City (989 Avenue of the Americas 12th floor) or elsewhere by invitation. John works extensively with the disadvantaged, and presents workshops (Intensive Courses) in other parts of the country as well. Needless to say, John teaches a process strictly in accord with the principles described in Chapters 4–7 of this book. Phone: (516) 627–8802.

Job Forums. These are run in various cities by the Chamber of Commerce, service organizations, sales executives clubs, advertising clubs. These are usually run on a weekly or bi-weekly basis, at some central location, and afford an opportunity for some expert to speak on some phase of marketing, plus an opportunity for questions from those attending on any phase of the marketing process. (Some cities call them *man marketing clinics,* or such like — instead of *job forums.*) Usually there is no charge for these forums, or only a nominal one. Consult your Chamber for information as to what exists in *your* city.

Shea Yablonsky Associates, Inc., 3045 North Federal Highway, Bldg. No. 7, Fort Lauderdale, FL 33306, (305) 564-2999. Corporate outplacement services, workshops, and individual and group sessions for men and women facing career decisions. Fees vary.

Center for Career Transition, Continuing Education Building, University of Florida, 2102 West University Avenue, Gainesville, FL 32603. A no-fee career consultation program, specializing in the personal and career concerns of persons forty and over.

The Key — Center for Creative Living and Spiritual Growth, 219 Grove Avenue, NW, Huntsville, AL 35801, (205) 539-0641. Rev. Luther Kramer, Director. John Haley, Staff Associate. Offers individual counseling and group programs of guidance, self-assessment, job-hunting tactics, resumes, and interviewing. Also helps non-profit and religious groups to identify and obtain organizational priorities.

Career Workshops, Inc., Executive Office Building, 1801 East Franklin Street, Chapel Hill, NC 27514, (919) 929-8338. Patricia Grandstaff and Daniel Grandstaff, Directors. Workshops, seminars, and individual counseling on Creative Job Hunting. Fees vary.

Career and Life Planning, 372 Reedwood Drive, Nashville, TN 37217, (615) 367-1816. Marshal Cooper, M.Ed., Director. By appointment only.

Career development, testing and tape recording of counseling sessions. Fixed fee.

Swenholt Associates, Inc., 3414 Barger Drive, Falls Church, VA 22044, (702) 256-2383. Frankie P. Swenholt, President. Workshops and seminars in creative job search, career development, career/life planning, retirement planning, and creative leisure. Individual counseling. Fees vary.

Georgetown University, School for Summer and Continuing Education, 36th and N Streets, N.W., Washington, DC 20057, (202) 625-3003. Offers the following courses: Mid-Life Crisis and Career Change, Creative Job Search for Women, A New Look at Retirement, and Career Development for Supervisory Personnel.

Harold G. and Marilyn J. Shook, Life Management Services, Inc., 6825 Redmond Drive, McLean, VA 22101, (703) 356-2630. Offers orientation sessions, or complete ten-session courses on days or evenings; also intensive one-week courses.

Womanscope, 222 Long Reach Village Center, Columbia, MD 21045, (301) 997-2916. A non-profit career counseling center offering workshops and individual counseling to women and men.

The Mid-Atlantic Career Center, formerly of Washington, DC, was discontinued as of the end of 1977. Bart Lloyd, its excellent director, is now with the New England Career Development Center (see page 261).

Center For the Study of Adult Development, affiliated with Dept. of Psychiatry, University of Pennsylvania, Suite 260, 3401 Market Street, Philadelphia, PA 19104, (215) 662-4080. Monday-Friday, 9 a.m.-10 p.m., some weekend workshops. Career Counseling, career consulting with profit and not for profit organizations. Special services include client marketing programs and preparation of resumes and presentation letters. Fees vary.

Walter Goldschlager & Associates, 8D Appletree Lane, Old Bridge, NJ 08857, (201) 679-8086. Provides individual counseling and small group and organizational career pathing workshops. Fee.

FJN Career Development Program, Francis J. Nead, Professional Career Consultant, 14 Eggert Avenue, Metuchen, NJ 08840, (201) 494-6280. Formerly Senior Career Consultant at Mainstream Associates and at Bernard Haldane Associates, both in Manhattan. Individual counseling. Fees vary.

The Counseling Service of the Metropolitan Hartford YMCA, Inc., 160 Jewel Street, 3rd Floor, Hartford, CT 06103, (203) 522-4183. Offers personal vocational counseling to all ages, both sexes. Fees vary; scholarship aid available for those unable to afford the full counseling fee.

People Management Incorporated, 10 Station Street, King's Head Row, Simsbury, CT 06070, (203) 658-1800. Arthur F. Miller, Jr., President. Works with individuals, groups and organizations, assisting them in identifying their strengths, translating their gifts into viable career/job objectives, and teaching them how to identify and land a job suitable for their gifts. Experiences in motivational patterns, and in use of the technique Miller calls SIMA (System for Identifying Motivated Abilities). Fees vary.

Life Career Counselor, Ellen Wallach, 8 Sherburne Road, Lexington, MA 02173, (617) 862-0997. Offers individual counseling, workshops and small group participation. Fees vary.

Communication Resources, 75 Parker Road, Wellesley, MA 02181, (617) 237-3599. John C. Zacharis, Counselor. Program of career counseling. Fees vary.

New England Career Development Center, 40 Washington Street, Wellesley Hills, MA 02181, (617) 237-2228. Barton M. Lloyd, Associate Director. Offers career planning services and job-finding guidance either individually or in groups, for men and women facing any major career problem or decision. Individual programs involve a systematic review of experience along the lines of chapter 5, and much of the work before and between counseling sessions can be done by correspondence. Group programs, for 10-25 participants, can be arranged anywhere in the East, with fees according to services needed.

Changes, Carl Schneider, 7 Woodbridge Street, Cambridge, MA 02140, (617) 876-5085. Training to identify new careers, and to locate employment. Therapeutic counseling to resolve problems hindering work effectiveness, career changes, or job hunting. Evening and weekend hours available. Fees vary.

Adult Education and Career Counseling Center, Montgomery County Community College, Walnut and Penn Streets, Pottstown, PA 19464, (215) 323-1939. Individual and group counseling, skill-identification and values clarification, vocational testing, career and college information. No fee for counseling; minimal fees for some printed materials.

Career Focus Counseling Service, Inc., 311 Pinevue Drive, Monroeville, PA 15146, (412) 372-4564. Mike and Betty Fonfara, Counselors. This service empowers individuals and groups to set career goals, evaluate present career progress, change careers, see how faith influences vocational choices and how work affects interpersonal relationships. Formats include individual counseling and workshops. Fees vary.

The University of Akron, Adult Resource Center, Akron, OH 44325, (216) 375-7448. Monday-Friday, 8 a.m.-5 p.m. Educational and occupational information, guidance, referral and lifespan and career planning. No registration fee.

Walt Hopkins, Ph.D., Learning Consultant, 2017 Calvin Cliff, Cincinnati, OH 45206. Walt works with individual clients and also offers short seminars, one-day or weekend workshops, and full-length courses. He has designed an introduction to the *Quick Job-Hunting Map* process called *How High Is Your Castle?* which enables people to get started on what, where and how within an hour.

Career Planning Services, 2777 Colony Road, Ann Arbor, MI 48104, (313) 973-9286. Catherine E. Schwarz, Vocational Advisor. Services include personal interest survey; flexible, individualized counseling; occupational information and exploring; information about education and training programs in Michigan; and decision-making assistance. Fees.

Job Information and Seeking Training Program, 1001 West Tenth Street, Indianapolis, IN 46202, (317) 630-6971. A program to teach people how to assess their own career goals, define their own skills, and find their own, satisfying jobs.

Midtown Community Mental Health Center, Wishard Memorial Hospital, 1001 West Tenth Street, Indianapolis, IN 46202, (317) 630-7606. A mental health clinic with special vocational services, including interest testing, vocational exploration, workshops on how to get a job or make a career change, job-finding assistance, individual counseling, and help with resumes, interviewing skills, how to fill out applications, dress and grooming suggestions. Fees vary, based on ability to pay.

Career Potential, 1318 East State Street, Rockford, IL 61107, (815) 962-6777. Linda Ream and Mary-Stuart Carruthers, Consultants in career and life renewal. Work with men and women individually and in workshops. Fees vary.

The Disier Group, Institute of Applied Academics, Career Advancement Center, 625 N. Michigan Avenue, Suite 500, Chicago, IL 60611, (312) 944-0990. Weekly four-hour seminars for degreed and paraprofessional people on non-traditional job-hunting methods. No individual counseling. $35.00. (Formerly Institute of Applied Academics . . .)

David Swanson, Career Seminars & Workshops, Inc., 7235 W. Wells Street, Milwaukee, WI 53213. (414) 774-4755. Conducts workshops nationwide in career planning & motivation for government, universities & colleges. CETA, corporation. Based on "Parachute" process. Individual counseling. Fees vary. Teaches some free or low-cost courses in career planning at WCTI, Pewaukee, WI. (414) 548-5270.

Human Renewal Center, 2720 West 43rd Street, Minneapolis, MN 55410, (612) 925-0330. Richard Leider and Janet Hagberg, Directors. Career-transition and "inventuring" workshops, individual counseling, self-directed computer, videotape and audiotape services. Fees vary.

Colorado Growth Center, Inc., 965 Humboldt St., Suite 105, Denver CO 80218, (303) 831-9578. Arthur F. Smith, Jr., Counselor. Consultation individually or in groups on Life/Work planning. Job seeking strategy, Career Development, executive relocation. Fees vary.

Kirk, Putney & Associates, 1418 S. Race Street, Denver, CO 80210, (303) 722-3629. Samuel M. Kirk and Richard Putney, Counselors. Offers individual counseling, workshops and small-group participation. Fees vary.

Cochran Chapel United Methodist Church, Life/Work Planning Workshop. 9027 Midway Road, Dallas, TX 75209. Rev. Wallace Chappell and Rev. Bill Johnson. Sessions on two successive Thursday nights plus all-day Saturday workshop.

Life/Work Design, 109 East 48th Street, Austin, TX 78751, (512) 458-2807. Jeanne Quereau, Counselor. Life/work planning and personal growth counseling. Workshops, support groups, and individual counseling. By appointment. Fees vary.

Creative Careers, Jon Patrick Bourg. 3206 Cripple Creek, 32-G, San Antonio, TX 78209, (512) 822-8672. Classes, workshops, individual counseling.

Southwest Institute of Life Management, Theodore Donald Risch, Director, 2500 North Pantano Road, Suite 120, Tucson, AZ 85715, (602) 296-4764. An educational facility, specializing in career guidance and self-management.

Aware Advisory Center, YWCA South Lounge, Second Floor, 2019 14th Street (near Pico Blvd.), Santa Monica, CA 90405, (213) 392-1303. Aware support groups, career planning classes, and individual counseling. Mondays and Wednesdays, 10 a.m.- 5 p.m., and 7 p.m.- 9 p.m. No appointment necessary. Donation: $3.00 per visit (may be waived).

Margaret Anstin, 10405 Mann Drive, Cupertino, CA 95014, (408) 245-0702. Career counseling.

Right Livelihood Associates, 1152 Sanchez Street, San Francisco, CA 94114, (415) 285-8112. A career firm runs "The San Francisco Job Rap," an open drop-in group meeting every Tuesday evening 8-10 p.m. at the Network Coffeehouse, 1036 Bush Street, San Francisco, and the "Berkeley Career Forum," every Monday evening 8-10 p.m. at the Unitarian Center, 1924 Cedar Street, Berkeley. Also offers individual consultation at low-cost support groups while job-hunting, and "Next Job Workshops" as well as "Career-Transition Workshops." Low fees, based on current income.

Withers, Wendy C., LCSW, Center for Evaluation and Service, Suite 107, 2020 North Broadway, Walnut Creek, CA 94596, (415) 930-6454. Offers workshops and individual counseling services for vocational planning, career change and coping with job stress; specializing in mid-life and re-entry career issues. Consulting services available for in-service staff training and program development. Fees vary.

The Berkeley Center for Human Interaction, 1820 Scenic Avenue, Berkeley, CA 94709. Ann MacKinlay, Director. This center is developing a whole series of Professional and Career Workshops, including Career Clinics, and workshops on "Careers in Transition," "Career Options for Women," etc. These range from ten to eighteen hours in length, and sometimes are run on weekends, or may be spread over six weeks. Fees vary.

Life/Career Development, 4035 El Macero Drive, Davis, CA 95616, (916) 756-8637. Russel A. Bruch, Director. Career consultant to business, government, industry, and education. Individually designed workshops, seminars, and programs. Fees vary.

Guidance Plus, 1107 9th Street, Room 1037, Sacramento, CA 95814, (916) 446-0533. Individual consultation on career change, resume and proposal writing, skill-identification, interviewing, and research/targeting strategies. Also conduct career development and upward mobility planning workshops for industry. Hourly fee.

Criket Consultants, P.O. Box 323, Rancho Cordova, CA 95670, (916) 362-1682. A life and career development program, offering individual and group counseling, interviewing and job hunting skills training, skills identification, vocational rehabilitation, and comprehensive testing.

Sylvan Psychological and Counseling Services, 215 Skyline Building, 2041 SW 58th Avenue, Portland, OR 97221, (503) 292-9867. Joseph A. Dubay, Life/Work Counselor. Offers workshops helping the individual find an enriched life-style and fulfillment in the world of work and of leisure.

Bernard Haldane, 4502 54th Avenue N.E., Seattle, WA 98105. (206) 525-8141. Independent of the agency which bears his name, Bernard offers seminars for clergy and layperson on career planning and on career-changing/job-finding. He is one of the original pioneers in this whole field.

CAREER COUNSELOR CATALOGS

I think I perceive a trend beginning, for enterprising souls in a particular city or area to put together a guide to all the career counselors (or many of them, at any rate) in that city. While such books, unless they are revised annually, are bound to become outdated rather rapidly (ah, how well I know) due to places moving, folding, or rising Phoenixlike from their own ashes in a different form and place, nonetheless these books have a real value if you are looking for counseling help. Five such works have been brought to our attention, so far:

Adams, Robert Lang, ed., *The Boston Job Bank.* You can order it from the editor, at 30 Kinross 2, Brookline, MA 02146. Primarily entry level positions, primarily at major firms (in size), primarily for new college graduates. 1980. $5.95.

Levine, Renee, *How to Get a Job in Boston,* Resources, networks and tips on finding a job in you-can-guess-where. This is the third edition of this 90 page book/pamphlet. You can order it from: Vocations for Social Change, P.O. Box 211, Essex Station, Boston MA 02112. $3.95, paper.

O'Callaghan, Dorothy, *The Job Catalog: Where to Find That Creative Job in Washington.* c/o Mail Order USA, P.O. Box 19083, Washington, DC 20036. Includes job information in publishing and the fast news media, communications and arts-related fields, tourism and public relations, and how to meet the people who do the hiring. 1979. $6.00.

Help Wanted: A Guide to Career Counseling in the Bay Area, by Florence Lewis. You can order it from: Two Step Books, 2490 Channing Way, No. 210, Berkeley, CA 94704. 1978. $4.95, paper. It covers San Francisco, Marin County, the East Bay, and Santa Clara County.

Portland Career Hunter's Guide, A sourcebook of Local Resources for the Serious Career Planner and Job-Hunter, by Sheri Raders. You can order it from: Victoria House, Publishers, 2218 NE 8th Avenue, Portland, OR 97212. 1977. $3.95, paper.

In addition to the above resources, the National Career Development Project has trained some 300 people — in the U.S. and Canada — in the particular techniques described in chapters 5, 6 and 7 of this book. Each of these people has had over 120 hours of training with Ye Olde Author.

Should you desire a list of the people in your state or in adjoining areas, who have been so trained, you may secure that list by sending a check for $1.00, payable to The National Career Development Project, attn: Referral List, Box 379, Walnut Creek, CA 94596. This request *must* be made by mail, not by phone, as we are not equipped to handle phone requests.

II. GROUP-SUPPORT FOR THOSE WHO ARE UNEMPLOYED

Forty-Plus Clubs. Not a national organization, but a voluntary group of autonomous non-profit clubs, manned by members, paying no salaries, supported by initiation fees and monthly dues of members. Clubs now operating in New York City (Manhattan), Philadelphia, Washington, DC, Chicago, Milwaukee, Houston, Denver, Los Angeles, the Bay Area (Oakland) of California, and Hawaii. (See phone book for exact addresses.) *Normally only open to those who are forty years or older, unemployed, seeking employment, making an average of at least $12,000-15,000 (varies from one club to another) for the preceding five years, and able to pass a screening process.* Screening procedures of all these 'Forty-Plus' type groups may also vary, but usually they involve personal interview, checking out of business references, and informal meeting with representative active members. Process may take two to three weeks, in normal course. Insiders say it takes the average member about three months to find placement, and one (at least) alleges that about one-third leave without finding placement — or hang around for indefinite periods. Members must agree to give (typically) sixteen hours a week or two and one-half days to the club. Fees and dues vary from club to club.

NE-VEST (New England Volunteer Employment Services Team), 400 Totten Pond Road, Waltham, MA 02154, (617) 890-7150. An organization of unemployed professionals who help themselves and each other to find jobs. Basic, Advanced and Career Planning Workshops, plus videotape workshops, and others for special interest groups: men over forty-five, women, etc. There are no fees; the only requirement is that for every hour you attend a workshop, you volunteer an hour of your time to NE-VEST. Orientation every Friday, 1 - 2 p.m.

Talent Bank Associates, 475 Calkins Road, Henrietta (near Rochester), NY 14467, (716) 334-9676. An organized form of the "Job-Hunters Anonymous" idea described on page 57. A non-profit organization comprised of unemployed persons of various professions and skills working together on a volunteer basis to find themselves meaningful, permanent employment. Free of charge.

Experience Unlimited. An organization for unemployed professionals, based in California. Contact: Mr. Herman L. Leopold, Experience Unlimited Coordinator, Department of Human Resources Development, 1111 Jackson Street, Room 1009, Oakland, CA 94607, (415) 464-1337.

Civic Center Volunteers, Marin County Personnel Office, Administration Building, Civic Center, San Rafael, CA 94903, (415) 479-1100. Placement in county jobs of volunteer re-entry women, career-experimenters and students wishing to gain experience. Volunteers sign a contract for each specific job, and receive supervision and evaluation. The purpose of this program is to give work experience in various jobs and provide a place to gain confidence in one's skills, new self-esteem, etc.

T-I-E (Together in Employment). Offered in the Seattle-Tacoma area. Seven individualized group sessions over two weeks. Small fee. Sponsored by the Episcopal Diocese of Olympia, the specially-trained volunteers (trained by Bernard Haldane) offer their programs through neighborhood churches. The seminars are however ecumenical, open to all. To register: (206) 235-4200.

III. HELP FOR COLLEGE STUDENTS
OR GRADUATES

As we stated earlier (page 28), most of the colleges in this country — two-year or four-year — have some kind of Career Planning or Placement Office. Usually the office on a particular campus can be found under the above title, although sometimes it is "buried" in the Counseling Department, or in the Dean of Student Services Office. How helpful the Career Planning office is, on the particular campus you are attending, depends on the staffing, philosophy, and funding of that office — and this may vary from year to year (and even from season to season). So, go explore for yourself.

A Directory of these offices is published, and is available for perusal in most Placement Offices. It is called the *Directory of Career Planning and Placement Offices*, and is published by the College Placement Council, Inc., Box 2263, Bethlehem, PA 18001. It costs, incidentally, $8.00 to non-CPC members, $5.00 to members. This Directory is not a complete listing of all such offices in the country. The Career Planning and Placement Office (c/o Office of Counseling and Testing) at Western Nevada Community College, for example, has asked us to point out that they exist, even though they are not in this Directory. (7000 Sullivan Lane, Reno, NV 89505, (702) 673-4666.)

Now, if you are not only a college graduate but also a hopeless romantic, you will have a vision of blissful cooperation existing between all of these placement offices across the country. So that if you are a graduate of an East Coast college, let us say, and subsequently you move to California, and want help with career planning, you should in theory be able to walk into the placement office on any California campus, and be helped by that office (a non-altruistic service based on the likelihood that a graduate of that California campus is, at the same moment, walking into the placement office of your East Coast college — and thus, to coin a phrase, "one hand is washing another"). Alas and alack, dear graduate, in most cases it doesn't work like that. You will be told, sometimes with genuine regret, that *by official policy*, this particular placement office on this particular campus is only allowed to aid its own students and alumni. One Slight Ray of Hope: on a number of campuses, there are career counselors who think this policy is absolutely asinine, so if you walk into the Career Planning office on that campus, *are lucky enough to get one of Those Counselors*, and you don't mention whether or not you went to that college — the counselor will never ask, and will proceed to help you just as though you were a real person.

This restriction (to their own students and graduates) is less likely to be found at Community Colleges than it is at four-year institutions. So, if you run into a dead end, try a Community College near you. For high school students considering college, there are various agencies that help, such as:

Educational Talent Search, Spanish Education Development Center, 1840 Kalorama Road NW, Washington, DC 20009, (202) 462-8782. Funded by H.E.W. to provide career counseling, and information on career and vocational opportunities to minority and low-income individuals between the ages of 14 and 27.

You'll have to ask what there is in your particular geographical area. Your high school guidance counselor may know.

IV. HELP FOR WOMEN

Resource centers for women are springing up all over the country, faster than we can record them. We are listing here *only a sampling* of same, as sent in to us by Betsy Jaffe at CATALYST, or by other interested readers. If you have a favorite, not listed here, send us the pertinent information — in format similar to the next pages — and we'll list it in the next edition. (Don't, however, bother to send us college services which are available only to the students and alumnae of that college. We try not to list such places, since such a listing only frustrates non-alumnae. If, inadvertently, any such place already listed here is thus restricted, please let us know, and we'll gently remove them from the next edition.) Incidentally, the centers which are listed here will know (in all probability) what other centers or resources there are in your geographical area. Also, try your telephone book's yellow pages: "Women's Organizations and Services," or "Vocational Consultants."

In all of this you will remember won't you, our earlier description (page 251) of all career counseling professionals, as falling into one of three groups: (1) Sincere and skilled; (2) Sincere but inept; and (3) Insincere and inept? Well, dear friend, groups or organizations or centers which have been organized specifically to help women job-hunters or career-changers are not — by that act — made immune to the above distinctions. Think about it, before you agree to put your (vocational) life into somebody else's hands. Remember: the numbers game (chapter 2), even if it is expressed in beautifully non-sexist language, is still the numbers game.

RESOURCES
FOR
WOMEN

ALABAMA

Enterprise State Junior College, Women's Center, Career Development Center, Highway 84 East, P.O. Box 1300, Enterprise, AL 36330, (205) 347-7881 or 5431. Monday and Tuesday, 8 a.m.-6 p.m. Wednesday and Thursday 8 a.m.-4:30 p.m. Friday 8 a.m.- 4 p.m.

University of Alabama, Career Planning and Placement, 1300 8th Avenue South, Building 5, Room 110, Birmingham, AL 35294, (205) 934-4324 or 4470. Monday-Friday, 8:30 a.m.-5 p.m.

ALASKA

University of Alaska, Anchorage Educational Opportunity Center, 2533 Providence Avenue-K-101, Anchorage, AK 99504, (907) 279-6622, Ext. 451. Monday-Friday, 8 a.m.-5 p.m.

ARIZONA

University of Arizona, Student Counseling Service, 200 W. Old Psychology Building, Tucson, AZ 85721, (602) 884-2316. Monday-Friday, 8 a.m. to noon and 1-5 p.m.; Tuesday and Wednesday, 6:30-9 p.m. at Continuing Education Office. Official college office. Restricted to students. Educational and career counseling, and personal and marital counseling, continuing education courses. No fees.

CALIFORNIA

Advocates for Women, Inc., 256 Sutter Street, 6th Floor, San Francisco, CA 94105, (415) 495-6750. Monday-Friday, 8:30 a.m.-4:30 p.m. Independent nonprofit agency. Career counseling, job referral, placement. No fees. Offices also in Berkeley and Hayward.

Alumnae Resources, 3979 Washington Street, San Francisco, CA 94118, (415) 387-9960. For alumni of Barnard, Mills, Mount Holyoke, Radcliffe, Scripps, Smith, Vassar, Wellesley and Wells Colleges. Offers career and job files, career counseling, support, programs and workshops for re-entry women. Fridays, 9.30 a.m.-4 p.m.; Saturdays, 9:30 a.m.-noon; fees vary from small to none. Appointments suggested.

American River College, College Opportunity Center, 4700 College Oak Drive, Sacramento, CA 95841, (916) 484-8391. Monday-Friday, 8:30 a.m.-4 p.m.

Career Design, An Affiliate of Ranny Riley & Assoc., 2398 Broadway, San Francisco, CA 94115, (415) 929-8161 / 929-8150. Offers a variety of intensive seminars and comprehensive workshops. Fees vary.

Career Planning Center, 1623 South La Cienega Blvd., Los Angeles, CA 90035, (213) 273-6633. Monday-Friday, 10 a.m.-4 p.m.; Thursday, 7-9 p.m. Independent nonprofit office. Labor market/career information and counseling, job referral, placement, resume preparation. Continuing education programs. No registration fee. Other fees vary.

Careerwise, 3174 Turk St., No. 3, San Francisco, CA 94118, (415) 387-9045. Ann Morton, Career Development Specialist. Offers variety of evening and Saturday workshops. Fees vary.

The Claremont Colleges, Special Academic Programs and Office for Continuing Education, Harper Hall 160, Claremont, CA 91711, (714) 626-8511. Monday-Friday, 9 a.m.-5 p.m. College-sponsored office. Educational and career counseling, job referral, continuing education courses. Registration fee.

Crossroads Institute for Career Development, 2288 Fulton Street, Berkeley, CA 94704, (415) 848-0698. Monday-Friday, 9 a.m.-5 p.m.

Cypress College, Career Planning Center, 9200 Valley View Street, Cypress, CA 90630, (714) 826-2220, Ext. 221. Monday-Friday, 8 a.m.-4 p.m.; Monday-Thursday, 6-9 p.m. Official college office. Educational and career counseling. No fees.

Displaced Homemakers Center, Inc., Mills College, Box 9996, Oakland, CA 94613, (415) 632-4600. Designed for the person over 35, who has worked without pay as a homemaker for one's family, and is not gainfully employed at present.

Foothill College, Continuing Education for Women, 12345 El Monte, Los Altos Hills, CA 94002, (415) 948-8590, Ext. 363. Monday-Friday, 10 a.m.-3 p.m. Official college office. Educational and career counseling, job referral, continuing education courses. No fees.

Anita J. Goldfarb, 19434 Londelius Street, Northridge, CA 91324, (213) 885-7653. Monday-Friday, 9:30 a.m.-4 p.m. Independent, private office. Educational and career counseling, class in Transitional Woman. Fees vary.

Information Advisory Service, UCLA Extension, 10995 Le Conte Avenue, Room 114, Los Angeles, CA 90024, (213) 825-2401, Ext. 250 or 261. Monday-Friday, 9 a.m.-5 p.m. College-sponsored office. Educational and career counseling, job referral information, continuing education courses. No fees.

Information Advisory Service, UCLA Extension, 1100 S. Grand Ave., Room 115, Los Angeles, CA 90015, (213) 747-2433/748-7079. Monday-Friday, 9 a.m.-4 p.m. Educational and career counseling, job referral information, continuing education courses.

Susan W. Miller, 360 N. Bedford, Suite 312, Beverly Hills, Ca 90210, (213) 837-7768. Career Counselor, Educational Consultant, private practice. Career counseling for individuals and career/life planning workshops for small groups using a structured, action-oriented approach.

Professional Career Center, Mission Center Park, Suite 333, 5333 Mission Center Road, San Diego, CA 92108, (714) 291-5480. Weekday evenings until 9 p.m. Independent, private agency. Offers workshops, training seminars and individual consultation designed to help women master the basics of career planning and development. Career tests, resume service, personal consultation, career advancement modules, or an affiliation of career-oriented women with monthly meetings. Fees vary.

Resource Center for Women, 445 Sherman Avenue, Palo Alto, CA 94306, (415) 324-1710. Monday-Friday, 9 a.m.-5 p.m.; Saturday, 10 a.m.-1 p.m. Independent non-profit agency. Educational and career counseling, adult education courses, job referral. Fees for workshops.

San Jose State University, Re-Entry Advisory Program, Old Cafeteria Building, San Jose, CA 95192, (408) 277-2188. Monday-Friday, 8 a.m.-5 p.m.; Wednesday, 8 a.m.-7 p.m. Official college program. Educational and career counseling, continuing education courses, referral to other services. No fees.

Aliyah Stein, M.F.C.C., Integrated Counseling Services — For Career and Personal Development, 50 Montell Street, Oakland, CA 94611 and 141 Belvedere Street, San Francisco, CA 94117, (415) 658-2963. Offers a comprehensive program of career and personal counseling, with special programs for homemakers and others concerned with re-entry or career change. Fees on a sliding scale.

University of California, Berkeley, Women's Center for Continuing Education of Women, T-9 Building, Berkeley, CA 94720, (415) 642-4786. Monday-Friday, 9 a.m.-5 p.m. College sponsored office. Educational and career counseling, research library. No fees.

UCSD Extension Counseling Programs, University of California, San Diego, Box 109, La Jolla, CA 92037, (714) 453-2000, Ext. 2096. Monday-Friday, 8 a.m.-5 p.m. Official college office. Educational and career counseling, continuing education courses, job referral. Counseling available in relation to courses. Fees range from $10 up.

Caroline Voorsanger, Consultant for Volunteer Management and Re-entry Women, 2000 Broadway, No. 1108, San Francisco, CA 94115, (415) 567-0890. Career counseling, assistance with focusing and self-assessment.

West Los Angeles College, Career Planning Center, 4800 Freshman Drive, Culver City, CA 90230, (213) 836-7110, Ext. 355, Monday-Friday, 8 a.m. - 4:30 p.m., Tuesday and Thursday, 5:30 p.m.- 8:30 p.m. Educational, personal and career counseling; Women's Re-entry Center, Career Exploration Program. No fees.

Women Can Win! Seminars, 8383 Wilshire Blvd., Ste. 517, Beverly Hills, CA 90211, (213) 653-5991, also 17814 Gertrudes Circle, Fountain Valley, CA 92708, (714) 848-6177. Seminars and individual counseling to assist women with career and personal goals. Programs offered in Los Angeles, San Fernando Valley and Orange County.

The Women's Opportunities Center, Univ. of California Extension, 148C Administration Bldg., Irvine, CA 92717, (714) 833-7128. Monday-Friday, 10 a.m.-4 p.m. College sponsored office. Educational and career counseling, continuing education courses. No fees.

Woman's Place, Inc., 1901 Avenue of the Stars, Los Angeles, CA 90067, (213) 553-0870. Monday-Friday, 9:30 a.m.-2:30 p.m. Independent private agency. Career counseling, workshops, job referral, 5-hour day. Fees vary.

Woman's Way, 710 C Street, Suite 1, San Rafael, CA 94901. (415) 453-4490. Monday-Friday, 9 a.m. to 5 p.m.

COLORADO

Better Jobs for Women, 1038 Bannock, Denver, CO 80202, (303) 893-3534. Monday-Friday, 8:30 a.m.-6 p.m. Helps to place women in high-paying jobs which are traditionally done by men; e.g., small appliance repair, painting, etc. Accepts applicants from 18-30.

Carrol Denmark, Magnolia Star Route, Nederland, CO 80466, (303) 443-2017/258-7289. Independent, private office. Conducts workshops, courses. Fees vary.

Women's Resource Agency, 25 North Spruce Street, Suite 309, Colorado Springs, CO 80905, (303) 471-3170. Monday-Friday, 8 a.m.-5 p.m.

CONNECTICUT

Albertus Magnus College, Life Career Development Center, 700 Prospect Street, New Haven, CT 06511, (203) 777-3363. Monday-Friday, 9 a.m.-5 p.m.

Fairfield University, Women's Bureau, North Benson Road, Fairfield, CT 06430, (203) 255-5411. Monday-Friday, 9 a.m.-3 p.m.

Information & Counseling Service for Women, 301 Crown Street, Box 5557, New Haven, CT 06520, (203) 436-8242. Five days a week — by appointment only. Independent nonprofit agency. Career counseling, education and employment information, job referral. Registration fees, fees for career events.

Norwalk Community College, Counseling Center, 333 Wilson Avenue, Norwalk, CT 06854, (203) 853-2040. Monday-Friday, 9 a.m.-7:30 p.m.

University of Connecticut, Continuing Education for Women, U-56W, Storrs, CT 06268, (203) 486-3441. Monday-Friday, 8:30 a.m.-4:30 p.m. Official college office. Educational and career counseling, continuing education courses. Fees vary.

Young Women's Christian Association, Career and Educational Counseling Center, 422 Summer Street, Stamford, CT 06901, (203) 348-7727. Monday-Friday, 9 a.m.-5 p.m.; and by appointment. National organization. Educational and career counseling, adult education courses. Registration fee.

DELAWARE

University of Delaware, Division of Continuing Education, Clayton Hall, Newark, DE 19711, (302) 738-8432. Monday-Thursday, 8:30 a.m.-9 p.m.; Friday, 8:30 a.m.-5 p.m.; Saturday, 9 a.m.-noon. Official college office. Educational and career counseling, continuing education courses. No registration fee. Other fees vary.

DISTRICT OF COLUMBIA

George Washington University, Continuing Education for Women, 2130 H Street NW, Suite 621-624, Washington, D.C. 20052, (202) 676-7036. Monday-Friday, 9 a.m.-5 p.m. College sponsored. Educational and career counseling, continuing education courses, job referral. Fees vary.

Wider Opportunities for Women, 1649 K Street NW, Washington, D.C. 20006, (202) 638-4868. A national non-profit organization. Maintains a national directory of women's employment programs, a national resource and advocacy network for women's employment organizations, a community outreach program which takes "suitcase seminars" to community groups, training programs for low-income women, a handbook (Working for You) to help employers who want to hire women in "non-traditional" jobs, and a women's professional, managerial and administrative talent tank for the D.C. area.

FLORIDA

Council for Continuing Education for Women of Central Florida, Inc., Valencia Community College, Downtown, 1 West Church Street, Third Floor, Orlando, FL 32801, (305) 423-4813. Monday-Friday, 9 a.m.-5 p.m. Independent non-profit agency. Educational and career counseling, adult education courses, testing. No fees.

Face Learning Center, Inc., 12945 Seminole Boulevard, Building 2, Suite 8, Largo, FL 33540, (813) 586-1110 / 585-8155. Monday-Friday, 9 a.m.-5 p.m. and by appointment.

The Greater Miami Council for the Continuing Education of Women, Miami-Dade Community College, 300 NE Second Avenue, Miami, FL 33132, (305) 577-6840. Monday-Friday, 8:30 a.m.-5 p.m. College sponsored office. Educational and career counseling, limited job referral, continuing education courses. No registration fee. Other fees vary.

Stetson University, Counseling Center, North Woodland Boulevard, Deland, FL 32720, (904) 734-4121, Ext. 215. Monday-Friday, 8:30 a.m.-4:30 p.m.

Valencia Community College, Center for Continuing Education for Women, P. O. Box 3028, Orlando, FL 32802, (305) 423-4813. Monday-Friday, 9 a.m.-5 p.m. Other hours arranged.

ILLINOIS

Applied Potential, Box 19, Highland Park, IL 60035, (312) 432-0620. Monday-Friday, 9 a.m.-5 p.m. Non-profit educational corporation. Professional counselors. Educational, career and personal counseling. No registration fee. Other fees vary.

Flexible Careers, Loop Center YWCA, 37 South Wabash Avenue, Suite 703, Chicago, IL 60603, (312) 263-6028. Monday, Tuesday, Wednesday, Friday 10:30 a.m.-2:30 p.m. Independent non profit organization. Career Information Center. Job Development Project. Registration fee.

Harper College Community Counseling Center, Palatine, IL 60067, (312) 359-4200. Monday-Thursday, 8:30 a.m.-4:30 p.m. and 6-10 p.m.; Friday, 8:30 a.m.-4:30 p.m. College sponsored office. Educational and career counseling. No registration fee. Other fees.

Jean Davis, Career Counseling, 540 Sheridan Road, Evanston, IL 60202, (312) 492-1002. Offers career assessment/design, resume and marketing strategies, job interview preparation, individual consultation and workshops.

Kishwaukee College, Career Guidance Center for DeKalb and Kane Counties, Malta IL 60150, (815) 825-2086, Ext. 348. Monday-Friday, 8:30 a.m.-4:30 p.m.

Moraine Valley Community College, Adult Career Resource Center, 10900 South 88th Avenue, Palos Hills, IL 60465, (312) 974-4300. Monday-Thursday, 9 a.m.-9 p.m.; Friday, 9 a.m.-5 p.m. Official college office. Educational career and personal counseling. No registration fee.

Oakton Community College, Women's Outreach Resource Center, 7900 N. Nagle, Morton Grove, IL, (312) 967-5120, Ext. 350. Monday-Friday, 9 a.m.-5 p.m.; evenings and weekends vary. Rotating center located in six community facilities. Call for location. College sponsored. Educational and career counseling, continuing education courses. Free counseling to district residents. Other fees vary.

Southern Illinois University, General Studies Division, Office of Continuing Education, Campus Box 44, Edwardsville, IL 62025, (618) 692-2242. Monday-Friday, 8 a.m.-5 p.m. Official college office. Educational and career counseling, continuing education courses. No fees.

Southern Illinois University, Women's Programs Office, Woody Hall, B-244/245, Carbondale, IL 62901, (618) 453-3655. Monday-Friday, 8 a.m.-5 p.m. Individual advising, group discussions. No appointment needed.

Thornton Community College, Counseling Center, 15800 S. State Street, South Holland, IL 60473, (312) 596-2000, ext. 306. Monday-Thursday, 8 a.m.-8:30 p.m.; Friday 8 a.m.-5 p.m. Career Information Center.

University of Illinois Urbana Champaign, Student Services Office for Married Students and Continuing Education for Women, 610 East John Street, Champaign, IL 61820, (217) 333-3137. Monday-Friday, 8 a.m.-5 p.m. Official college office. Educational and career counseling. No fees.

Women's Employment Counseling Center, YWCA, 1001 South Wright, Champaign, IL 61820, (217) 344-0721. Monday-Friday, 9 a.m.-5 p.m. Independent, nonprofit office. Educational and career counseling, job referral and placement. No fees.

Women's Inc., 15 Spinning Wheel Rd., Suite 14, Hinsdale, IL 60521, (312) 325-9770. Monday-Saturday, 9 a.m.-9 p.m. Independent private agency. Educational and career counseling, job referral and placement. No registration fee. Other fees vary.

INDIANA

Ball State University, Student Services, Office of Admissions, Muncie, IN 47036, (317) 285-4248. Monday-Friday, 8 a.m.-5 p.m.

Continuing Education Services, Indiana University/Purdue University, 1301 East 38th Street, Indianapolis, IN 46205, (317) 923-1321. Monday-Friday, 8 a.m.-5 p.m. Official college office. Educational and career counseling, continuing education courses. Fees vary.

Indiana University, Continuing Education for Women, Owen Hall, Bloomington, IN 47401, (812) 337-1684. Monday-Friday, 8 a.m.-5 p.m. Official college office. Educational and career counseling, continuing education courses. Fees vary.

University Center for Women, Counseling and Academic Development Division, Purdue University, 2101 Coliseum Blvd. East, Fort Wayne, IN 46805, (219) 482-5393. Monday-Friday, 8 a.m.-noon, 1 p.m.-5 p.m. College sponsored office. Educational and career counseling, continuing education courses, job referral. Fees vary.

Woman Alive! Inc., YWCA, 229 Ogden Street, P. O. Box 1121, Hammond, IN 46325, (219) 931-2922. Wednesdays (or by appointment).

Women's Career Center, Inc. YWCA, 802 N. Lafayette Boulevard, South Bend, IN 46601, (219) 233-9491 or 287-8356. Monday-Friday, 9 a.m.-5 p.m.

IOWA

Drake University, Community Career Planning Center for Women, 1158 27th Street, Des Moines, IA 50311, (515) 271-2916. Monday-Friday, 9 a.m.-5 p.m. Official college office. Educational and career counseling, continuing education courses. No fee for individual counseling. Fee for group sessions.

University Counseling Service, Iowa Memorial Union, University of Iowa, Iowa City, IA 52242, (319) 353-4484. Monday-Friday, 8 a.m.-5 p.m. College sponsored office. Educational, vocational and personal counseling. Fees vary for non-students.

University of Iowa, Office of Career Planning and Placement, Iowa City, IA 52242, (319) 353-3147. Monday-Friday 8 a.m.-5 p.m.; Wednesday, 5:30-7:30 p.m. Official College office. Educational and career counseling, job referral, placement. Fee for job placement only.

Women's Work/Work Associates, 820 First National Building, Davenport, IA 52801, (319) 326-6249. Monday-Friday, 9 a.m.-4 p.m. Independent, private agency. Job referral and placement. Fees vary.

KANSAS

University of Kansas, Student Services, Extramural Independent Study Center, Division of Continuing Education, Lawrence, KS 66044, (913) 864-4792. Monday-Friday, 8 a.m.-noon and 1-5 p.m. College sponsored. Educational and career counseling, continuing education (independent study, classes). No registration fee. Other fees vary.

Adult Life Resource Center, Division of Continuing Education, 1246 Mississippi Street, Annex A, Lawrence, KS 66045, (913) 864-4794. Monday-Friday, 8 a.m.-5 p.m.; other times by appointment. College-sponsored. Educational and career counseling, independent study, workshops and activities programmed around life-cycle change. Free Inward WATS information for Kansans, 1-800-532-6772. No fee for initial contact; other fees vary.

MARYLAND

Baltimore County Work Counseling Center for Women, Baltimore County Commission for Women, Courthouse Room 126, Towson, MD 21204, (301) 494-3403. Monday-Friday, 8:30 a.m.-4:30 p.m.; other times by appointment. Government agency. Offers educational and career counseling for individuals and groups, workshops and courses, information on apprenticeship training opportunities, self-help resources; job-finding support groups, and referral to other services. No fees.

Baltimore New Directions for Women, 2517 N. Charles Street, Baltimore MD 21218, (301) 366-8750. Monday-Thursday, 10 a.m.-2 p.m. Government agency. Educational and career counsel-ing, continuing education courses, job referral, placement. Information center. No fees.

College of Notre Dame of Maryland, Continuing Education Center, 4701 N. Charles Street, Baltimore, MD 21210, (301) 435-0100. Monday-Friday, 9 a.m.-4:30 p.m. College sponsored. Educational and career counseling, continuing education courses, job referral. Fees vary.

Goucher Center for Educational Resources, Goucher College, Towson, Baltimore, MD 21204, (301) 825-3300. Monday-Friday, 9 a.m.-4:30 p.m. College sponsored. Counseling to women considering a return to school. Non-credit and credit courses for adults. Referrals for career and volunteer work.

MASSACHUSETTS

Civic Center and Clearing House, Inc., 14 Beacon Street, Boston, MA 02108, (617) 227-1762. Monday-Friday, 10 a.m.-4 p.m. Independent non-profit agency. Educational and career counseling, job information. Fee for consultation of the Career and Vocational Advisory Service.

Continuum, Inc., 785 Centre Street, Newton, MA 02158, (617) 964-3322. Internship Program for Re-Entry Women. Monday-Friday, 9 a.m.-3 p.m.

Resource Center for Educational Opportunities, 19 Fort Hill Street, Hingham MA 02043, (617) 749-7445. Monday-Friday, 9:30 a.m.-11:30 a.m. and by appointment. Branch action project of American Association of University Women.

Smith College, Career Development Office, Pierce Hall, Northampton, MA 01063, (413) 584-2700. Monday-Friday 8:30 a.m.-4:30 p.m. Official college office. Educational and career counseling. No fees.

Widening Opportunity Research Center, Middlesex Community College, Division of Continuing Education, P. O. Box T, Bedford, MA 01730, (617) 275-8910, ext. 291. Monday-Friday, 9 a.m.-2 p.m. College sponsored office. Educational and career counseling, continuing education courses. Fees vary.

Wider Opportunities for Women, 413 Commonwealth Avenue, Boston, MA 02215. (617) 261-2060. Monday-Saturday (except Wednesday) 10 a.m.-2 p.m.; Wednesday, 10 a.m.-8 p.m. A private, non-profit organization, serving career counseling to women on a self help basis. A membership organization, charging an annual fee, which entitles members thereafter to unlimited drop-in career counseling and use of job-listings. Also offers workshops.

Women's Educational & Industrial Union, Career Services, 356 Boylston Street, Boston, MA 02116, (617) 536-5651. Monday-Friday, 9 a.m.-5 p.m. Independent non-profit agency. Career counseling, job referral and placement. No registration fee. Placement fees vary.

Why Not? Program, YWCA, 2 Washington Street, Worcester, MA 01608, (617) 791-3181. Monday-Friday, 9 a.m.-5 p.m.; evenings by appointment. Fees vary.

YWCA Women's Resource Center, 66 Irving Street, Framingham, MA 01701, (617) 873-9781. Monday-Friday, 9 a.m.-5 p.m. Individual career counseling. Free.

MICHIGAN

Every Woman's Place, 23 Strong Avenue, Muskegon, MI 49441, (616) 726-4493. Monday-Friday, 9 a.m.-5 p.m.

Michigan Technological University, Center for Continuing Education for Women, Room 301A, Administration Building, Houghton, MI 49931, (906) 487-2270. Monday-Friday, 8 a.m.-5 p.m. Official college office. Educational and career counseling, continuing education courses. No registration fee. Other fees vary.

Macomb County Community College, Community Resource Center 14500 Twelve Mile Road, K-332, Warren MI 48093, (313) 779-7417, 779-7422. Monday-Friday, 8:30 a.m.-5 p.m.

Montcalm Community College, Career Information Center, Sidney, MI 48885, (517) 328-2111. Monday-Friday, 8 a.m.-5 p.m.; evenings by appointment. College sponsored office. Education and career counseling. No fees.

C. S. Mott Community College, Guidance Services and Counseling Division, 1401 East Court Street, Flint, MI 48503, (313)

762-0356. Monday-Thursday, 8 a.m.-8:30 p.m.; Friday, 8 a.m. - 4:30 p.m. Health counseling and vocational testing.

Northern Michigan University, Women's Center for Continuing Education Marquette, MI 49855, (906) 227-2219. Monday-Friday, 8:30 a.m.-4:30 p.m. Official college office. Educational and career counseling, job referral, continuing education courses. Fees vary.

Oakland University, Continuum Center for Adult Counseling and Leadership Training, Rochester, MI 48063, (313) 377-3033. Monday-Friday, 8 a.m.-5 p.m. College affiliated. Personal, educational and career counseling, continuing education courses. Fees vary.

Schoolcraft College, Women's Resource Center, 18600 Haggerty Road, Livonia, MI 48152, (313) 591-6400, Ext. 430. Monday-Friday, 9 a.m.-3 p.m. Continuing Education Community Services; Educational and career counseling courses, workshops, referral to other agencies, and peer counseling. For widowed, displaced homemakers and re-entry women and men. Fees for courses and workshops only.

University of Michigan, Center for Continuing Education of Women, 330 Thompson Street, Ann Arbor, MI 48108, (313) 764-6555.

Western Michigan University, Center for Women's Services, Kalamazoo, MI 49008, (616) 383-6097. Monday-Friday, 8 a.m.-5 p.m. Official college office. Educational and career counseling, continuing education courses. Fees vary.

Women's Resource Center, 226 Bostwick NE, Grand Rapids, MI 49503, (616) 456-8571. Monday, 9 a.m.-8 p.m.; Tuesday-Friday, 9 a.m.-5 p.m. Independent non-profit agency. Educational and career counseling, job referral. Fees vary.

MINNESOTA

Minnesota Women's Center, University of Minnesota, 306 Walter Library, Minneapolis, MN 55455, (612) 373-3850. Monday-Friday, 7:45 a.m.-4:30 p.m. Official college office. Educational and career counseling. No fees.

Southwest State University, Personal Development Center, 268 CAB, Marshall, MN 56258, (507) 537-7150. Monday-Friday, 8 a.m.-4:30 p.m.; evening schedule varies. Official college office. Educational and career counseling, job referral and placement, continuing education courses. Placement fee only.

Working Opportunities for Women, 65 East Kellogg Boulevard, Room 437, St. Paul, MN 55101, (612) 227-8401. Monday, Wednesday, Thursday, Friday, 8 a.m.-4:30 p.m.; Tuesday 8 a.m.-9 p.m. Displaced Homemaker Center.

MISSISSIPPI

Mississippi State University, Placement and Career Information Center, Drawer P, Mississippi State, MS 39762, (601) 325-3344. Monday-Friday, 8 a.m.-5 p.m.

MISSOURI

University of Missouri, St. Louis, Extension Division — Women's Programs, 8001 Natural Bridge Road, St. Louis, MO 63121, (314) 453-5511. Monday-Friday, 8 a.m.-5 p.m. Official college office. Educational and career counseling, adult education courses, limited job referral. No registration fee. Other fees vary.

Washington University, Continuing Education for Women, Box 1099, St. Louis, MO 63130, (314) 889-6759. Monday-Friday, 8:30 a.m.-5 p.m. Official college office. Educational and career counseling, continuing education courses. Fees vary.

The Women's Resource Service, University of Missouri, Kansas City, 5325 Rockhill Road, Kansas City, MO 64110, (816) 276-1442. Monday-Friday, 10 a.m.-2 p.m. Official college office. Educational and career counseling, job referral, continuing education courses. No fees.

MONTANA

Focus on Women, 9 Hamilton Hall, Montana State University, Bozeman, MT 59717, (406) 994-2012. Monday-Friday, 8 a.m.-5 p.m. Workshops, seminars. Fee varies.

Women's Bureau, 35 S. Last Chance Gulch, 202 Capitol Station, Helena, MT 59601, (406) 449-5600. Monday-Friday, 8 a.m.-5 p.m. An agency of' the State Department of Labor and Industry. An information clearinghouse, they also conduct career planning and job awareness workshops for women, as well as counseling of women in search of employment. No fee.

Women's Resource Center, Nontraditional Job Counselor, University of Montana, Missoula, MT 59801. Nontraditional career counseling, and job referral. No fee.

Job Counselor, Missoula YWCA, 1130 W. Broadway, Missoula, MT 59801. Job counseling, career counseling, job referral, resume preparation. Works with displaced homemakers. No fee.

NEW JERSEY

Adult Service Center, 112 Main Road, Montville, NJ 07045, (201) 335-4009, 335-4420. Monday, Tuesday, Thursday, Friday, 9 a.m.-1 p.m.; Wednesday, 7 p.m.-10 p.m.

Bergen Community College, Division of Community Services, 295 Main Street, Hackensack, NJ 07652, (201) 489-1556. Monday-Friday, 9 a.m.-5 p.m. College sponsored office. Educational and career counseling, adult education courses. No fees.

Caldwell College, Career Planning and Placement, Caldwell, NJ 07006, (201) 228-4424, Ext. 60. Monday-Friday, 9 a.m.-4:30 p.m. College-sponsored office. Educational and career counseling, limited job referral. No fees.

College Counseling and Education Center, 369 Forest Avenue, Paramus, NJ 07652, (201) 265-7729. Monday-Saturday, 9 a.m.-9 p.m.

Douglass College, Douglass Advisory Services for Women, Rutgers Women's Center, 132 George Street, New Brunswick,

NJ 08903, (201) 932-9603. Monday-Friday, 9 a.m.-noon and 1-4 p.m. Educational and career counseling. No fees.

Fairleigh Dickinson University, Center for Women, Madison Ave., Madison, NJ 07940, (201) 377-4700, ext. 377. Monday-Friday, 9 a.m.-5 p.m. Official college office. Educational and career counseling, continuing education courses, job referral and placement. No fees.

Eve, Kean College of New Jersey, Administration Building, Union, NJ 07083, (201) 527-2210. Monday-Friday, 9 a.m.-4:30 p.m. College sponsored. Educational and career counseling. No registration fee. Other fees vary.

Jersey City State College, The Women's Center, 70 Audubon, Jersey City, NJ 07305, (201) 547-3189. Monday-Friday, 9 a.m.-5 p.m. Official college office. Educational and career counseling, continuing education courses. No fees.

Jewish Vocational Service, 454 William Street, East Orange, NJ 07017, (201) 674-6330. Five days, thirty-seven hours. Independent, non-profit office. Educational and career counseling, job referral and placement. Fees vary.

Middlesex County College, Women's Career Information Center, Woodbridge Avenue, West Hall Annex, Edison, NJ 08817, (201) 548-6000, ext. 411. Monday-Friday, 10 a.m.-2 p.m.

Montclair State College, Women's Center, Valley Road, Upper Montclair, NJ 07405, (201) 893-5106. Monday-Friday, 8:30 a.m.-4:30 p.m.; evenings by appointment. College-sponsored office. Educational and career counseling. No fees.

The Professional Roster, 5 Ivy Lane, Princeton, NJ 08540, (609) 921-9561. Monday-Friday, 10 a.m.-1 p.m. Independent, non-profit organization. Educational and career counseling, job referral. No fees.

Reach, Inc., Box 33, College of St. Elizabeth, O'Connor Hall, Convent Station, NJ 07961, (201) 267-2530. Monday-Friday, 9 a.m.-noon. Independent non-profit office. Educational and career counseling, job referral. Fees vary.

Union County Technical Institute, Women's Center for Career Planning, 1776 Raritan Road, Scotch Plains, NJ 07076, (201) 880-2000. Monday-Friday, 8:30 a.m.-4:30 p.m.

NEW YORK

Academic Advisory Center for Adults, Turf Avenue, Rye, NY 10580, (914) 967-1653. Monday-Thursday, 9 a.m.-4 p.m., some evenings.

Adelphi University, Women's Center, Linen Hall, Garden City, NY 11530, (516) 294-8700, Ext. 7490. Monday-Friday, 9:30 a.m.-4:30 p.m. Official college office. Educational and career counseling, legal and health referrals, etc. No fees.

Career Counseling for Women, Box 372, Huntington, NY 11743, (516) 421-1948. Monday-Friday, 9 a.m.-5 p.m.; some evenings. Independent, private agency. Educational and career counseling, life-planning. Fees vary.

Career Services for Women, Inc., 382 Main Street, Port Washington, NY 11050, (516) 883-3005. Tuesday, Wednesday, Thursday, 9:30 a.m.-2:30 p.m. Independent non-profit agency. Educational and career counseling, job referral. Fees vary.

Columbia University, Womanspace, School of General Studies, 306 Lewisohn Hall, Broadway and 116th Street, New York, NY 10027, (212) 280-2820. Monday-Thursday, 9 a.m. to 5 p.m. One evening a week.

Counseling Women, 14 East 60th Street, New York, NY 10022, (212) 486-9755. Monday-Friday, 9:30 a.m.-7 p.m. Assertiveness training.

County Counseling Center, 2242 Central Park Avenue, Yonkers, NY 10710, (914) 946-0333. Hours by appointment. Independent, private agency. Educational and career counseling. Fees vary.

Hofstra University, Counseling Center, Hempstead, NY 11550, (516) 560-3565. Monday-Friday, 9 a.m.-5 p.m.; Monday, Thursday, 6-10 p.m. Official college office. Educational and vocational counseling, testing, continuing education courses. Fees vary.

Human Relations Work-Study Center, New School for Social Research, 66 West 12th Street, New York, NY 10011, (212) 675-2700, Ext. 348/349. Monday-Friday, 9 a.m.-5 p.m. Official college office. Educational counseling, continuing education courses. Special training for human services. Fees vary.

Kingsborough Community College, Office of Career Counseling and Placement, 2001 Oriental Boulevard, Room C102, Brooklyn, NY 11235, (212) 934-5115. Monday-Friday, 8 a.m.-5 p.m.

Janice La Rouche Assoc., Workshops for Women, 333 Central Park West, New York, NY 10025, (212) 663-0970. Monday-Saturday, 9 a.m.-6 p.m. Independent private agency. Career counseling. Assertiveness training. No registration fee. Other fees vary.

Mercy College, Career Counseling and Placement Office, 555 Broadway, Dobbs Ferry, NY 10522, (914) 693-4500. Monday-Friday, 9 a.m.-5 p.m. Evenings by appointment. Official college office. Career counseling. Fees.

More for Women, Inc., 52 Gramercy Park So., New York, NY 10010, (212) 674-4090. Monday-Friday, 9 a.m.-9 p.m.; Saturday, 9 a.m.-4 p.m. Independent private agency. Educational and career counseling, workshops. Fees vary.

New Options, 26 West 56th Street, New York, NY 10019, (212) 541-4114. Monday-Friday, 9 a.m.-5 p.m.

New School for Social Research, Human Relations Center, 66 West 12th Street, New York, NY 10011, (212) 741-5684 /5 /6. Monday-Friday, 9 a.m.-5 p.m.

NYCTI'S Educational & Career Headquarters, 225 Park Avenue South, Suite 505, New York, NY 10003, (212) 677-3800, /4 /5. Monday-Friday, 9 a.m.-5 p.m.

Orange County Community College, Office of Community Services, 115 South Street, Middletown, NY 10940, (914) 343-1121. Monday-Friday, 9 a.m.-5 p.m. Official college office. Educational counseling, continuing education courses. Fees vary.

Personnel Sciences Center, 341 Madison Avenue, New York, NY 10017, (212) 661-1870. Monday-Saturday, 9 a.m.-5 p.m. Independent private agency. Educational and career counseling. Fees vary.

Placement 500, A Womanschool Affiliate, 424 Madison Avenue, New York, NY 10017, (212) 688-4606. Monday-Friday, 9:30 a.m. to 5:30 p.m.

Potential Unlimited, 214 East 49th Street, New York, NY 10017, (212) 421-1157. Monday-Friday, 9 a.m.-5 p.m. Evening and Saturday workshops.

Professional Skills Roster, 410 College Avenue, Ithaca, NY 14850, (607) 256-3758. Monday-Friday, 9:30 a.m.-12:30 p.m. Independent non-profit agency. Job referral, limited educational and career counseling. No fees. Suggested donation.

Regional Learning Service Center of New York, 405 Oak Street, Syracuse, NY 13203, (315) 425-5262. Monday-Friday, 8:30 a.m.-4:30 p.m. Independent non-profit agency. Educational and career counseling, education courses. Registration fees vary.

Ruth Shapiro Associates, Career Development and Self-Marketing Workshops, 200 East 30th Street, New York, NY 10016, (212) 889-4284. Monday-Saturday, 9 a.m.-5 p.m. Monday and Wednesday evening groups.

Suny at Buffalo, University Placement and Career Guidance, 14 Capen Hall, Buffalo, NY 14260, (716) 636-2231. Monday-Friday, 8:30 a.m.-5 p.m. Official college office. Educational and career counseling, job referral and placement. No fees.

Suny at Stony Brook, Mid-Career Counseling Center, Sociology and Behavioral Sciences Bldg., Room N235, Stony Brook, NY 11794, (516) 246-3304. Monday-Friday, 9 a.m.-8 p.m. Official college office. Educational and career counseling, continuing education courses. Fees vary.

Syracuse University/University College, Women's Center for Continuing Education, 610 East Fayette Street, Syracuse, NY 13202, (315) 423-3294. Monday-Friday, 9 a.m.-5 p.m. College sponsored office. Educational and career counseling, continuing education courses. No fees.

Vistas for Women, YWCA, 515 North Street, White Plains, New York, NY 10605, (914) 949-6227. Monday-Thursday, 9 a.m.-5 p.m.

Women's Career Center, Inc., 121 North Fitzhugh Street, Rochester, NY 14614, (716) 325-2274. Monday, Tuesday, Wednesday, Friday, 10 a.m.-2 p.m.; Tuesday, Thursday, 5:30 p.m.-9:30 p.m.

NORTH CAROLINA

Duke University, Office of Continuing Education, 107 Binns, Durham, NC 27708, (919) 684-6259. Monday-Friday, 8:30 a.m.-5 p.m. Official college office. Educational and career counseling, continuing education courses, for men as well as women. Fees vary.

Fayetteville Family Life Center, North Carolina Baptist Hospital, Bordeaux Shopping Center, Fayetteville, NC 28304, (919) 484-0176. Monday-Friday, 8:30 a.m.-5 p.m. Tuesdays and Thursdays in evening.

Salem College, Lifespan Center for Women, Lehman Hall, Box 10548, Salem Station, Winston-Salem, NC 27108, (919) 723-7961. Monday-Friday, 8:30 a.m.-4:30 p.m. College sponsored office. Lifespan planning, educational and vocational, personal and social counseling. Fees vary.

OHIO

Baldwin-Wallace College, Experience CUE, Counseling and Advising Center, Administration Building - No. 118, Berea, OH 44017, (216) 826-2188. Monday-Friday, 8:30 a.m.-5 p.m.; Tuesday and Thursday, 5:30 p.m.-9 p.m.

Bowling Green State University, Center for Continued Learning, 194 S. Main Street, Bowling Green, OH 43402, (419) 372-0363. Monday-Friday, 9 a.m.-5 p.m.

Cleveland Jewish Vocational Service, 13878 Cedar Road, University Heights, OH 44118, (216) 321-1381. Monday-Friday, 9 a.m.-5:30 p.m.; Thursday, 9 a.m.-6:40 p.m. Independent non-profit agency. Educational and career counseling, job referral, placement. No registration fee. Other fees vary.

Lifelong Learning/Women's Programs, Cuyahoga Community College, 2900 Community College Avenue, Cleveland, OH 44115, (216) 241-5966. Monday-Friday, 9 a.m.-5 p.m. Community service. College-sponsored office. Individual educational and career counseling, no fee. Group series and programs, fees vary.

Ohio State University, Women's Programs, Division of Continuing Education, 1800 Cannon Drive, Columbus, OH 43227, (614) 422-8860. Monday-Friday, 8 a.m.-5 p.m. Career services, continuing education for mature women. Individual counseling, no fee. Career planning courses, special programs and workshops, fees vary.

Pyramid, Inc., 1642 Cleveland Avenue, NW, Canton OH 44703, (216) 453-3767. Monday-Friday, 8:30 a.m.-4:30 p.m.

Women the Untapped Resource Inc., 1258 Euclid Avenue, Cleveland, OH 44115, (614) 422-8860. For professional development of women with one year of college or more. By appointment only. Fee on sliding scale to $35.

Wright State University, Women's Career Development Center, 140 East Monument Avenue, Dayton, OH 45402, (513) 223-6041. Monday-Friday, 8:30 a.m.-5 p.m.

University of Akron, Adult Resource Center, Akron, OH 44325, (216) 375-7448. Monday-Friday, 8 a.m.-5 p.m. Educational and career counseling, adult education courses, job referral, placement. No registration fee.

OKLAHOMA

Women's Resource Center, Inc., 207½ East Gray, P. O. Box 474, Norman, OK 73070, (405) 364-9424. Monday-Friday, 8 a.m.-5 p.m., plus emergency answering service. Independent non-profit agency. Educational and career counseling, job referral and placement. $5 registration fee.

OREGON

Women's Programs, Division of Continuing Education, Oregon State System of Higher Education, 1633 SW Park Avenue, (mail) Box 1491, Portland, OR 97207, (503) 229-4849. Monday-Friday, 8:30 a.m.-4:30 p.m. Official college office. Educational and career counseling, continuing education courses. No registration fee. Other fees vary.

PENNSYLVANIA

Bryn Mawr College, Office of Career Planning, Bryn Mawr, PA 19010, (215) 525-1000, Ext. 397. Monday-Friday, 9 a.m.-5 p.m. Official college office. Educational and career counseling, job referral and placement. No fees.

Career Resource Center, Harcum Junior College, Morris and Montgomery Avenues, Bryn Mawr, PA 19010, (215) 525-4100, Ext. 268. Monday-Friday, 9 a.m.-5 p.m. Career counseling, job referral and placement.

Cedar Crest College, Career Planning Office and Women's Center, Allentown, PA 18104, (215) 437-4471. Monday-Friday, 8:30 a.m.-4:30 p.m. Official college office and community center. Educational and career counseling, continuing education courses, job referral, alumnae placement. No fees for alumnae; other fees vary.

Community College of Allegheny County, Displaced Homemakers Program, College Center North, 111 Pines Plaza, 1130 Perry Highway, Pittsburgh, PA 15237, (412) 366-7000, ext. 35. Official college office. Individual and group counseling and workshops on various subjects including Preparing to Work, Nontraditional Career Options and Assertiveness Training. No fees.

Indiana University of Pennsylvania, Women's Center, Uhler Hall, Indiana, PA 15701, (412) 357-2227, Ext. 18. Monday-Friday, 8:30 a.m.-4:30 p.m. Educational counseling, workshops, continuing education for women. No fees.

Institute of Awareness, 401 South Broad Street, Philadelphia, PA 19147, (215) 545-4400. Monday-Friday, 9 a.m.-5 p.m. Independent non-profit agency. Educational and career counseling, adult education courses, special workshops, training programs. Fees vary.

Job Advisory Service, Chatham College, Beatty Hall, Woodland Rd., Pittsburgh, PA 15232, (412) 441-8200, Ext. 256. Monday, Tuesday, Thursday, 10 a.m.-2 p.m. Independent non-profit office. Job counseling and referral, workshops. Fees.

Lehigh County Community College, Alternatives for Women, 2370 Main Street, Schnecksville, PA 18078, (215) 799-2121, Ext. 177. Sponsored by college community service office. Workshops. Fees vary.

Options for Women, 8419 Germantown Avenue, Philadelphia, PA 19118, (215) 242-4955. Monday-Friday, 9 a.m.-5 p.m. Independent non-profit agency. Individual career counseling, day and evening hours by appointment. Career development workshops for employed women. Consult on Affirmative Action and Career Development for Business. Fees vary. Free weekly orientations.

Spring Garden College, 102 Mermaid Lane, Phildelphia, PA 19119, (215) 242-3700. Kay Root, Coordinator of Women's Programs.

Temple University, Career Services, Mitten Hall, Philadelphia, PA 19122; or 1619 Walnut Street, Philadelphia, PA, (215) 787-1503. Monday-Friday, 8:30 a.m.-4:30 p.m. College-sponsored offices: (215) 787-7981. No registration fee.

University of Pennsylvania, Resources for Women, Houston Hall, Philadelphia, PA 19104, (215) 243-5537. Monday-Thursday, 9:30 a.m.-12:30 p.m. College sponsored. Educational and career counseling center, job referral and placement. Fees vary.

Villa Maria College, Counseling Services for Women, 2551 West Lake Road, Erie, PA 16505, (814) 838-1966. Monday-Friday, 9 a.m.-4 p.m. Official college office. Educational and career counseling, job referral, placement, adult education courses. No fees.

Wilson College, Office of Career Planning and Placement, Chambersburg, PA 17201, (717) 264-4141. Monday-Friday, 9 a.m.-5 p.m. Official college office. Educational and career counseling, job referral and placement. No fees.

SOUTH CAROLINA

Converse College, Women's Center, Spartanburg, SC 29301, (803) 585-6421. Monday-Friday, 8 a.m.-5 p.m. Free to students and alumnae.

Greenville Technical College, Center for Continuing Education for Women, Greenville, SC 29606, (803) 242-3170. Monday-Friday, 8:30 a.m.-5 p.m.

TENNESSEE

Scarritt College, Center of Women's Studies, 1008 19th Avenue South, Nashville, TN 37203, (615) 327-2700. Monday-Friday, 8 a.m.-4:30 p.m. Displaced Homemaker's Center.

Women's Services of Knoxville, Inc., 4931 Homberg Drive, Knoxville, TN 37919, (615) 584-0092. Monday-Friday, 9 a.m.-2 p.m. Independent, private agency. Educational and career counseling, continuing education courses, psychotherapy, job referral and placement. Fees vary.

YWCA of Nashville, Career/Life Planning Center, 1608 Woodmont Boulevard, Nashville, TN 37215, (615) 385-3952. Monday-Saturday, 8 a.m.-12 noon.

TEXAS

Amarillo College, Women's Programs, P. O. Box 447, Amarillo TX 79178, (806) 376-5111, ext. 320. Monday-Friday, 8 a.m.-5 p.m.

Brookhaven College, Brookhaven College Counseling Center, 3939 Valley View Lane, Farmers Branch, TX 75234, (214) 746-5230. Monday-Friday, 8:30 a.m.-9 p.m.

The University of Texas at Austin, Services for Returning Students, Office of the Dean of Students, Student Services Building, Room 10-E, Austin, TX 78712,

(512) 471-3305. Monday-Friday, 8 a.m.-5 p.m. College-sponsored office. Educational and career counseling. No fees.

Vocational Guidance Service, Inc., 2525 San Jacinto, Houston, TX 77002, (713) 659-1800. Monday-Thursday, 8:30 a.m.-7 p.m.; Friday, 8:30 a.m.-5 p.m. Nonprofit organization. Educational and career counseling, job referral and placement. Fees based on sliding scale.

Women for Change Center, 3220 Lemmon, Suite 290, Dallas, TX 75204, (214) 522-3560. Monday-Thursday, 9 a.m.-3 p.m. Independent non-profit agency. Educational and career counseling, adult education courses, job referral. Fees vary.

Women's Center of Dallas, 197 The Quadrangle, 2800 Routh, Dallas TX 75201, (214) 651-9795. Monday, Wednesday, Thursday, 10 a.m. - 3 p.m., Tuesday, 5-9 p.m.

Women's Counseling Service, 1950 West Gray, Suite 2, Houston, TX 77019, (713) 521-9391. Small group sessions in personal autonomy, vocational direction, financial self-sufficiency; also individual vocational, divorce adjustment and educational counseling.

UTAH

The Phoenix Institute, 989 East 900 South, Salt Lake City, UT, (801) 532-5080. Monday-Saturday, 10 a.m.-12 p.m. and by appointment.

Women's Resource Center, 293 Union Building, University of Utah, Salt Lake City, UT 84112, (801) 581-8030. Monday-Friday, 8 a.m.-5 p.m. Evening groups. Conferences, discussion programs, groups and referral information open to the community.

VIRGINIA

Career Planning Division, Psychological Consultants, Inc., 1804 Staples Mill Road, Richmond, VA 23230, (804) 355-4329. Monday-Saturday, 8:30 a.m.-5:15 p.m. Independent private agency. Educational and career counseling. No registration fee. Other fees vary.

Hollins College, Career Counseling Center, Administration Building, Hollins College, VA 24020, (703) 362-6364. Monday-Friday, 9 a.m.-4:30 p.m.

Mary Baldwin College, Career & Personal Counseling Center, Staunton, VA 24401, (703) 995-0811, Ext. 294/333. Monday-Friday 9 a.m.-1 p.m. and 2-5 p.m. College affiliated office. Educational and career counseling. Fees vary.

University of Richmond, Women's Resource Center, University College, VA 23173, (804) 285-6316. Call for appointment.

University of Virginia, Office of Career Planning & Placement, 5 Minor Hall, Charlottesville, VA 22903, (804) 924-3378. Monday-Friday, 8 a.m.-4 p.m. Official college office. Educational and career counseling, limited job referral and placement. No fees.

Virginia Commonwealth University Evening College, 901 West Franklin Street, Richmond, VA 23284, (804) 770-6731. Monday-Friday, 8:30 a.m.-9:30 p.m.; Saturday, 9 a.m.-1 p.m. Official university office. Educational counseling, referral to university career and personal counseling services, continuing education courses.

WASHINGTON

Individual Development Center, Inc. (I.D. Center), Career and Life Planning, 1020 East John Street, Seattle, WA 98102, (206) 329-0600. Monday-Friday, 9 a.m.-4 p.m. Evening counseling and appointments. Independent private agency. Career and life decision counseling, career development workshops for company and government agency employees, awareness seminars for managers and supervisors of women employees. Partial scholarships available.

University of Washington, Career and Life Plan, 1209 NE 41st, Seattle, WA 98105, (206) 543-4262. Monday-Friday, 8 a.m.-5 p.m. Official college office. Educational and career counseling, testing, job referral, free resume register. Counseling, testing, course fees vary. Scholarships available.

Women's Resource Center, Box 1081, Richland, WA 99352, (509) 946-0467. Monday-Saturday, noon -4 p.m. Independent, private agency. Educational and career counseling, job referral, placement. Resume preparation. Fees vary.

Williams & Associates, Inc., 400 E. Evergreen Blvd., Vancouver, WA 98660, (206) 695-4800. Monday-Friday, 9 a.m.-5 p.m.; Saturday, by appointment. Independent private agency. Women-owned agency working with women in transition, career development counseling and guidance, testing and evaluation, seminars, management consulting, staff training and development. Fees vary.

WEST VIRGINIA

West Virginia University, Placement Service, Mountain Lair, Morgantown, WV 26506, (304) 293-2221. Monday-Friday, 8:15 a.m.-5 p.m. Official college office. Restricted to alumnae. Educational and career counseling, job referral. Registration fee.

WISCONSIN

Reserch Center on Women/Community Services, Alverno College, 3401 South 39th Street, Milwaukee, WI 53215, (414) 671-5400. Monday-Friday, 8:30 a.m.-5 p.m. Official college office and public facility. Educational and career counseling by appointment. Continuing education courses. Counseling fees.

Skilled Jobs for Women, Inc., 111 South Hamilton Street, Madison, WI 53703, (608) 257-4373. Monday-Friday, 8:30 a.m.-6 p.m. Evening and weekend appointments arranged.

Women's Development Center, Waukesha County Technical Institute (WCTI), 800 Main Street, Pewaukee 53072. Career, vocational and personal counseling; free seminars and workshops on decision making, coping, career planning and job seeking skills. Special emphasis on non-traditional employment. All services free. Appointments and reservations advised. All services open to men also.

WYOMING

University of Wyoming, Placement Service, P. O. Box 3915, University Station, Laramie, WY 82071, (307) 766-2398. Monday-Friday, 8 a.m.-5 p.m. Official college office, restricted to students and alumnae. Educational and career consulting, job referral. No fees.

CANADA

University of Calgary, Student Counseling
Services, Calgary, Alberta T2N 1N4,
Canada, (403) 284-5893. Monday-Friday,
8:30 a.m.-4:30 p.m.

OVERSEAS

American College in Paris, Women's Institute for Continuing Education, 31 Avenue Bosquet, Paris, France 75007,
551-21-57 or 705-30-66 - Paris. Monday-
Friday, 9 a.m.-12 noon. Closed summers.

V. HELP FOR CLERGY & RELIGIOUS

Probably no profession has developed, or had developed for it, so many
resources to aid in career assessment as has the clerical profession. Nonetheless, the warning sounded at the introduction to the last section (IV.
Help for Women) should be read at this point, for it applies with equal
force to this section of resources. Where you run into a clerical counselor
who is sincere but inept, you will probably discover that the ineptness
consists in a failure (thus far) to grasp the distinction between career
assessment — roughly comparable to taking a snapshot of people as they
are in one frozen moment of time — vs. career *development* — which is
roughly comparable to teaching people how to take their own motion
pictures of themselves, from here on out.

Having issued this caution, however, we must go on to add that at some
of these centers, listed on the next page, are some simply excellent counselors who fully understand this distinction, and are well trained in that
empowering of the client which is what career *development* is all about. If
you ask the right questions before you sign on the dotted line (see chapter
4), you will be able readily to identify them.

The centers listed at right are all accredited and coordinated by the
Career Development Council, Room 760, 475 Riverside Drive, New York,
NY 10027. Some of them are accepting directors of Christian Education,
ministers of music, and others in their program; some centers are open to
all applicants, and not merely church-related professionals.

ALSO DOING WORK IN THIS FIELD:

The Judicatory Career Support System, 3501 Campbell, Kansas City, MO
64109, (816) 931-2516. The Rev. Eugene E. Timmons.

The Episcopal Office of Pastoral Development, 116 Alhambra Circle, Suite
210, Coral Gables, FL 33134. The Rt. Rev. David E. Richards.

Bernard Haldane, 4502 54th Avenue N.E., Seattle, WA 98105 (206)
525-8141. One of the pioneers in the clergy career management and assessment field, Bernard works through seminars and in training of volunteers
to do job-finding counseling.

THE OFFICIAL INTERDENOMINATIONAL
CAREER DEVELOPMENT CENTERS

Career Development Center
St. Andrews Presbyterian College
Laurinburg, NC 28352
(919) 276-3162
Alfred E. Thomas, Director

American Baptist
Center for the Ministry
40 Washington Street
Wellesley Hills, MA 02181
(617) 237-2228
Harold D. Moore, Director

Career Development Center
Eckerd College
St. Petersburg, FL 33733
(813) 867-1166
John R. Sims, Director

American Baptist
Center for the Ministry
7804 Capwell Drive
Oakland, CA 94621
(415) 635-4246
John R. Landgraf, Director-
Counselor

Counseling Center
Davis and Elkins College
Elkins, WV 26241
(304) 636-1900
C. Joseph Martin, Director

Lancaster Career Development
Center
561 College Avenue
P. O. Box 1529
Lancaster, PA 17604
(717) 393-7451
Thomas E. Brown, Director

New England Career
Development Center
40 Washington Street
Wellesley Hills, MA 02181
(617) 237-2228
Barton M. Lloyd,
Associate Director

North Central Career
Development Center
3000 Fifth Street NW
New Brighton, MN 55112
(612) 636-5120
Dr. John Davis, Director

Northeast Career Center
40 Witherspoon Street
Princeton, NJ 08540
(609) 924-4814
Robert G. Foulkes, Director

Midwest Career Development Center
66 East 15th Avenue
Columbus, OH 43201
(614) 294-2587
Frank C. Williams, Director

Midwest Career Development Center
176 West Adams, Suite 1400
Chicago, IL 60603
(312) 263-2714

Southwest Career Development
Center
Suite 712
2723 Avenue E East
Arlington, TX 76011
(817) 265-5541
William M. Gould, Jr., Director-
Counselor

Western Career Development Center
109 Seminary Road
San Anselmo, CA 94960
(415) 453-7000
Don Falkenberg, Director-
Counselor

VI. HELP FOR THOSE WHO CONCLUDE
THEY WANT TO DEAL WITH
THEIR INTERIOR FURNITURE

In dealing with people in career transition, three types of problems have surfaced:

1. The problems people have carried for a long long time, and which slumbered relatively quietly (maybe), but cry aloud when they are considering career transition. These would be hangups such as dependency, feelings of inadequacy, a need for status, a fear of competing, extreme guilt feelings — and the somewhat more exotic problems such as sexual hangups, marital conflict, alcoholism, depression, etc.

2. The problems that appear to come to a person only as the years go on, particularly those that are characteristic of "middle life." Edmund Bergler's classic, *The Revolt of the Middle-Aged Man* (Grosset & Dunlap, New York, NY. 1954. $1.25) about "those dangerous years when men decide to 'get more out of life' and the erotic games they play with their women" (*that* should sell) is filled with over-generalizations, but it applies to enough middle-aged men to warn us of some false solutions to "the generativity issue," as Erik Erikson calls it. Other middle-age problems: change within the self over the years, in the direction of health, that make

the work environment no longer appropriate; or change in the environment over the years (the new introduced, the old taken away) that makes it no longer appropriate to that particular Self.

3. The problems that characterize transition from one career system to another. Experts are amassing an impressive amount of data regarding this; for example, let us look at ex-military and ex-clergy: both have been members of a closed social system, somewhat isolated from the mainstream of society, in which roles and status positions were defined, paternalism was encouraged, and security was promised; also, both have worn distinctive uniforms, which they now must shed. In a study reported in *The American Journal of Psychiatry,* McNeil & Giffen found that the transition from military to civilian took (typically) five years, and problems appeared for two years prior to transition, and *could* continue for three years afterward. They included: reduced efficiency, psychosomatic symptoms (chest or intestinal), loss of energy, interest, confidence, and sometimes a singular incident of flagrantly unacceptable behavior. Findings of psychiatrists dealing with ex-clerical patients (or a cleric contemplating transition) parallel the military findings. The point is, *these* symptoms are often comparatively temporary, for any career transitionist, attending — as they do — the temporary period of role confusion, and role transition. Brawer teaches that temporary symptoms (typical of regression) are ways in which the Ego finds its way around obstacles, regroups energies, and then goes on — *even more rapidly because of the temporary regression.*

Now the three different kinds of problems outlined above and on the previous page are, to be sure, intertwined. Problems showing up in middle-age, for example, are often merely accentuated versions of problems which have long been present. Still, the distinguishing of these three kinds of problems *may afford some clue* as to how earnestly help is needed, and what kinds of help.

The ideal of emotional health to which (presumably) we all aspire has been variously described.

Would you prefer: acceptance of reality; self-acceptance, interest and direction; acceptance of ambiguity and uncertainty; tolerance; flexibility and risk-taking?

Or would you prefer: maleness and femaleness both given acceptance in the self; acceptance of my own weaknesses (not wasting time keeping them hidden); living in the here and now; security, satisfaction and fulfillment found for the self and shared with others?

Or: good reality testing; energy and creativity; providing the ego with opportunities for growth; ability to delay gratification; tolerance of internal and external ambiguity; ability to rebound from challenging experiences; ability to tolerate regression when necessary for ultimately greater development?

Call it emotional health, self-love, or ego strength, or whatever. There is your checklist (or checklists). There are many more around.

Those wishing to feel their psychological pulse (privately) will probably want to grapple with Max Luscher's *The Luscher Color Test*, Random House, New York, 1969. $6.95. Quite fascinating. Max has also written *The Four-Color Person*, (Simon & Schuster). A personality evaluation system keyed to four basic colors, each of which represents an aspect of self-awareness, including checklists, guidelines and color charts to recognize character and behavior patterns in ourselves and others. 1979. $8.95.

Now, suppose you decide you want help in this area?

This has been called the field of psychological counseling, traditionally. However, this whole field has been undergoing radical changes. The people who decide they need some professional help with their own personal growth have a decision to make about what kind of help they want, and accordingly we here categorize the professionals instead by the type of help that they offer and that you may want. Basically, this is

INSTRUCTION,
EXPLORATION, and
PSYCHOTHERAPY

We will deal briefly with each of these categories on the next few pages.

- **PROFESSIONAL HELP (FOR A FEE)
  BY MEANS OF INSTRUCTION:**

1. Local college or university: cf. courses in the psychology department, and adult education.

2. Free universities (informal experimental colleges) have grown to life in a number of communities across the country, and if you know of one, it may be worth investigating to see if they have instructional types of personal growth seminars. Example: Entropy, 1914 Polk Street, Suite 205, San Francisco, CA 94109.

3. Many of the growth centers (see below, under *Exploration*) also have lectures, seminars, etc., which offer help by means of instruction.

- **PROFESSIONAL HELP WITH PERSONAL GROWTH
  BY MEANS OF EXPLORATION:**

> This covers a wide range of techniques designed to produce new awareness and/or change in the self, in one's relations to others, and in one's relation to God. In general, they are explorations of new experiences which then become (hopefully) challenges to all of the rest of one's experiences, day by day. Techniques include *sensitivity training, encounter groups, gestalt therapy, marathons, sensory awareness, bio-energetics, meditation (including Yoga), auto-analysis (games people play), simulation games, reality-therapy* — and even some very exotic stuff like group nudity, "psychological karate," etc. These techniques are virtually without exception, group techniques, for use by and in groups.

The Association for Humanistic Psychology, 325 Ninth Street, San Francisco, CA 94103. AHP produces a list of Growth Centers with corrections and updatings in its *AHP Newsletter*. Includes other countries' centers, as well as this one's. You can order both the list and the *Newsletter* from the Association, at the address above. You can then find the center, or centers, nearest you, and ask them for their catalog and/or schedule of events.

NTL Institute for Applied Behavioral Science, P.O. Box 9155, Rosslyn Station, VA 22209. As of 1967, an independent non-profit corporation associated with the National Educational Association. It certifies competency of leaders; an inquiry to the Institute may secure names of competent leaders in your area of the country, who (likely as not) offer various events. Ask for their list of publications, also.

Dialogue House, 80 East 11th Street, New York, NY 10003, conducts some 400 Intensive Journal workshops throughout the country, under the local auspices of churches, retreat centers and mental health centers, helping individuals to do personal growth through exploration of themselves in a self-directed journal. Those wishing to know more about such exploration, can write directly to Dialogue House for their schedule. You may also want to read their founder's book: *At A Journal Workshop*, by Ira Progoff. Obtainable directly from Dialogue House. $6.95, paper, prepaid.

- **PROFESSIONAL HELP WITH PERSONAL GROWTH BY MEANS OF PSYCHOTHERAPY:**

1. *The 1979-80 Directory of Counseling Services* lists accredited places which offer psychotherapy. You can obtain it from International Association of Counseling Services, Inc., Two Skyline Place, Suite 400, 5203 Leesburg Pike, Falls Church, VA 22041. 1979. $6.00.

2. The Psychology Department of your local college or university may be able to suggest places or persons which offer psychotherapy.

3. Consult also your local physician for referral suggestions, and/or your local or state psychiatric association, psychologists' association, and psychoanalytic institute (see "Professional Organizations" in your telephone book's yellow pages), for recommendations or lists of accredited personnel. See also your community mental health association or center.

If you decide to consult a psychologist, psychiatrist, psychotherapist, analyst, or psychoanalyst, here are a few suggestions, or guiding principles for choosing one:

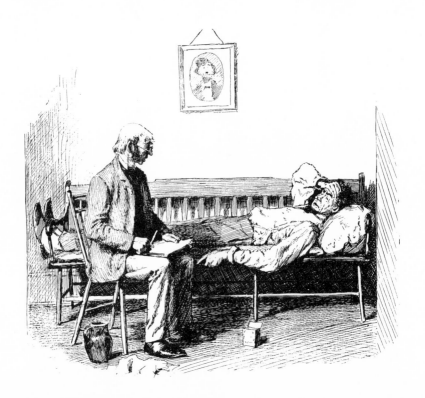

1. Get suggestions of names (see below).

2. We recommend you choose three to go see for a one-hour exploratory visit. You will almost certainly have to pay the going rates for this hour, with each therapist. It's well worth it.

3. Guidelines in evaluating therapists: a) Do you like them? (Lack of rapport can kill therapy.) b) How much personal therapy have they had? (You have a right to ask. An answer in terms of years doesn't count; hours does. Like, 200-300, or more.) c) Do you feel they are real people? (If they come across as pasteboard, maybe that's their ideal for you, too.) d) Do they assiduously avoid giving you advice? Hope so. (You need someone living their life out through you like you need a hole in the head.) Beware of the therapist who gives lots and lots of advice. (Like this!) On the other hand, give them three stars if they come across as clarifiers.

4. Choose one, after you have weighed your impressions of all three. Give serious consideration to committing yourself to say, six-eight sessions with the therapist you've chosen, after which each of you will evaluate whether or not to continue. That way, if you chose badly, you can terminate it gracefully; if you chose wisely, you have an impetus to begin working immediately.

5. If you have done the exercises in this book, you may have an idea of what goals you have for your own personal therapy: things you want to work on, hangups you want to get rid of, etc. Part of your arrangement with your therapist should be to clarify why you want therapy, so that you will have goals by which to measure progress. With this one proviso: you should feel free to revise these goals, if you want to, as therapy progresses. But therapy without any definition of what you are working toward *can be deadly. Or innocuous* — the way in which lonely people simply *purchase* friendship.

6. A book which summarizes the various options — the different sorts of therapies that are available — is Ehrenberg, Otto and Miriam, *The Psychotherapy Maze: A Consumer's Guide to the Ins and Outs of Therapy,* Holt Paperback. 1977. $3.95.

7. There is also Mishara, Brian, and Patterson, Robert, *Consumer's Guide to Mental Health.* Times Books. 1977. In addition to how to rate your therapist, it includes specific data on the various modalities of therapy. Highly recommended! And: Adams, Sallie and Orgel, Michael, *Through the Mental Health Maze: A Consumer's Guide to Finding a Psychotherapist.* Health Research Group, 2000 P Street, NW, Washington, DC 20036. 1975. $2.50, (prepaid). And: Wiener, Daniel N., *A Consumer's Guide to Psychotherapy.* Hawthorn paperback. 1975, revised edition. $4.95

All men dream… but not equally.
They who dream by night in the dusty recesses
of their minds wake in the day to find that
it is vanity; but the dreamers of the day are
dangerous men, for they act their dream with
open eyes, to make it possible.

T. E. LAWRENCE

Supplement:

Research
Notes
for
Career
Changers
(and Others)

NOTES ON PARTICULAR FIELDS OF WORK

People who change their careers have gone into just about every field of endeavor that you can name — including being a secretary, politician, doctor, psychiatrist, lawyer, and so forth.

Readers often write us, asking why we do not have information about their favorite field (such as travel agencies, sales, nursing, computer programming hotel/motel management, tourism, medicine, secretarial). I can only assume such readers leaped immediately to this section, from the table of contents, without reading the rest of the book. If you are in their company, then please — dear reader — read the book, and especially chapter 6. You will thus see that we have given you, in this book, a method whereby you can gather your own information about the field that interests you. There are a number of good books out, also, on various fields, as your librarian or local bookstore can show you. Thus can you supplement your own interviewing for information.

But, there are certain fields of work that career-changers (esp. professionals) seem to choose more often than others, for understandable reasons.

- **BUSINESS**
  - **SOCIAL SERVICE OR CHANGE**
    - **EDUCATION**
      - **GOVERNMENT**
      - **SELF-EMPLOYMENT**

We are therefore including special notes about these fields and one or two others that people have asked frequently about. *These notes are intended as merely primers for your own research (pump). Most of the research you are still going to have to do yourself.*

SOME RESEARCH NOTES ABOUT
THE FIELD OF BUSINESS

Career-changers who aspire to management positions in the business world usually despair of their unfamiliarity with the business world, and wonder if anyone wants them. Isn't the field crowded already?

Mason Haire, professor of organizational psychology and management at M.I.T. says that before the end of this decade there will be a 40% shortage of people needed to fill management positions that will exist at that time.[1]

In filling management positions, most companies have a penchant for *generalists* who can see "the whole picture" rather than for *specialists* who may suffer from "tunnel vision."

What the businesses need are executives with *people skills.* First of all, this is the way history has moved. The history of the industrial enterprise

---

1. "The Management of Human Resources: A Symposium" (See Bibliography), p. 24. Haire is the source of the statistic (p. 19) that human resources comprise about two-thirds of the value of a typical company.

has focused successively on Production, Marketing, and Distribution, and finally (these days) on the needs of the people making up the organization or being served by the organization.[1]

Most of the problems that an organization faces today are *people problems*. A survey revealed that, in 177 organizations, for every manager who failed to make the grade because of insufficient knowledge, seven failed because of personality problems.[2] Or, as we might prefer to say, because of a lack of "adaptive skills" for that particular environment.

The higher position a man or woman holds, the more he or she has to deal with people. A top executive's major job is to organize resources for the accomplishment of goals. Two-thirds of the average company's resources are *human resources*, i.e., people. It is hardly surprising, therefore, that experts say top executives rarely have more than five minutes to themselves in between their dealing with *people*, and their major task is — in the end — passing judgment upon people.

THE QUALITIES BEING LOOKED FOR IN NEW EXECUTIVES OR MANAGERS ARE:

- *authority* — the only authority which succeeds, today, being comprised of (overall) competence + compassion
- *ability to work with others*
- *communicative skills* — studies[3] have shown that effectiveness is directly correlated with the extent to which a man or woman can express his or her own convictions and feelings and at the same time also express consideration for the thoughts and feelings of others
- *intelligence and ability to solve problems*
- *perseverance* — the ability to deliver continuously, and not just in spurts; inner motivation
- *character, dependability, integrity, maturity*

In other words, intangible assets rather than technical knowledge. Career changers lacking business experience nevertheless offer what business needs in these areas, as *The Wall Street Journal* observed (April 28, 1969).

Ex-pastors, for example, are *generalists*, and they usually possess *people skills* in abundance. If they come out of parish backgrounds, they are accustomed to exercising authority, working with others, and certainly, *communicative skills*. They also usually have intelligence, perseverance and character.

Above all else, they have *clear thinking* and the ability *to get others to accomplish results* — which, as experts like John Crystal have observed, are the only skills really needed at more senior levels in management.

---

1. In *Dun's Review,* February 1969.
2. Uris, *Action Guide,* p. 196.
3. Saxenian (See Bibliography), p. 57. He suggests this as a helpful criterion for interviewers to use, in the process of hiring. It should be equally a criterion for job-hunters to use, in order to measure how much they ought to speak about themselves during an interview.

These are the assets all career-changers should stress (assuming you possess them indeed) when it comes time to zero in on the organizations you *want* to work for.

There are few, if any, management positions that are closed. General administration, community relations, manpower development, industrial relations are just some of those that, in the past, career-changers have aimed at, and gotten, in the business world.

▲▲

Cautions: Career-changers who have been through the mill caution men and women just beginning the process not to be taken in by the title: Executive. That can mean anything from $10,000 to $100,000, with or without a private office, with or without a private phone, with or without a secretary, with or without supervisory powers. *Titles are meaningless.*

▼▼

For additional research, read Jennings, Eugene E., "Mobicentric Man" in *Psychology Today*, Vol. 4, No. 2, July, 1970.

Also: Levinson, Harry, *The Exceptional Executive: A psychological conception*, Harvard University Press, Cambridge, MA. 1968. $7.25. And: Archer, Jules, *The Executive "Success,"* The Universal Library, Grosset & Dunlap, New York, NY. 1970. $1.95. A description of the executive "rat race" for any dreamers who think the business world is "just a step away from heaven."

SOME RESEARCH NOTES ABOUT THE FIELD OF SOCIAL SERVICE OR CHANGE

There are the obvious old-time occupations in this field, such as *social work, case work,* etc. Some of these have, however, changed radically in their nature over the years. Many who hold a Masters degree in social work are today working as psychotherapists in mental health clinics as well as in private practice. There are also new occupations in this field, broadly called *public service careers* or *human service occupations.*

Community colleges are spearheading this concern, since the concern is focused upon minorities and the disadvantaged. Information, consequently, can often be procured from the community colleges division of your State Department of Education.

Public service careers may be with government (federal, or state, or local), with non-profit organizations, with agencies (independent of state or local government, but often cooperating with them) with colleges (particularly community colleges), etc.

Public service careers include such varied occupations as *Community Services Officer* at a community college, *recreation educator, city planner, social service technician* (working with any or all agencies that deliver social services), *welfare administration, gerontology specialist* (for further information, contact — among others — your State Commission on Aging).

Other careers: *Workers with the handicapped, public health officials* (see your State Department of Public Health, or the Chief Medical Doctor at the county Public Health Agency — the Doctor being the best informed person about *opportunities*), *officials dealing with the foster parent program for mentally retarded persons, workers in the child welfare program,* and so forth.

If you are interested in this general field of social service, you ought to do extensive research, including talking with national associations in the fields that interest you, state departments, county, city. And do not forget college people. They have a whole bag of positions, themselves, such as: *Division Director in Human Service Careers, Director of the Department of Human Services* (write Vermont College's Department of Behavioral Science, Montpelier, VT, for further information).

Do not overlook the fact that it is very possible to create your own job. For example, in California, before Proposition 13 hit, the state used to collect an override tax of 5¢ per person, which was designated for the one or more community colleges that were in each particular county, *to be used for community services.* Many of the one hundred community colleges in that state could therefore at that time be approached by career changers who could sell themselves for the job of Community Services Officer at that college, a new job which was paid for out of these designated tax funds.

Thorough research on your part will often reveal other ways in which *funding can be found for positions not yet created if you know exactly what it is you want to do,* and find out who knows something about this.

Potential employers for social or public service occupations include social welfare agencies, public health departments, correctional institutions, government offices, economic opportunity offices, hospitals, rest homes, schools, parks and recreation agencies, etc.

As a research aid, there is *Human Service Organizations: A Book of Readings,* The University of Michigan Press, 615 East University, Ann Arbor, MI 48106. $7.95, paper. Deals with an analysis of the structure of schools, employment agencies, mental health clinics, correctional institutions, welfare agencies and hospitals. If you're thinking about going to work in one of these human service organizations, this could help your research.

For those interested in working in state and local government, a most helpful resource is the Western Governmental Research Association, 109 Moses Hall, University of California, Berkeley, CA 94720. They have monthly compilations of employment opportunities in *The Jobfinder,* as well as much other helpful material. They are trying to attract people with integrity into local government.

Now, for those interested more particularly in *working for social change,* your first and most helpful resource has got to be Vocations for Social Change, at P.O. Box 211, Essex Station, Boston, MA 02112. It produces a number of extremely helpful publications, including "Boston People's Yellow Pages" ($2.60).

There is also: *Good Works: A Guide to Social Change Careers,* Edited by Karen Aptakin, with a preface by Ralph Nader. It's produced by Nader's organization, The Center for Study of Responsive Law, Box 19367,

Washington, DC 20036, and a check payable to the Center, in the amount of $22.50, must accompany your order.

If it's Christian opportunites for service that you're interested in, you'll want to know about Intercristo, 19303 Fremont Avenue N., Seattle WA 98133. They have a job-matching system they call "Intermatch." You can call 800-426-1342 for information.

If you are interested in social change *personally* — that is to say, you are interested in exploring Alternatives not merely in your choice of Work, but also in your lifestyle, choice of technologies, use of resources, etc., there are — as you may be aware from visiting any "Alternatives Book-store" or "Headshop" — a whole library of helpful books and catalogs to help you out. A comparatively new one is *Rainbook: Resources for Appropriate Technology*, published by a group of people in Portland, Oregon who have been experimenting with "living better with less," for some years now. It costs $7.95, paper, and is available from RAIN, 2270 NW Irving, Portland, OR 97210, (503) 227-5110. They also publish a magazine called *Rain*, which updates the book.

But if it's more specifically in the area of your work, that you are interested in social change, there are resources to help you do your research *before* you come down to that more immediate decision as to which places interest you the most. One such resource is *Profiles of Involvement* (Human Resources Corporation, Philadelphia, PA. 1972. $50.00) which describes and evaluates the social involvement of corporations, organizations, government agencies, banks, non-profit organizations, etc. Very helpful to anyone doing research on the social involvement of potential employers. See your local library.

There is also *Open The Books: How To Research A Corporation.* Available from: The Midwest Academy, 600 W. Fullerton, Chicago, IL 60614. 1974. How to research a multinational corporation, banks, insurance companies, mutual funds, foundations, churches, universities, real estate companies, subsidiaries, cab companies, etc. Very thorough and helpful.

Then, there is the *Corporate Action Guide* published by the Corporate Action Project, 1500 Farragut St. NW, Washington, DC 20011 (1974) which is an information guide about corporate power and how it works. ($2.95, with postage.)

Finally, there is: *What's Happening To Our Jobs?* by Steve Babson and Nancy Bingham, published by Popular Economics Press, Box 221, Somerville, MA 02143. 1976. $1.45, paperback. An anti-establishment radical analysis of the job-market in toto.

SOME RESEARCH NOTES ABOUT THE FIELD OF EDUCATION

Types of positions typically sought by job-hunters who are new to this field — whether fresh out of college or coming to it later in life — are in the traditional teaching positions in school situations, etc. This is especially true of Ph.D.s. When they run into a tight labor market, as has been the case thus far in the '70s, they often quickly conclude they must abandon their desire to teach, and go hunting for some other kind of employment altogether.

You would do well not to make this error. The range of places that use people with teaching skills is mind-boggling: but as just a sampling, there are — as experts like John Crystal point out — training academies (like fire and police); corporate training and education departments; local and state councils on higher education; designers and manufacturers of educational equipment; teachers associations; foundations; private research firms; regional and national associations of universities, etc.; state and congressional legislative committees on education; specialized educational publishing houses; professional and trade societies. An indication of some of the possibilities you may want to research, can be found in *Education Directory: Education Associations*. It's available in your local library, or from the Superintendent of Documents, U.S. Government Printing Office, Washington, D.C 20402. Stock Number: 017-080-01714-8. $2.75.

Moreover, the range of jobs that are done within the broad definition of Education are multitudinous and very varied; just for openers, there is: *teaching* (of course), *counseling* (an honorable teaching profession, where it isn't just used by a school system as the repository for teachers who couldn't 'cut it' as teachers), *general administration, adult education programs, public relations, ombudsman, training,* and such. If the latter — i.e., training — is of particular interest to you, you will find out that the Ontario Society for Training and Development has put out a very helpful guide, entitled *Competency Analysis for Trainers: A Personal Planning Guide.* It is available from O.S.T.D., P.O. Box 537, Postal Station K, Toronto, M4P 2G9, Ontario, Canada, for $5.00, plus $1.50 for postage and handling. It outlines the kinds of skills which people who are entering this field ought to possess, and provides a checklist against which one can compare one's own skills.

All of which is to say, just because you have defined your dream of life for yourself as "teacher" doesn't mean you have even begun to narrow that down sufficiently to go looking for a job. You still have more research, and information gathering to do, before you have defined exactly what kind of teaching, with what kind of groups, in what kind of place. In other words, chapters 4-7 in this manual apply to you as much as, or even more than, anyone else.

Along the way in your research, if you are particularly interested in community colleges (which in many ways are good places for career-changers to begin), you will want to order a copy of the fact sheet "Teaching in the Community-Junior College" from the American Association of Community and Junior Colleges, One Dupont Circle NW, Washington, DC 20036. It lists a number of places to pursue in your research. If you want to know what community colleges are in your chosen geographical area, ask the AACJC for their Community, Junior, and Technical College Directory ($10.00).

If you decide to look elsewhere than teaching, there are aids produced for various teaching specialties, that you may want to seek out, e.g., for history majors there is: "Careers for Students of History," from the American Historical Association, 400 A Street SE, Washington, DC 20003. 1977. $3.50, paper. While, for English majors, there is: *Aside from Teaching English, What in the World Can You Do?* by Dorothy K. Bestor, available from: University of Washington Press, Seattle, WA 98105. 1977. $5.95, paper. There are also more general helps. Two recent ones are: Miller, Jean M., and Dickinson, Georgianna M., *When Apples Ain't Enough: Career Change Techniques for Teachers, Counselors and Librarians.* Jalmar Press, Inc., 6501 Elvas Avenue, Sacramento, CA 95819. 1980. $4.95, paper. Miller, Anne, *Finding Career Alternatives for Teachers: A Step-by-Step Guide to Your New Career.* Apple Publishing Co. Inc., Box 2498, Dept. R, Grand Central Station, New York, NY 10017. 1979. $7.95 plus $.75 postage and handling, paper.

SOME RESEARCH NOTES ABOUT THE FIELD OF GOVERNMENT

The diversity of jobs in government (or public service) is very great. You must decide, first of all, whether you want to work for *Federal, State, County, Municipal,* or *Other Agencies of a quasi-governmental nature* (redevelopment agencies, regional councils of governments, special district governments, etc.).

Each of these employs personnel in a great variety of occupations, including *administrative assistant, human relations specialist,* and others.

All government budgets today are suffering from tight constraints, the like of which have not been encountered for many years. To the extent that you go through traditional routes to governmental positions (civil service examinations, etc.) you are going to face stiff competition. If you go this route, find out all you can about it first (Warren Barker in Washington has pointed out that there are special things that ex-clergy in particular should know: e.g., "How many people were you in charge of?" — *put down total number of volunteers, and not just paid full time staff under you*).

- If you have identified your skills at a high enough level, however, and go to see the one person who has the power to hire you (Chapter Seven), you may avoid all of this level of competition, examinations, etc. Many *have* done this successfully.

INFORMATION SOURCES (AMONG MANY):

United States Office of Personnel Management (formerly called the Civil Service Commission), *Guide to Federal Career Literature,* U.S. Government Printing Office, Superintendent of Documents, Washington, DC 20402. 1975. $1.05.

Federal: Your nearest Office of Personnel Management; pamphlet entitled *Working for the USA,* from the above office.

State: Contact your State Personnel Board for beginning clues for your research. Do your research extensively. Follow the techniques of chapter 6.

County: Personnel departments of the individual counties, again for beginning clues. Lots of interviewing, done by you, to find out what you want to know, is essential before deciding what field you want to aim at and *campaign for.*

Municipal: Personnel departments of individual cities. Also your state may have some association of them (California has the League of California Cities, 1108 O Street, Sacramento, CA 95814 — for example), where you can pick up clues.

Some regions have organizations or "house organs," for municipalities, e.g., the western part of the country has *Western City Magazine* — see your local library, or 702 Hilton Center Bldg., Los Angeles, CA 90017. ($2/yr.)

Government fields include antipollution enforcement, education, welfare, day care, beautification, probation and parole, public works, recreation and parks, health and hospitals, urban renewal, and countless others.

SOME RESEARCH NOTES ABOUT THE FIELD OF SELF-EMPLOYMENT

The idea of going the self-employment route is exceedingly attractive to many job-hunters and career-changers. If you are presently employed, and can move gradually into moonlighting — testing out your own enterprise, as you would a floorboard in a very old house, stepping on it cautiously without putting your full weight on it at first, great.

If you are not presently employed, and it will be your only means of support, beware. Many men and women have starved very slowly (or not so slowly) in this kind of activity. Others have done quite well. Odds against new businesses remain depressing; 51% fail during the first five years. And some claim that figure is quite conservative.

You will do well to do as much reading-up on running your own business as possible. See Peter Weaver's *You, Inc. A detailed escape route to being your own boss* (Doubleday. 1973). Other materials are listed on page 238 — "For Those Going Out On Their Own." This will give you a helpful background.

You will want to decide exactly what you want to do. And this may mean putting several different activities together: for example, if your skills are in helping people, this might mean *private practice, teaching* at the nearby community college, or university extension division, *consulting*, etc.

If in preparation for this kind of "self-employment" you yourself want to go back to college to get additional training, see page 302.

If you need to get accredited, licensed or whatever, do *intensive questioning* of others in your kind of work, before you falsely conclude there is "only one route."

If your interest is in *sensitivity,* etc., you should include the Association for Humanistic Psychology (address p. 287) as contacts to make along the way, in your research. AHP has a newsletter with listings of growth centers (possible leads on employment) and Positions Wanted. Dues: $15/yr.

There is also the *Journal of Humanistic Psychology*, which you can search through at your local library, or get a subscription to (325 Ninth St., San Francisco, CA 94103; $10/yr.).

Self-employment can be "the pits" if you have to go out and convince people, one by one, to buy your product, services, or whatever. No wonder, then, that a number of (hopefully) soon-to-be self-employed persons find the idea of a foundation grant or government grant, tremendously attractive and winsome. How, they ask — in letter after letter — can I find such a grant? Well, basically the same way you find a job. Thorough-going research. To get you started, consult your library (or else your banker) for one of the directories of grants (already) given. Such directories as:

Annual Register of Grant Support, published by Marquis Academic Media, 200 East Ohio Street, Room 5608, Chicago, IL 60611. If you have to buy it (ouch), it's $57.50, plus $2.00 for postage and handling, plus state tax (where applicable). Makes your local library look absolutely *wonderful,* doesn't it? The directory or register covers 2300 current grant programs, and has four helpful indexes. There's also the *Foundation 500*, published by the Foundation Research Service, 39 East 51st Street, New York, NY 10022. Hopefully, your local library has this only-slightly-less-expensive volume, too. There is also: Lefferts, Robert, *Getting a Grant*. Prentice-Hall, Spectrum. 1979. $4.95.

If your idea of self-employment runs in the direction of *the arts (writing, etc.)* you may be interested in a $13.95 listing of operating foundations, businesses, unions, associations, educational and professional institutions, which give support (thru grants or other kinds of aid) to *writers, painters, filmmakers, musicians,* etc.: "Grants and Aid to Individuals in the Arts" from *Washington International Arts Letter,* 325 Pennsylvania Avenue, Box 9005A, Washington, D.C. 20003. They have other lists (private foundations active in the arts, federal monies available, etc.) and their *Letter* itself is $13.95/yr. (or see your local library to see if it has it).

On the other hand, if you've always dreamed about being a consultant, there are books about consultancy available through the mails, or at your library, or at your bookstore, such as Shenson, Howard, *How to Establish and Operate Your Own Consulting Practice*. Prentice-Hall Spectrum. 1979. $17.50. OR: Bermont, Hubert, *How to Become a Consultant in Your Own Field*. Bermont Books, 815 Fifteenth St., N.W., Washington, DC 20005. $20.00 Money-back guarantee available. But I need to tell you that some of our readers have not found books very helpful. We recommend, in such a case, that you go talk to some consultants of the type which interests you (see the yellow pages in your phone book) to see what they regard as the virtues and pitfalls of your intended profession. If you like to do consulting or training, but prefer to hitch up with an already established firm, go to your library and peruse Wasserman, Paul, and Watson, Marlene A., eds., *Training & Development Organizations Directory*, Gale Research Company, Book Tower, Detroit, MI 48226. 1978. $45.00, hardcover. This is a reference work describing 985 individuals, institutions, firms, and other agencies offering training programs for business, industry, etc.

IF YOU WANT TO BUY IN ON YOUR OWN BUSINESS, there is an endless number of franchises (you put up $x of your own, and in return you get equipment, know-how, and — sometimes — national advertising campaigns to help you). You can also get taken to the cleaners by supposedly reputable companies.

For a sampling of the kind of franchises available you may want to get your hands on *Franchise Opportunities Handbook*. Produced by the United States Department of Commerce, Industry and Trade Administration, and Office of Minority Business Enterprise. Available from: Superintendent of Documents, U.S. Government Printing Office, Washington, D.C. 20402. 1978.

Somewhat more detailed is: Finn, Richard P., *Your Fortune In Franchises*. Contemporary Books. Details the steps involved in acquiring a franchise, including financing, site selection, franchisor's rights and promotion. 1979. $9.95.

Caution: Some experts warn that the successful entrepreneur and the successful organization-person are two entirely different breeds of cat, and the longer a man or woman has been at one, the less likely he or she will succeed at the other.

Other experts, of course, have a good word for franchises and running your own business. In any event, you had better be aware of the fact that businesses are failing at the rate of 900-1000 a month (33% higher than a year previous). "A Franchise is a Hard Way to Get Rich," as Michael Creedman said in *Money* magazine, September 1973 (see your local library, to get a look at this very apt warning).

To repeat, the odds against new business are very depressing: 51% fail during the first five years.

Conclusion: *Be sure you're not tempted to go this route just because you can't stand the*

*job-hunt process. (Say it again Sam.) If you decide to go this route, have
a lawyer at your elbow constantly, have enough cash for the first five years
to tide you over, and be sure to hire people who have the expertise in areas
you lack.* In other words, for most of us: forget it.

SOME RESEARCH NOTES ABOUT
GOING BACK TO SCHOOL

    ☐ Your first problem is *what you want to go back to school for.*

    ☐ Your second problem is *where you want to go, and why?*

    ☐ Your third problem is *how to finance it.*

As for the first: *There are five reasons why most people go back to
school:*

1. To learn more about the world in which we are called to do our
mission, e.g., *business, astronomy, black culture,* etc.

2. To pick up additional skills for the work we are presently doing
full-time, e.g., *Counseling,* or for the work we intend to move into.

3. To pick up a degree in our present or future field; i.e., to prepare for
"that day," e.g., *business administration.*

4. To broaden the horizons of our mind, *e.g., some authorities (probably math teachers) maintain that mathematics is a means of making the
mind more elastic and receptive to change.*

5. To postpone decision, and create a never-never land between one's
past and any future career. The "eternal student" is becoming a more and
more familiar figure in our land.

If you want to go back for the third reason, dear friend, please be very
sure you have done the exercises in chapter 5, in detail, because you can
get to taking some courses that are, in retrospect, a waste of time — in
terms of your priority goals and skills.

Read the rash of books (e.g., Berg, Ivar, *Education and Jobs: The Great
Training Robbery,* The Center for Urban Education, Department NM, 105
Madison Avenue, New York, NY 10016. $7.50) and articles (e.g., "Let's
Break the Go-to-College Lockstep" in *Fortune,* November 1970) that have
appeared in recent years *if your only reason for going back is to get a
degree. ("That ol' black magic.")*
Confirmation of the futility of degrees is found in a study done by
Richardson of 367 Air Force officers who got full-time secular jobs. They
agreed that *"higher" education credentials were asked of them in order to
get hired, than were necessary for the actual performance of the job.* (See
Appendix B, page 243.) You can get around this, if you faithfully follow
all of chapters 6 and 7. If you want to know what colleges are available,
see the *College Blue Book* (three volumes) or *The Blue Book of Occupational Information* (Macmillan) at your local library. If you are interested
in working part-time toward a degree, you may want to get your hands on:
On-Campus/Off-Campus Degree Programs for Part-Time Students, edited
by Linda W. Gordon and Judy H. Schub, and published by the National
University Extension Association, One Dupont Circle, Suite 360, Washing-

ton, DC 20036. ($4.00, which must accompany your order.) For overseas opportunities (if that interests you), there is: *International Education: A Directory of Resource Materials on Comparative Education and Study in Another Country* by Lily von Klemperer. (Garrett Park Press, Garrett Park, MD 20766. $5.95, if payment is enclosed with order.)

If you have done private study, and feel you could pass equivalency examinations without taking (at least some) courses, write: The College Entrance Examination Board, Box 592, Princeton, NJ 08540 or Box 1025, Berkeley, CA 94701 and ask for details of their College-Level Examination Program.

If it's a *doctorate* you want, viable ones are in business administration (even a Masters in same is highly regarded from one of the *great* schools), economics, and computer-related sciences (but beware of *useless* computer schools — see *The Wall Street Journal,* June 10, 1970 at your local library).

If you don't care about a degree, but *you just want to gain some knowledge,* a good introductory volume to help you choose the *method* of learning is: *The Lifelong Learner* by Ronald Gross ($8.95, hardcover), which you can order from Simon and Schuster, 1230 Avenue of the Americas, New York, NY 10020. See especially pages 88-89 and following, for an overview of your options. Among the possibilities, there are:

1. *Seminars, workshops,* etc. Get your hands on *The Weekend Education Source Book* by Wilbur Cross. $6.95, paper. You can order it from Harper and Row, Publishers, Inc., 10 East 53rd Street, New York, NY 10022. Lists various types of organizations (with addresses) that offer seminars or workshops.

2. *Independent study at home: guided by others.* Get your hands on *Guide to Independent Study Through Correspondence Instruction,* published by National University Extension Association; you can order it from: Petersen's Guides, 228 Alexander Street, Princeton, NJ 08540. $2.00, plus $1.00 for postage and handling. Or: you may want *Directory*

of Accredited Private Home Study Schools, from National Home Study Council, 1601 18th St. NW, Washington, DC 20009.

3. *Independent study at home: guided by yourself.* If you want to do it the traditional way, i.e., by reading a bunch of books in a particular subject, but you don't know which books to choose, you'll want to consult *College On Your Own: How You Can Get a College Education at Home* by Gail Thain Parker and Gene R. Hawes ($6.95, paper), in your library, bookstore, or ordered directly from Bantam Books, Inc., 666 Fifth Avenue, New York, NY 10019. It lists various subjects, and then the recommended books in that field.

Or, if you prefer to listen, rather than to read, try learning by means of cassettes. This is getting to be an extremely popular way to learn.

4. *Study at a community college, college extension division, university, etc.* In case you don't know, *The Education Directory, Part 3 (Higher Education)* will tell you which schools of this nature are near you (or near the area where you would like to go and live). Consult the directory at your local library.

You should also know that many communities or geographical areas have regional clearinghouses of information about educational opportunities. I am thinking of such places as the Educational Information and Referral Service which Atlanta, Georgia, has (3393 Peachtree Road, NE, (404) 233-7497). For other places, in your area, read pages 78-83 in *The Three Boxes of Life*, or consult the National Center for Educational Brokering, 405 Oak Street, Syracuse, NY 13203.

For non-school type learning, you know "places that will let you get your hands dirty and places that will leave you alone to work out the struggle between you and whatever hunk of the world you're grappling with," there are 400 such places listed in the Center for Curriculum Design's *Somewhere Else: a living-learning catalog* (The Swallow Press Inc., 811 West Junior Terrace, Chicago, IL 60613). It was published back in 1973, but the list is still useful. $3.00, or see your local library.

As for your *finances,* there are three possible ways to get finances: a) Consult your university or college office to see what resources they have for aiding people in financial binds (like you); b) Consult your local service clubs (in town) to see if they have, or know of, similar kinds of aid: scholarship or whatever; c) Get your hands on: *Catalog of Federal Domestic Assistance,* Supt. of Documents, U.S. Government Printing Office, Washington, DC 20402. $7.00.

You can also get financed, by various ingenious methods, on your own. One cleric, for example, wrote to all the clergy whom he knew in large parishes, and asked for gifts from their *discretionary funds or other special funds.* He secured enough money to cover his whole study program.

The government, incidentally, has "guaranteed loans" in a program which enables banks to lend you money at lower rates. But this program has run into real difficulty recently, and many students were left high and dry. Consult your local college for details about the viability of this program, and any others that may exist.

AND FINALLY SOME RESEARCH NOTES ABOUT WORKING OVERSEAS

Mandatory reading for anyone contemplating overseas living is Hopkins, Robert, *I've Had It: A Practical Guide to Moving Abroad*, Holt, Rinehart & Winston, New York, NY. 1972. Unfortunately, it is apparently out-of-print, so you'll have to depend on your friendly neighborhood public library. (If they don't have it, and you definitely want it, ask them to get it for you on an inter-library loan.) Also, there is:

Kocher, Eric, *International Jobs: Where They Are, How To Get Them.* Addison-Wesley Publishing Co., Jacob Way, Reading, MA 01867. 1979. $5.95, paper.

We still advise following the techniques of chapters 4-7, in the end.

If you want to know the kinds of places you might target in on, overseas, there is the *Dictionary of American Firms Operating in Foreign Countries*, by Juvenal L. Angel (World Trade Academy Press. 1971; look it up, in your local library, and ask your librarian for similar directories).

Index

Author Index

Update

To: PARACHUTE
Box 379
Walnut Creek, California 94596

☐ I think that the information in the '81 edition needs to be changed regarding (or, the following resource should be added):

_____

_____

_____

_____

_____

☐ I cannot find the following resource:

_____

_____

_____

_____

_____

Name _____

Address _____

_____

Hotline

To: PARACHUTE
Post Office Box 379
Walnut Creek, California 94596

I HAVE READ YOUR ENTIRE BOOK AND HAVE
COMPLETELY FILLED IN *THE QUICK JOB-HUNTING
MAP* EXERCISE IN APPENDIX A, but I am still having
trouble with the following part of the career-change /
job-hunting process:

_____

_____

_____

_____

_____

_____

_____

_____

_____

_____

_____

If there is a resource in my area, from whom I could get
help with this, please let me know.

Name _____

Address _____

_____

Mailing List

Richard Bolles is the Director of the National Career Development Project, located in Walnut Creek, California.

This Project maintains a mailing list. Those who are on this list receive notification of new books or other creations from the pen of Richard Bolles; as well as of workshops which he conducts around the country, from time to time.

If you wish to be on this mailing list, please fill out the form below, and send it to:

Mailing List
NCDP
P.O. Box 379
Walnut Creek, CA 94596

If you wish also to receive the bi-monthly Newsletter written by Richard Bolles, and published by the Project, that is a separate matter for which it is necessary for us to ask you to fill out (also) the order blank on the other side of this form. Thanks.

To: Mailing List, NCDP, P. O. Box 379, Walnut Creek, CA 94596

Dear Folks:

Please add me to your mailing list, so that I may receive periodic announcements of your newly-published works, your workshops, etc.

NAME_____

ADDRESS_____

CITY, STATE AND ZIP_____

Organization (optional): _____

To: **Newsletter**

P.O. Box 379
Walnut Creek, CA 94596

Yup, we publish a Newsletter (bi-monthly) for job-hunters and professionals in career-counseling. (A professional is someone who is not currently hunting for a job.) The charge for the six issues a year is $10. Check payable to: National Career Development Project.

Subscriptions *must* run from January through December, for a given year. So, if you send us a check in, say, June, we will send you all the issues that have already come out in the period January–June of this year, and then continue your subscription through the end of December, only. Then you have to re-subscribe, if you wish the Newsletter for the next year.

In the Newsletter (its formal name is *Newsletter about life/work planning*) we run articles about special problems that job-hunters are encountering, which are not covered (so far) in *Parachute*; *plus* descriptions of new research or publications concerning the job-hunt or career-change; *plus* news of the project and what we are up to lately.

If you want this Newsletter, tear out this page please, fill in your address below, attach your check or money order, and send it on in.

Name _____

Address that you want on the mailing label:

_____

_____

_____
City   State Zip Code